D0847422

# CIRCUMFERENCE

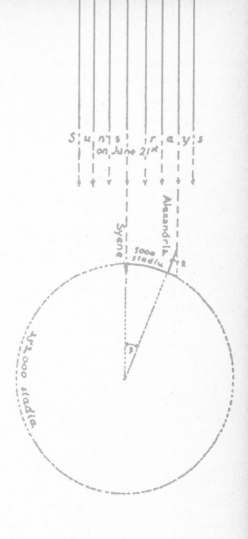

FICTION BY NICHOLAS NICASTRO

*Antigone's Wake: A novel of Imperial Athens*

*The Isle of Stone: A novel of Ancient Sparta*

*Empire of Ashes: A novel of Alexander the Great*

*Between Two Fires: A novel of John Paul Jones*

*The Eighteenth Captain: A novel of John Paul Jones*

Nicholas Nicastro

# CIRCUMFERENCE

ERATOSTHENES
*and the*
ANCIENT QUEST
TO MEASURE
THE GLOBE

ST. MARTIN'S PRESS
NEW YORK

www.stmartins.com

Book design by Jonathan Bennett

Library of Congress Cataloging-in-Publication Data

Nicastro, Nicholas.
    Circumference : Eratosthenes and the ancient quest to measure the globe / Nicholas Nicastro.
        p. cm.
    Includes bibliographical references and index.
    ISBN-13: 978-0-312-37247-7
    ISBN-10: 0-312-37247-7
    1. Arc measures.  2. Earth—Figure—Measurement.  3. Eratosthenes.
4. Weights and measures, Ancient.  5. Mathematics, Greek.  I. Title.
QB291.N53 2008
526'.1092—dc22

                                                              2008025773

First Edition: November 2008

10  9  8  7  6  5  4  3  2  1

*Dedicated with love to my daughter, Nell Nicastro,*
*who gave me life*

# CONTENTS

PREFACE    *ix*

1. THE PHILOSOPHER'S RUN    *1*

2. A ZOO OF UNIVERSES    *29*

3. MR. BETA AND THE ANCIENT PLAN B    *59*

4. GREEKS AND BARBARIANS    *104*

5. ECLIPSE    *144*

NOTES    *193*

BIBLIOGRAPHY    *205*

INDEX    *213*

# PREFACE

The muse of history has been grudging in her attention to the ancient scientists. The catalog of the eight-million-volume Cornell University Library, where much of this book was researched, lists twenty-eight books with the keyword *Archimedes* as a subject, but only two slim biographies (neither in English). The keyword *Cleopatra,* by contrast, calls up 227 listings (many fictional) and no fewer than thirteen biographies. Even Diogenes the Cynic gets forty-nine listings and a couple of biographies. As of this writing, the figures for Eratosthenes of Cyrene, one of the greatest minds of antiquity, are twelve general book listings, zero biographies, and nothing in English.

Not all of this can be blamed on the paucity of direct evidence of our man. The historical development of science is arguably of epochal importance to all our lives. Unlike the exploits of sexy queens and scandalous philosophers, however, appreciating the achievements of ancient scientists demands a degree of comfort with science. For the majority of classicists in academia, whose training is overwhelmingly in Greek and Latin languages and literatures, such comfort is exceptional.

Something similar might be said of the Hellenistic era in general, which stretched roughly from the end of the fourth century BCE* to

---

*This book uses the abbreviations BCE (Before the Common Era) and CE (Common Era), which have generally replaced the older BC and AD.

the end of the first century BCE. We've seen a steady stream of popular books on the Trojan War and its beguiling cast, on the classical era, and on the reign of Caesar, but short shrift paid to what is sandwiched in between. Yet the Hellenistic period is arguably more relevant to the modern condition than any of these others. The military and cultural dominance of the West, the clash of cultures, urbanism, the tension between political fission and fusion, the advent of rationalism and the rise of new structures of belief—these are the themes of Eratosthenes' times, and of our time as well.

True, our knowledge of Eratosthenes himself is tantalizingly limited. Only scraps of his voluminous written output have survived, mostly in quotations by other writers. We know of no verifiable likenesses. His personal background is known only in outline, and our sources conflict on the circumstances of his death. Yet none of this has been an obstacle for those determined to write about other important but obscure figures from antiquity. We have even less direct evidence for Helen of Troy and Solon of Athens than we have for Eratosthenes, yet those two are the subject of seven and twenty-four monographs in the Cornell library collection, respectively.

One of the occupational hazards of writing about such material, even in a book for a general audience like this one, is that just about every categorical statement has been or will be challenged by specialists. Nonetheless, I prefer not to encumber the text with qualifiers, such as *as far as known records indicate, for the most part, probably, presumably,* and *it appears.* Let the reader be forewarned: our knowledge of even as well attested a period as this one is provisional only. To minimize my errors, Prof. Duane W. Roller (Ohio State University), Prof. David Hollander (Iowa State University), and one anonymous expert in ancient science graciously agreed to examine the manuscript. I am much indebted to them for their advice; the fault for any mistakes that remain is entirely my own.

Thanks as well to my editor at St. Martin's Press, Michael Flamini, whose questing intellect gave this book a home, and to Jeff Gerecke, my endlessly patient agent.

Greek words have been transliterated into Latin orthography for the convenience of the general reader. Greek spellings have been used for less well-known terms, such as the Serapeion. Insisting on Museion instead of Museum, however, or Alexandros instead of Alexander, verges on the pedantic. All ancient dates are BCE unless otherwise noted. For brevity's sake, the phrase "circumference of the earth" will occasionally be referred to simply as $E$.

# CIRCUMFERENCE

# 1. THE PHILOSOPHER'S RUN

IN 245 BCE, Eratosthenes of Cyrene left Athens to take up his position as head librarian at the Museum in Alexandria. Though long-distance travel in antiquity was never a trivial undertaking, a summer voyage to Egypt would have been a pleasant journey. Eratosthenes would no doubt have first made inquiries at Athens' port of Piraeus for passage aboard a freighter. In his time, there was no specialized passenger trade spanning the Aegean: a traveler would simply go down to the waterfront, or perhaps the storefront offices of a reputable shipping company, and ask for passage on a vessel heading toward his destination. For obscure places or sailings out of season, he had to make do with passage to someplace near his destination and complete his journey aboard smaller coastal craft or overland. But in the case of the Athens–Alexandria run, he would have had little trouble finding passage; the route in the mid-third century BCE would have been well plied, with frequent direct sailings by shippers making a good profit.

Vessels leaving Alexandria were weighted down with the wares of the greatest entrepôt in the Mediterranean world: grain and papyrus from the Egyptian countryside; wine from the vineyards around Lake Mareotis; textiles, glass, goldwork, faience, papyrus, unguents, and perfumes from the city's factories; spices, incense, aromatic woods, and other luxuries from Arabia and points east. Athens herself by the mid-third century had already been supplanted by Rhodes as the leading mercantile democracy in the

Aegean. Because Athenian bulk exports to Egypt would have been far more limited than her imports, Alexandrian cargo ships would come home far higher in the water than when they set out. Indeed, Athens' most important exports to Ptolemy's kingdom would not have been her signature products, such as wine, honey, and olive oil, or even books for the Great Library, but intellectuals like Eratosthenes himself.

Ships of the time were small by modern standards: the only Hellenistic-era merchant vessel known to archaeology, the so-called Kyrenia ship discovered off the north coast of Cyprus in 1967, was a four-man island hopper that measured only forty-seven feet long and fifteen wide. Dwarfing that would have been the big grain ships that plied the Egypt–Italy route in Roman times, such as the 180-foot-long, 44-foot-wide *Isis* described by Lucian of Samosata in the second century CE. But such leviathans appeared only late in antiquity, and were exceptional. Most likely Eratosthenes would have booked passage on something far more modest.

The right price bought space on deck to lay a bedroll or perhaps pitch a small tent. Cabins, which were few, expensive, and undoubtedly cramped, were more suited to the wives and daughters of the wealthy, who needed privacy away from the crew and the other passengers, almost all of whom were male. (This, notwithstanding the effect on milady's stomach: an ancient merchantman with its round bottom and small sails—the Kyrenia ship had only about sixty-four square meters of canvas—would have pitched and rolled terribly. This effect would have seemed far worse to those confined onboard in a tiny cubicle.)

To a man in his prime such as Eratosthenes, there would have been no reason to avoid spending his time under the open sky. Moderns can hardly imagine the contrast of breathing clean sea air after sampling the conditions in a typical ancient Greek city, with no internal plumbing, few allowances for public sanitation, and animals and their waste everywhere. Narrow streets cut city dwellers off from sky and sun; insecurity at night kept them indoors, away from the stars.

But on a quiet sea, with lungs and nostrils unburdened, no responsibilities, and much time on his hands, the traveler with a philosophic bent could find his imagination enlarged. Presented with the night sky, Eratosthenes might have contemplated the cosmological speculations of Thales, Anaximander, Leucippus, and the Pythagoreans. He might have considered the popular theory that the Milky Way, which glowed so brightly at sea, was the remnant of a path through the sky abandoned by the sun. Or he might simply have been impressed with how little was truly known about what he saw above him.

Passage to Africa during the fair-sailing season—roughly, May to October—would have put the seasonal winds behind the ship's sails. After a few days afloat, a different sort of star would have appeared near the southern horizon: a steady gleam that would shine day and night, never setting but rising subtly as the vessel neared shore. At the sight of it most of those aboard would have begun their obeisances to the gods who had secured their safe passage. The beacon of the Lighthouse of Alexandria was, after all, the passengers' first direct glimpse of their destination.

### TOWER OF SIGNIFICANCE

*There is an island washed by the open sea*
*lying off the Nile mouth—seamen call it Pharos—*
*distant a day's sail in a clean hull*
*with a brisk land breeze behind. It has a harbor,*
*a sheltered bay, where shipmasters*
*take on dark water for the outward voyage.*

—*The Odyssey,* book IV

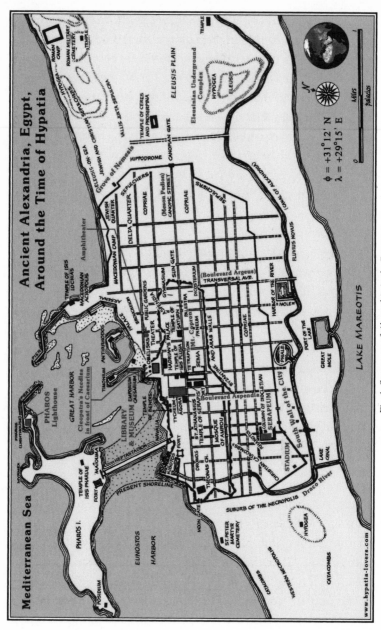

Fig. 1. Street map of Alexandria in the Roman era

The Great Lighthouse (in Greek, Pharos) was for centuries one of the tallest human-made structures on earth. Based on contemporary illustrations and descriptions of its remains, historians know that it was sited on a small natural island (also called Pharos) that was connected to the mainland by a mole (breakwater causeway) that, in turn, separated the east and west harbors of the city (see figure 1). Built of white limestone and pink Aswan granite, the Pharos had a tripartite structure based on a vaguely Pythagorean geometric theme, with a square-sided base, octagonal middle, and circular upper stage. At its very top was mounted a lantern that included a mirror for reflecting sunlight during the day, and for an oil-fed fire at night. At a height of 384 feet, its beacon would theoretically have been visible some thirty miles out to sea—more than a day's sail away. If the Pharos had somehow been plucked off the North African shore and placed on Lake Michigan, it would have topped the Chicago skyline until the construction of the Wrigley Building in 1922.

Dedicated in the early third century at a cost of eight hundred talents, the Lighthouse was one of the first monumental structures completed after the city's founding. Its manifest purpose was to compensate for the lack of landmarks for navigating the northwest Egyptian coast, though its utility as a lookout (and, if legend is to be believed, for burning ships at a distance with its great mirror) would have been a useful bonus. As such it represented an innovation: while towers had been built elsewhere, and human-made landmarks, such as the gleaming bronze helmet of Athena Promachos on the Athenian Acropolis, had incidental uses in navigation, the Pharos was probably the first structure expressly designed for that purpose. There was nothing in mainland Greece to compare to it.

It therefore comes as something of a surprise that the first known catalog of the Seven Wonders of the ancient world, that of

Antipator of Sidon (c. second century BCE), did not include the Pharos. Instead, Antipater preferred to list the Walls of Babylon. It wasn't until the first century CE that the practically minded Romans, specifically Pliny the Elder, included the Lighthouse among the canonical seven (along with the Pyramids of Giza, the Hanging Gardens of Babylon, the Mausoleum of Halicarnassus, the statue of Zeus at Olympia, the Colossus of Rhodes, and the Temple of Artemis at Ephesus). The Lighthouse was so well constructed, however, that it was among the last Wonders to vanish: Arab travelers describe at least part of the tower surviving well into the medieval period. The rest of the Pharos finally succumbed to earthquakes in the early fourteenth century CE. Underwater surveys of the area northeast of the island clearly show remnants of the tower toppled in that direction, with more than two thousand of its blocks littering the harbor bed.

Yet, like many landmark structures in history, the Lighthouse towered as much in symbol as in physical height. It was a practical expression of the self-aggrandizing impulse that inspired other mega-structures in the new Hellenistic kingdoms, such as the renovated Temple of Apollo at Didyma, or the Mausoleum of Halicarnassus. Like the buildup of super-tall skyscrapers along the Asian rim in our own time, architectural gigantism followed the accumulation of sufficient money and political confidence to make such gestures. Sure enough, the Pharos's visibility was fully exploited to advertise the splendor of the Ptolemaic state: much of what we know about its appearance is based on its representation on coins, lamps, and other souvenirs, where it was reproduced as frequently as the Statue of Liberty is today (see figure 2). More to the point, its ingenious design, which anticipated the setback designs of modern masonry skyscrapers by more than twenty centuries, might have represented the first practical fruit of research done at the institution Eratosthenes had come to join—the Museum.

*Fig. 2. Bronze coin from the reign of the Roman emperor Hadrian, depicting the Pharos, right, and Isis, the patron goddess of sailors*

The beacon would have had another significant implication to an informed mind like Eratosthenes'. Its visibility from far out at sea, when the rest of the coast appeared to lie below the horizon, was as graphic a demonstration as possible of the curvature of the earth's surface. This would (or should) have ruled out competing models of the planet's shape, such as Thales' disk, Anaximander's flat-topped column, and Leucippus's kettledrum. One of the key assumptions of Eratosthenes' measurement of the earth's circumference—that the planet is spherical—would have been reinforced in his mind even before he set foot on Egyptian soil.

### INTO THE BIRDCAGE

*Many are feeding in populous Egypt, scribblers on papyrus, ceaselessly wrangling in the birdcage of the Muses.*

—TIMON OF PHLIUS (c. 320–230)

The final approach to the city would have presented the ship's passengers with a panorama of Greek ingenuity. The city's *Greek* character deserves emphasis: though Alexandria was located in the enviably rich kingdom of Egypt, and Egypt had been respected for centuries (along with Babylonia) as the font of all ancient wisdom, there never seemed any prospect of constructing a capital that actually *looked* authentically Egyptian. The ambiguous relationship of the capital to the rest of the country was obvious even to outsiders: the Romans, who knew a thing or two about the geography of power, called it Alexandria ad Aegyptum, or "Alexandria *near* Egypt," not in it.

To be sure, the Ptolemies did commission massive new temples in the ancient style, largely to help the Macedonian rulers ingratiate themselves with their native subjects. But those constructions stood upriver, at such places as Dendera, Edfu, and Philae. The Greeks had also plundered interior sites, such as Heliopolis, for sphinxes, obelisks, columns, and so on, with which to decorate their public spaces. These appear to have been spread about, out of context, like titanic bric-a-brac, in a manner that would have struck the natives as highly irreverent—Egyptianizing instead of Egyptian. (The twin seventy-foot "Cleopatra's Needles"—obelisks—were first installed in Alexandria just after the Ptolemaic period, and subsequently shipped to the West. They are now mounted on the Thames embankment and in Central Park in New York, largely for the same reasons the Ptolemies had for displaying them.)

Strabo offers the best surviving description of the city in its heyday. Approaching from the north, Eratosthenes' ship would likely have made for the mouth of the eastern or Great Harbor, which was bound by Pharos Island on the west and on the east by the promontory of Lochias. The pilot would have had to proceed carefully around the rocks that either stuck their heads above the water or lay just below the surface—Strabo makes a point of mentioning the violence of the sea in the vicinity. As the ship entered protected waters and proceeded along one of three channels (nicknamed Steganos, Posideos, and Tauros) to the docks, Eratosthenes would have seen the Lighthouse towering over him on his right, clad in marble and graced with monumental statuary, the trident of the bronze Poseidon (or Zeus or Proteus) at its peak gleaming in the sun.

Before him, the city's waterfront would have stretched in a crescent: starting from the east, where the Lochias peninsula (today, sunk below sea level) joins the mainland, he would have seen the royal compound—a sprawling complex of "various dwellings and groves" so sprawling that it "occup[ies] a fourth or even a third part of [the city's] whole extent. For as each of the kings was desirous of adding some embellishment to the places dedicated to the public use, so, besides the buildings already existing, each of them erected a building at his own expense; hence the expression of the poet may be here applied, 'one after the other springs.'" Strabo notes that the buildings of the royal pleasure dome were "all connected with one another and with the harbor, and those also which are beyond it"—a scheme that Fraser likens to the Topkapı palace in Istanbul, but that also suggests the mazelike arrangement that Caesar would find so frustrating in his attempts to barricade himself in the palaces two hundred years later.

Below the palaces would have lain the royal anchorage, and beyond that, the small island (since vanished) that in Strabo's time boasted "a palace and a small port" and was known somewhat grandiosely as Anti-Rhodes. Behind, on higher ground, stood a splendid theater, a compulsory feature in any Greek city, and to its west, the Emporion, a complex of docks and customshouses where every ship was inspected. Farther east was the Serapeion, a vast temple complex six hundred feet long and one hundred wide, dedicated to Alexandria's patron deity. Serapis was an amalgam of Apis, the native bull god, and Osiris, the anthropomorphic lord of the dead—an instant "designer god" fashioned by the Ptolemies to give Greeks and Egyptians a deity in common.

The inspections at the Emporion had their pecuniary purpose, of course. Much of the state's revenue was derived not from direct taxation, but from duties placed on goods moving in and out of the port. But they had another mission: since the foundation of the Museum, the Ptolemies had a standing policy of confiscating any valuable books that arrived by ship in the town, copying them, and returning the copies to the owner. The originals were retained in a special section of the Great Library called "the ships' collection." In this and other ways the Ptolemies were able, in just a few decades, to amass the largest collection of books in the Greek world. We can be sure, then, that if Eratosthenes brought any of his own books from Athens, they would have been thoroughly examined by the king's officials.

The Great Harbor was deep enough for the biggest ships to come right up to the edge of the street grid. As the passengers waited for the royal inspectors to complete their work, we can imagine that Eratosthenes was close enough to hear the bustle of the merchants' quarter, and to smell the city's fragrant treasures—the half-fruity, half-balsamic complexity of frankincense, cinnamon's sweet bite, the tang of pepper.

Cleared at least to proceed into the city, the visitor would soon encounter a spectacle of urban grandeur widely celebrated in its time. Achilles Tatius, a second-century CE native of Alexandria, included an ecstatic description in his novel, *Leucippe and Clitophon,* which should sound familiar to many a modern tourist trying to encompass the abundant wonders of Rome or Paris. It is worth quoting at length:

> As I entered through the so-called "gates of the Sun," I was immediately confronted with the brilliant beauty of the city, and my eyes were filled with pleasure. Two opposing rows of columns ran in straight lines from the gates of the Sun to the gates of the Moon. . . . Many a road crisscrossed this part: you could be a tourist at home. . . . I divided my eyes between all the streets, an insatiable spectator incapable of taking in such beauty in its entirety. There were sights I saw, sights I aimed to see, sights I ached to see, sights I could not bear to miss . . . my gaze was overpowered by what I could see before me, but dragged away by what I anticipated. As I was guiding my own tour around all these streets, lovesick with the sight of it, I said to myself wearily:
>
> "We are beaten, my eyes!"
>
> I saw two extraordinary novelties, grandeur competing with splendor and the populace striving to exceed their city. Both

sides won: the city was bigger than a continent and the people more numerous than an entire race. When I considered the city, I could not believe that it could be filled with people; when I beheld the people, I was amazed that a city could hold them. The scales were that finely balanced.

The Arabs, who gained possession of the city by treaty in 641 CE but ultimately neglected it in favor of their own foundation at Cairo, were unnerved by Alexandria's splendor. The well-traveled Abd al-Malik Ibn Juraij offered the slightly impious encomium "if God had suffered me to stay a month in Alexandria and pray on its shores, that month would be dearer to me than the sixty [Mecca] pilgrimages which I have undertaken." Amrou ibn el-Ass, the occupying general, wrote a letter to the caliph explaining that he had "taken a city of which I can only say that it contains 4,000 palaces, 4,000 baths, 1,200 greengrocers and 40,000 Jews." The embarrassment of riches is palpable. Another Arab visitor reported, even at a late date in Alexandria's ancient career, that

the city was all white and bright by night as well as by day. By reason of the walls and pavements of white marble the people used to wear black garments; it was the glare of the marble that made the monks wear black. So too it was painful to go out by night . . . a tailor could see to thread his needle without a lamp. No one entered without a covering over his eyes.

History does not record if Eratosthenes arrived in the city with the proper eyewear. In all likelihood, he did look toward the king's palaces, fringed with shade trees and gardens; perhaps it occurred to him that somewhere in that maze, very likely invisible from the water, were the private apartments of Ptolemy III Euergetes ("the Benefactor")—the man who had hired him as head librarian.

## BENEFACTOR

Eratosthenes must have had occasion to question Egypt's reputation for stability during his first days in Alexandria. Just before he arrived, the third war between the Ptolemies and the Seleucid Empire broke out, this time over a succession dispute.

The perennial "sick man" of the Hellenistic world, the kingdom of the Seleucids had been coming apart almost since its inception. The crisis this time was occasioned by the death of the Seleucid king Antiochus II, in Asia Minor. His ex-wife, Laodice, insisted that the old king, with his dying breath, had named as successor her son Seleucus II. The sitting queen, Berenice Syra, rejected Laodice's claim and announced the ascension of her own son. She then called on her brother, Ptolemy III Euergetes, for support.

Ptolemaic kings were nothing if not devoted to their sisters. Euergetes, himself but newly crowned, rushed to Antioch at the head of a large military force. Entering his sister's private apartments, he made a grisly discovery: Berenice and her son had already been murdered by allies of Laodice.

Euergetes salvaged the situation by going on a rampage of conquest. As his army marched east, city after city surrendered before him, until by 245 he reached Babylon without encountering serious resistance. By the time the smoke cleared his rule extended deep into what is now Afghanistan; one source even asserts—dubiously—that his sway ran straight to the gates of India. Euergetes was now sovereign over a swath of territory nearly as large as Alexander's. He had to cut his victory tour short, however, when troubling news arrived from home: his Egyptian subjects were in revolt.

Proclaiming victory, Euergetes rushed back to Alexandria with a mountain of loot, including as many as twenty-five hundred Egyptian cult statues originally taken by the Persians back in the sixth century. It is likely that the rebels were emboldened by the king's long absence in Asia. A famine caused by an inadequate Nile flood in 245 aggravated native resentment against the Greek monarchy and the burdensome cost of its imperial rivalries. In any case, Euergetes acted decisively, defeating the dissidents and importing vast amounts of grain to feed the people. According to one source, he also pivoted north in time to repulse a Seleucid counterattack against Egypt. The king's Asian empire, alas, proved even more ephemeral than Alexander's: within six months all his appointed governors were deposed, and Seleucus II was crowned in Babylon.

Considering his youth and inexperience, Euergetes survived this early crisis well. We have many likenesses of all the early Ptolemies on coins and statues (see figures 3 and 4). From his portraits, old Ptolemy I Soter appears to have been a beetle-browed, droopy-eyed fellow with a jaw

Fig. 3. Left: Silver tetradrachm coin depicting Ptolemy I, third century BCE

Fig. 4. Right: Gold coin depicting Ptolemy III Euergetes BRITISH MUSEUM

thick enough to gnaw a new tip on his spear; this is clearly the battered face of a onetime grunt who had marched thousands of miles at Alexander's side. The face of his grandson, by contrast, is that of a bud-lipped aesthete.

Euergetes' baby face belied an intellect capable of heartbreaking deception. According to an account by Galen, it was Euergetes who was responsible for one of the most notorious acts of bait and switch in ancient history. After extensive negotiations, the king convinced the government of Athens to lend him what amounted to state treasures: the definitive editions of the plays of the three great dramatists: Aeschylus, Sophocles, and Euripides. To secure the loan, the Athenians demanded a deposit of fifteen talents, or approximately nine hundred pounds of solid gold. But once in possession of the manuscripts, Euergetes simply wrote off his deposit as money well spent. Like the books confiscated from foreign ships, the originals stayed in the library, and the former owners had to be content with a handsome set of copies. Euergetes, it seems, valued the plays even more than the Athenians did.

Euergetes' self-interest had its civic benefits. One of the chronic problems of old Egypt was the calendar: based on a year of 365 days, it had the disadvantage of being about six hours shorter than the actual solar year (365.24 days). For this reason, Egyptian religious holidays had a tendency to slip backward relative to the seasons. By Euergetes' time, the situation was embarrassing—a spring planting festival, for instance, would actually take place in spring only once every 1,460 years.

The problem was well understood at the time. According to Geminos of Rhodes (c. 110–40), Eratosthenes himself treated this and similar topics in a work entitled *About the Eight-Year Cycle*. The cycle referenced in the title is a system for synchronizing the ritual and solar years by adding extra months to the calendar at intervals of two years, but not in the eighth year. As this method was clumsy, Euergetes—very possibly at the advice of his new librarian— proposed a simpler four-year cycle with three years consisting of 365 days each, plus a leap year of 366 days. This "Alexandrian" year was officially accepted by the Egyptian priesthood in 239. However, widespread local mistrust of the regime in Alexandria prevented the new calendar from being wholly implemented.

Enter Julius Caesar in 48. Faced with an old Roman calendar that was itself drifting out of sync with the solar year, he recognized the Alexandrian calendar as a worthy model for a proposed revision. His so-called Julian year retained some elements of the traditional Roman calendar (such as differing lengths for the months), but adopted the fundamentally Alexandrian features of a quadrennial cycle and a year averaging 365.25 days. Caesar's scheme, in turn, remained the standard in the Western world for some 1,600 years, forming the basis of the Gregorian calendar we use today.

That Eratosthenes was the architect of Euergetes' proposed calendar—and indirectly of ours as well—is not a proven fact. It is only a likely possibility, given that he wrote about the problem, and that a solution promptly followed his arrival in Alexandria. It would perhaps be unfair to say that the Romans cribbed their calendar from "decadent" Egypt, but not unfair by much. It is, in any case, another reason to extol, not begrudge, the fundamental innovativeness of the Ptolemaic state.

Under Euergetes, with the return of Cyrene to Ptolemaic control by marriage, and the retention of many Aegean islands, as well as of Thrace, Coele-Syria, Lycia, and Caria in Asia Minor, and expansion of trade outposts into Arabia and as far south as modern Eritrea in Africa, the Ptolemaic Empire reached its widest geographical extent. The failed expedition to Asia, meanwhile, was spun as a reprise of the fondly remembered but equally unavailing campaigns of the eighteenth- and nineteenth-dynasty pharaohs (c. 1500–1200). This notion placed Euergetes in the unquestionably legitimate company of Thutmose I and Ramses II. The Canopus Decree of 239, in which the native priesthood resoundingly affirmed its support for his kingship, is best understood in the context of those twenty-five hundred cult statues rescued from Persia. Despite its turbulent start, Euergetes' reign—and Eratosthenes' tenure as head librarian—was on a secure footing.


THE MERMAID

There is a slogan posted in English all over modern Alexandria that reads, "Alexandria is the mermaid of the Mediterranean Sea." The metaphor is blunt, but undeniable. Like a mermaid, the city is half fantasy, teasing us across a sea of myth. She is irresistible because we can't stop imagining the better parts she keeps hidden under the water.

I wanted to come to Alexandria as Eratosthenes had in 245. In March 2007 I was obliged to travel by plane instead of boat, because there is no longer any regular ferry service from Athens. This may be an economic inevitability in a time of discount air travel, but it is also a historical absurdity—not being able to sail into Alexandria is like not being permitted to drive into Los Angeles. The only direct flight from Greece, moreover, left in the middle of the night, and arrived at three A.M. And so, like an underworld courier delivering a bag of ill-gotten cash, the modern traveler must steal out of Athens in the dark, and slip into Alexandria when nobody is watching.

Flying in at night has one big advantage: my first glimpse of the city revealed her exactly as I had come to know her on the map. First come the scattered lights of the ships at anchor, massed at the city's doorstep like the campfires of an invading army. Then, with a thrill of recognition, I watched the curves of Alexandria's two harbors slide into view, their outlines looping like an Arabic epigram inked in incandescent gold. Though rightly known in her time as a city of lights, never in antiquity could she have shone quite like this.

But in most ways, time has not been kind to Alexandria. To appreciate what has been lost in twenty-three centuries, imagine a certain city in north-central France—and take away the Louvre, the Eiffel Tower, the Sorbonne, the Arc de Triomphe, Napoleon's Tomb, and Notre Dame. Take away the seat of national political power. Take away the intelligentsia, couture, and better restaurants (but keep the catacombs, the cemeteries, and a few broken columns from the Pantheon). Imagine that all the bridges over the Seine have been buried in silt and Île de la Cité is just a slight bump on the landscape. What would be left might be a perfectly charming provincial city, but would it still be Paris?

None of this is meant to cast blame on Alexandria's current residents. The city has now been Arab far longer than she was Greek, yet for sheer, stupefying destructiveness, the Arabs stand near the bottom of the list of the city's victimizers. At the very top come the mobs of early Christian fanatics—the ones who fought turf battles over the Caesareum, razed the Temple of Serapis, scattered the contents of the Great Library's daughter annex, and, with the brutal gang murder of the philosopher Hypatia in 411 CE, helped to snuff out a tradition of intellectual activity that stretched back seven centuries. Also on the list are the punitive armies of Rome, the fecklessness of Byzantium, Ottoman indifference, and British gunboats. Finally, we come to the jealousy and mostly benign neglect of her masters in Cairo, to whom Alexandria and her port were, at best, redundant, and at worst, a reminder of Egypt's foreign-dominated past.

Granted, no great capital is just the sum of her institutions and monuments. As I came to know Alexandria in my brief time there, I saw that something more important—the business of life—has not disappeared from the city. Sailors still tend their wooden boats in the Great Harbor, and gangs of line-fishermen still haul their catch from the shallows offshore. The Ptolemaic avenues with their grand colonnades are gone, but the streets of Alexandria are just as crowded and chaotic as the ancient accounts describe. The draperies and veils of today's Muslim women would not have been unfamiliar to their ancient counterparts—nor the way that some of these emblems of modesty are allowed to cling to the hips, complemented by fancy heeled shoes, or made moot by furtive glances. That Alexandria has survived at all represents a significant victory, given that the city, with a population of perhaps half a million in Cleopatra's time, was reduced to just four thousand souls in Napoleon's, clinging to just a fraction of its original area.

When I told people at home that I was traveling to Egypt in the spring of 2007, a few were intrigued, but most were concerned. "Travel safe," my agent wrote; asked others, "Aren't you afraid?" I had visited Cairo and Upper Egypt in 2000, and had some experience traveling in other parts of the Middle East, so I knew that the chances of suffering from crime were worse in almost any U.S. city, and that anti-American bias was more likely to be encountered in Athens than in Alexandria.

But the Alexandrines outdid even my rosy expectations of hospitality and courtesy. Walking down the street, the typical American with his sunglasses, bridal-white tennis shoes, and hopeful cluelessness is about as obvious as a stray giraffe. Yet the spectacle draws almost incomprehensible good will—"Welcome to Egypt!" and "Welcome to Alex!" come from all sides. Catch anyone's eye and you'll get a smile; stare into a crowded minibus and every passenger will wave. Learn a few words of Arabic and you're the Tadeusz Kościuszko of foreigners, perhaps worthy of enshrinement on the Corniche.

Perhaps this is all for show, and doesn't reflect what the average Egyptian really thinks of Americans. A useful rule of thumb in this regard is to forget the adults and pay attention to the behavior of the children. Below a certain age, kids don't have enough guile to filter what their parents tell them in private. From them, you get a peek into what's in the hearts of the grown-ups, buried under all the emotions and rationalizations that come with adult concerns.

Heading to Fort Qaitbey on my first morning in Alexandria, to the site of the legendary Pharos, I encountered scores of children out on school field trips. Most of them thought my presence was a good opportunity to try out their one or two English phrases: *What is your name?* and *Where are you from?* are the favorites. Before long I was signing autographs, posing for pictures, and being told how hand-

some I was by the more forward—yet somehow still outwardly
discreet—young women. This, it appears, is what it's like to lead
K-Fed's charmed life; for one brief hour, I could have been Marc
Antony, Cleopatra's Roman lover, or that other Marc Anthony, the
one attached to Jennifer Lopez.

PTOLEMYLAND

The point of my visit, though, was to see what I could see of
Alexandria's grand past. Thanks to an ongoing program of salvage
archaeology in the Great Harbor, such remnants are now easier
than ever to find. Fragments of pink Aswan granite from the
Pharos are built into the reconstructed Fort Qaitbey, which stands
on the site of the original lighthouse. Monumental statuary that
once graced the Pharos precinct has been raised from the harbor
floor and set up in various places in the city, such as the
fragments near the little Roman theater at Kom al-
Dikkah, and the colossal figure of Ptolemy II erected
outside the modern Biblioteca Alexandrina in the
old palace district (see figure 5). All of the salvaged
figures were scoured by the swirling currents near
the harbor mouth for centuries, and therefore have
the smoothed-over, hollow-eyed look of creatures
snatched, to their surprise, from the grip of
oblivion. But they do give us a sense of the
hardware that greeted visitors sailing in under the shadow of the Lighthouse. In his
time, Pompey passed these statues on the
way to his betrayal; Caesar, pursuing his rival, gazed at these faces too, and probably
pondered the quality of the monarchs they
represented.

*Fig. 5. Ancient monolithic statue of a Ptolemic ruler, salvaged* ▶
*from the harbor floor near the site of the Pharos. The colossus now*
*stands in front of the new Biblioteca Alexandrina.*

And what of the city's old topography? General subsidence of the waterfront, combined with a rise in elevation inland, have erased the city's original outlines. The broad sweep of the harbors remains, but the quays where Eratosthenes landed are now underwater. Today, where the treasure of continents once passed, divers and snorkelers swim the trash-strewn shallows in search of artifacts, and wrecks of fishing boats nod and rot in the gentle surf.

Likewise obscured is the city's legendary wealth. Augustus boasted that he found Rome a city of brick and left it one of marble; in Alexandria, history has taken a city of marble and left it one of tin, plaster, and tar paper. Disheveled piles surge toward the sea, shouldering each other for a place on the shore. A fine mist of pulverized concrete seems to cover everything, and the once salubrious climate is overwhelmed by smog. For some reason, I arrived when all the sidewalks had been pulled up, rendering the only refuge from the city's murderous traffic a shambling crater-scape. It's untidy, but at least it is genuinely so—thankfully, the twee, sanitized historic districts ("Ptolemyland") we mistake for downtowns in the West have not yet made it to Egypt.

Primary thoroughfares have a way of persisting through the indignities of time—though Manhattan Island has been entirely resurfaced by human hands, the old Indian trail through it persists as Broadway. Tradition has it that modern Sharia Nabi Danyal corresponds to the Street of the Soma, ancient Alexandria's primary north–south byway. It stands to reason, then, that somewhere along that street should be a spot corresponding to the ancient city's main crossing, the confluence of the Street of the Soma and the east–west-running Canopic Way.

Heading into Africa from my harborside hotel, I entered a warren of narrow streets throbbing with activity. Instead of the franchised blandness of American cities, Alexandria is a city of mom-and-pop stores, all with signage screaming for attention, their wares encroaching on the streets. Fiat taxis run the gauntlet, honk-ing promiscuously above Arabic monologs droning from speakers. Men watch from lawn chairs or stand, hands balled in their pock-ets. The heads of the women are almost universally covered, with a few completely draped, peering through their slitted abayas or ut-terly invisible under closed hoods. One wants to respect cultural differences, but the effect here is dismaying—the city that gave us Cleopatra now obliges women to hide their faces.

Reaching the train station, I realized I had gone too far. I doubled back toward the bookstalls, puzzled by the disparity between the map and what I saw. The mosque that was supposed to be on the site of Alexander's tomb, the Masgid al-Nabi Danyal, should be on the east side of the street. After a few trips back and forth, I realized my mis-take: the mosque was there all the time, but I had walked right past it.

Masgid al-Nabi Danyal is a low, modern, meringue-colored structure, set four shallow steps above street level and far back in a courtyard. It is easy to overlook, lying as it does in the shadow of a neighboring high-rise, which was then only a frame of reinforced concrete. To look at it, it's hard to believe this unobtrusive struc-ture may lie above the storied final resting place of Alexander the Great (and, perhaps, the biblical prophet Daniel as well). Kings and commoners alike made pilgrimages to this spot to gaze at the con-queror's unspoiled remains in their golden sarcophagus. Caesar prayed there, and as Augustus bent to kiss the great man's face, he accidentally broke the corpse's nose. Today, the setting is dwarfed by a cellular transmission tower.

The spot corresponding to the famous crossroads lies just a few yards north of the mosque. Since it was known as the Canopic Way, the city's main east–west artery has been renamed many times—a century ago, E. M. Forster complained that the previous name, the Rue de la Porte Rosette, was being changed to "the unmeaning Rue Fouad Premier, thus breaking one of the few links that bound

[the] city to the past." Though many of the locals still call it Fouad Street, it is now known variously as Tariq Abd el-Nasser, Tariq al-Hurriyyah, and Ishak Nadim Street. Whatever you call it, the street is still as arrow straight as it was twenty-three hundred years ago, when it ran between the Gate of the Sun in the east and the Gate of the Moon in the west. Today is it a speedway for black-and-yellow taxis taking advantage of limited pedestrian access. One can only imagine the speeds the drivers could have reached on the original Canopic Way, which was at least twice as wide as the existing thoroughfare.

There's a buff-colored neoclassical structure on the northwest corner of the intersection. Though the grand colonnade Achilles Tatius described is gone (see pages 10–11), the modern building has a few Ionic columns standing on massive volutes. Fetching my camera, I snapped a picture of what I took to be the last columns to stand on the old Canopic Way.

### THE WORLD RECKONER

The world known to the ancient Greeks was a tiny place. Geographical knowledge in the classical period of fifth to fourth centuries BCE—the times of Socrates, Plato, Pericles, Sophocles, and Aristotle—was not much broader than in Homer's day, four hundred years earlier. All told, the Greeks knew the Mediterranean Sea from Gibraltar to Syria; they knew that the European continent stretched north into an icy waste, and that Africa stretched south into a trackless, infernal desert. Of Asia they appreciated the vast extent of the Persian Empire, and they had an inkling of the Indian subcontinent beyond. But of the rest of the Old World, including central and southern Africa beyond Nubia, the northern half of Europe, and all of central and east Asia, they knew little or nothing (see figure 6).

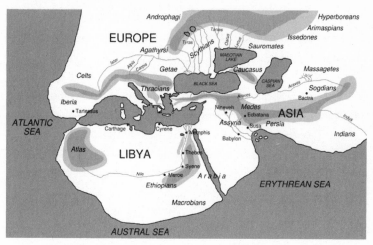

*Fig. 6. The world known to the Greek historian Herodotus, fifth century* BCE

The conquests of Alexander in the late fourth century gave the Greeks firsthand experience of Persia, India, and the Asian kingdoms lying between. The voyage of Nearchus, who was commissioned by Alexander in 325 to reconnoiter a possible sea route for the invasion of Africa, taught the Greeks much about the coastal regions of the Arabian Sea and the Persian Gulf. Around 300, an explorer named Pytheas sailed a ship through the Straits of Gibraltar, turned north, and circumnavigated the British Isles. He referred to other lands beyond, but scholars continue to dispute which places (Iceland? Norway? Denmark?) correspond to his descriptions.

Herodotus recounts an earlier voyage that surpassed Nearchus and Pytheas in audacity: around 600, a Phoenician fleet hired by Pharaoh Necho actually circumnavigated the African continent. The voyage supposedly took three years, with frequent stops in the foul-sailing season to build temporary settlements and sow crops for the next year's push.

Herodotus, who is not exactly renowned for his skepticism, relates the story but discounts it—he can't accept the idea that the Phoenicians sailed so far south that the sun rose and set in the northern half of the sky. But for us this is just the sort of key detail that makes the story convincing. Necho's expedition probably did happen, but Herodotus's guardedness suggests it added little to the store of Greek geographical knowledge. Most authorities, including Aristotle (384–322), continued to believe that India was somehow connected with Africa, rendering such a circumnavigation of the latter impossible from the Red Sea. The margins of the Greek world continued to remain dark, narrow, and filled with sea monsters, giant gold-digging ants, and men with faces in the middle of their chests.

It was not long after this that a certain Greek polymath named Eratosthenes of Cyrene (c. 285–204 BCE) calculated the circumference of our planet. Indeed, he did so accurately, coming at least to within 10 percent of the modern polar measurement of about 24,860 miles, and perhaps as close as 1 percent. He accomplished this without the complex surveying equipment available later to the Romans, let alone GPS receivers, laser range finders, or satellites. He did it, in fact, with nothing more than a sundial, a compass, and a scrap of paper (or, more likely, a scrap of papyrus) to make a simple calculation.

The Roman naturalist Pliny the Elder (23–79 CE) praised Eratosthenes as "a man who was peculiarly well skilled in all the more subtle parts of learning, and in this above everything else, and a person whom I perceive to be approved by everyone." He further declared that Eratosthenes' earth measurement was "supported by such subtle arguments that we cannot refuse our assent." Indeed, it was one of the greatest feats of practical geometric inference in history. Fortunately, it was also widely known in antiquity— we know about it in detail because one of Eratosthenes' successors, an otherwise obscure mathematician named Cleomedes, left a lengthy description (Eratosthenes' own treatise, *On the Measurement of the Earth,* has been lost.)

As we shall see, his work continued to have repercussions down to the eve of the Renaissance, as Columbus prepared to sail west to China. Geography didn't catch up to Eratosthenes until true ocean-going ships proved his calculations directly, almost two thousand years after he was born. To say what he found was "ahead of its time" would therefore be a squalid understatement. His experiment belonged to a different world entirely—a world light-years ahead of the floating disks and squat cylinders previous ancient authorities had imagined our planet to be.

GEODESY

There is virtually no math in this book. However, to put Eratosthenes' geodesy (a fancy word for "earth measurement") in context, it is essential to understand what went into his calculations.

Eratosthenes was a foreigner in Egypt, appointed as only the third head librarian since the founding of the Museum in Alexandria. The latter was an unprecedented institution in the Greek world—a place devoted not only to the religious cult of the Muses, but to advancing human knowledge in the broadest sense. The foundation, purpose, and organization of the Museum (and the associated Great Library) will be discussed in some depth below. What is most relevant here is that when Eratosthenes arrived in Egypt he must have heard a curious fact: somewhere near Syene (modern Aswan), there existed an open well into which the sun shone directly to its bottom but once a year—at noon on the summer solstice, when the sun was highest in the sky in the northern hemisphere.

The importance of this fact can be understood by looking at Box 1 on page 27 (geometriphobes should feel free to skip the details).

Eratosthenes' limpid inference does conceal a few additional assumptions, and some difficulties. It assumes that the well in Syene was sunk perpendicularly to the surface of the earth. It posits that Syene lies at the latitude where the sun is overhead on the summer solstice (that is, at the Tropic of Cancer), and that Syene and Alexandria lie on the same line of longitude, both of which suppositions are only approximately true. More crucially, it assumes that the earth is a sphere and that the sun's rays strike it in parallel lines—assumptions that seem safe today, but as we shall see below, were far from settled issues in Eratosthenes' time.

As for the difficulties, even this apparently simple procedure taxed the primitive measuring technologies of the period. Measuring angles amounted to eyeballing shadows on a compass, which might do for gross approximation but could not yield very accurate results. Fixing accurate distances between cities was a difficult proposition before the advent of modern surveying techniques. More often than not, such distances were expressed merely as approximations based on traveling speeds—that is, if it took a caravan ten days to reach its destination at one hundred stades a day, the distance must be one thousand stades. (As we shall see, Eratosthenes probably had a more firm basis for the distance he used between Syene and Alexandria.)

The most pedantic difficulty—and the one that has undoubtedly spilled the most scholarly ink—is the question of which version of the stade Eratosthenes used in his work. In the days before international standardization of such units, there were several candidates. There was a short stade, equivalent to one-fortieth of an Egyptian schoenus, three hundred royal cubits, or 157.2 meters; there was a somewhat longer Attic stade of 177.6 meters, and a so-called long stade of 185 meters. The figure of 252,000 Egyptian "short" stades is closest to the true circumference of the earth; even the Attic stade would have gotten Eratosthenes within 15 percent

## BOX 1: ERATOSTHENES' GEODESY

The essential principle behind Eratosthenes' reasoning can be understood by anyone with an elementary knowledge of geometry. On the scale of diffi-

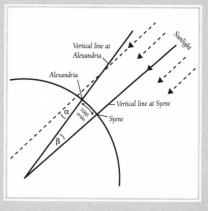

*Fig. 7*

culty seen in the math section of a typical college entrance exam, the problem probably would rank around the middle. But like many innovations, the solution is remarkable not for its inherent difficulty, but because it took one remarkable mind to apprehend its power.

If the sun is direct-ly overhead at Syene on the solstice, then the simultaneous angle of the sun's shadow back at Alexandria, α, must by definition be the same as the angle β between two lines drawn from the earth's center to Syene and Alexandria. If angle β is known, and we know that the complete circumference of a circle contains 360 degrees (a convention borrowed by the Greeks from the Babylonians), then we can set up a simple proportion:

$$\frac{\text{angle } \beta}{360} = \frac{\textit{Linear distance from Syene to Alexandria}}{\textit{Circumference of the earth}}$$

Eratosthenes took the distance from Syene to Alexandria to be 5,040 stades (a *stade* was an ancient unit of measure approximately equal to 600 modern feet). Using some vertically plumb object

*continued …*

at Alexandria on the day of the solstice, he measured angle α, and therefore angle β, at 7.2 degrees. Knowing three of the terms in the equation above, he was then in a position to calculate the final term, the circumference of the earth. His final result, 252,000 stades, works out to 24,662.2 miles—just under 1 percent shy of the modern polar measurement of about 24,859.8 miles.

of the true measurement. In any case, as we shall see below, there is good reason to think Eratosthenes used the Egyptian unit.

In the rest of this book we will explore these assumptions and difficulties. In some cases, we will find that Eratosthenes was prescient in his thinking; in others, that he was sloppy or mistaken, but that his errors had the fortuitous effect of canceling each other out. We will try to understand his choices by looking carefully at what is known about him and his world—his birthplace, his adoptive homes in Athens and Alexandria, his predecessors, colleagues, and enemies. Occasionally, we will not shy away from using some narrative imagination in reconstructing this background, both because little has come down to us about Eratosthenes himself, and because the truth is not always reducible to the literal facts. In this way, it will become clear that even the most transformative, elegant-seeming solution, appearing by inspiration two thousand years before its time, was the result of a struggle.

## 2. A ZOO OF UNIVERSES

*[Anaxagoras] was eminent for his noble birth and for his riches, and still more so for his magnanimity, inasmuch as he gave up all his patrimony to his relations . . . and at last he abandoned [his estate] entirely, and devoted himself to the contemplation of subjects of natural philosophy, disregarding politics. So that once when some said to him, "You have no affection for your country," "Be silent," said he, "for I have the greatest affection for my country," pointing up to heaven.*

—DIOGENES LAERTIUS, *Life of Anaxagoras*, II

THE ANCIENT Greeks were relative latecomers to the discipline of astronomy. Mesopotamia had a legacy of astronomical observation going back at least a thousand years before the classical era. Babylonian records for the movements of the sun, moon, and planets were impressively comprehensive by Eratosthenes' time. Their mathematical treatments of the motions of heavenly bodies were based on a sexagesimal (sixty) number system that is the root of our sixty-second minute, sixty-minute hour, and 360-degree circle. Babylonian astronomy displayed an arithmetical refinement that, in some ways, complemented the mostly geometrical approach of the Greeks. The deep antiquity of the Babylonian tradition is somewhat exaggerated, however: their most impressive work in mathematical astronomy dates after 300, roughly contemporaneous with developments in the Hellenistic world.

What seems to differentiate the Babylonians from the Greeks is that the former were primarily interested in using their observations to calibrate their religious calendar and to mine celestial events, such as star risings and eclipses, for their astrological significance. They seemed to have adopted a "black-box" approach to astronomy, being concerned primarily with visible phenomena, and to have paid little attention to formulating detailed systematic models of the mechanics that underlay what they could observe. "So far as we can interpret the somewhat mystical references that have come down to us," wrote a modern historian,

> the Babylonian cosmology would seem to have represented the earth as a circular plane surrounded by a great circular river, beyond which rose an impregnable barrier of mountains, and resting upon an infinite sea of waters. . . . But the precise mechanism through which the observed revolution of the heavenly bodies was effected remains here, as with the Egyptian cosmology, somewhat conjectural. The simple fact would appear to be that, for the Chaldeans [one of the dominant peoples of Babylonia] . . . despite their most careful observations of the tangible phenomena of the heavens, no really satisfactory mechanical conception of the cosmos was attainable.

Likewise the ancient Egyptians' approach to understanding celestial events remained primarily mythological (they believed that the sky goddess, Nut, was upheld by Shu, the god of the air). As a result, their attainments in astronomical theory seem to have paled in comparison to their achievements in engineering, medicine, and statecraft. A "universal" compendium of astronomical objects produced by one Amenhope around 1100 includes the stars in but five constellations; observed patterns in the risings of other star groups (called "decans") allowed the Egyptians to tell time at night to within an hour's accuracy. Though their use of stellar and solar observations to orient temples and pyramids has been a mainstay in Western pseudoscientific conjecture for centuries, such observations led to no known school or corpus of systematic cosmological thought. Possible reasons lie beyond the scope of this discussion, except to note that this in no way implies some deficiency in Egyptian genius or language. The pertinent point is worth emphasizing: though the Alexandrian Greeks such as Eratosthenes worked within the geographical confines of Egypt, they were not drawing from some deep well of native wisdom.

The Greek intellectual world, on the other hand, was almost frantically preoccupied with competing models of the ultimate configuration and substance of the cosmos. As Plato wrote in his *Timaeus,* "to attempt to tell of all this [the working of the cosmos] without a visible representation of the heavenly system would be labor in vain." The first of these representations emerged in the Ionian city of Miletus—a place on the far end of the Persian Royal Road from Mesopotamia, and therefore well positioned to receive astronomical inspiration from the east. Thales of Miletus (640–572) imagined that all things emerged from the element of water, and that the earth was a flat disk afloat on a universal ocean. His pupil, Anaximander (611–545), developed an idea that the habitable surface of the earth lay at the end of a squat disk, its diameter three times its height, which in turn floated in the middle of an infinite universe. The sun, in Anaximander's view, was not a spherical body, but a world-girdling wheel of fire; the bright orb we see in the sky is just a hole through which we glimpse the conflagration beyond. That Babylonian astronomy was not the only eastern influence on Anaximander is suggested by correspondences between his model and certain elements of native Persian religion, such as those preserved in Zoroastrianism.

Where old Thales saw water as the ultimate source of all matter, Anaximander's student Anaximenes (d. ~525) chose another elemental substance as the basis of his universe. His cosmological theory described a flat earth suspended in air, with the other celestial objects lofted above, like leaves blown on a universal wind. Leucippus (480–420) was the first to argue that the universe is made of tiny, indivisible particles (atoms); his cosmological model was geocentric, with a flat visible portion of the earth resting on a round base, somewhat like a covered bowl or drum, and his sun circling the earth in a sphere beyond that of the other planets. We know of Leucippus's work only through that of his student, Democritus of Abdera (450–370). Democritus, who further developed his master's atomist theories, also had his own pet cosmology, including a Thalian throwback to a flat-disk earth, floating in air.

With the emergence of powerful Greek city-states on the mainland and in "greater Greece" (Sicily and southern Italy) in the fifth century, the Ionian schools declined in importance. Perhaps the most important of their successors was Pythagoras (c. 580–500), a semimythical figure alleged to have studied under Thales before going on to start his own institution in the southern Italian city of Croton. The history of the Pythagorean School, including the question of how much Pythagorean philosophy can be attributed to the man himself or to followers in some cases generations removed, is too large a topic to do justice here. That the curriculum seems to be a strange agglomeration of geometry, myth, and mysticism may be blamed on the school itself, where lectures were said to have been delivered from behind a curtain and questioning the teacher was forbidden.

The Pythagoreans held that the universe can be apprehended entirely in terms of numerical relations (and more precisely, whole-number relations). Their cosmology developed over time, but was notable for positing a perfectly spherical earth either in the center of the universe, or rotating around an ideal central fire. Their preoccupation with numbers also inspired them to place the five known planets (Mercury, Venus, Mars, Jupiter, and Saturn) on an equal footing with the earth, sun, and moon. The rotation of each body, along its own proportionately scaled distance from the center, was likened to the intervals on a vast musical scale, and thought to give voice to the famous "music of the spheres."

Like that of the Babylonians, the Pythagorean universe seems more a construction based on mysticism and aesthetics than the result of empirical study. Most relevant here, though, is that the Pythagoreans were willing to entertain the notion of a spherical earth, and a nongeocentric cosmos. Nor was this the extent of their radicalism: a later Pythagorean, a certain Hicetas of Syracuse (400–335), not only argued against a static geocentric cosmos, but held that *only* the earth moved, with all the apparent motions of the planets and stars attributable to earth's rotation on its axis.

The theory of "homocentric spheres," attributed to Eudoxus of Cnidus (c. 390–340), has been called "the beginning of scientific astronomy," insofar as it attempted to supply a single consistent explanation for the observed motion of all heavenly bodies. Eudoxus held that the universe was a nested set of twenty-seven rigid (and presumably invisible) spheres rotating around the earth. The motions of sun, moon, stars, and planets were explained by assuming that each body was embedded in the surface of a rotating sphere that was furthermore connected to an enveloping sphere with a different axis and inherent motion. (A modern analogy might be the spacewalk simulators in some modern science museums, in which the visitor is strapped into a frame that rotates inside another free-turning frame, and subjected to wild gyrations.) Eudoxus argued that if enough nested spheres were assumed (in his system, four for each planet) even the most complex planetary motions could be accounted for.

Though clearly ingenious, the Eudoxan system was liable to the simple objection that some bodies, most evidently the moon and planets, change in size and/or brightness, suggesting they are not fixed in a rigid frame but move freely in space. Later thinkers attempted to salvage the model by adding more spheres (Aristotle argued for as few as forty-seven and as many as fifty-five), but these changes failed to address the fundamental problem that direct observation of the heavens contradicted the theory.

Still, support for the Eudoxan system was far wider and longer-lasting than for heliocentrism, which made its debut with Eratosthenes' older contemporary, Aristarchus of Samos (310–230). Aristarchus proposed a universe with the sun at its center and the stars set in a sphere that was unimaginably distant. Though he was a respected observer of the sky, and his model had the virtue of offering a simple way to explain many puzzling astronomical phenomena, his suggestion appears to have landed in learned society with an audible thud. The notion of the earth whirling and hurtling through the cosmos was, in the end, fatally counterintuitive to the ancient mind. How could the earth not lie at the center of the universe, critics asked, if all heavy objects on our planet tend to fall toward its center? If the earth rotates, why are the paths of flying objects, such as arrows, not visibly affected by its movement? We know of only one notable astronomer of the Hellenistic era, Seleucus of Seleucia (c. 190), who seems to have followed Aristarchus's lead; according to Plutarch, he even contrived to prove the heliocentric hypothesis, though his exact arguments are now lost to us.

Eratosthenes' contemporary, Apollonius of Perga (c. 262–190), was called "the Great Geometer" for his fundamental work on the properties of intersecting cones and planes (so-called conic sections). Many historians also credit him with at least one noteworthy contribution to astronomy—namely a universal model that put the planets in orbit around the sun, which in turn revolved around the earth. Indeed, his system precisely anticipated one put forward by Tycho Brahe some eighteen centuries later. What endured about it, however, was the recognition that envisioning the heavenly bodies as being in orbit around a point that, in turn, revolved around the earth (an "epicycle") had much utility in explaining the apparent back-and-forth motions of the planets against the background stars.

Naturally, Eratosthenes could have known nothing of what would eventually become perhaps the most highly developed of the cosmological models of antiquity, that of Claudius Ptolemaeus★ (85–165 CE). Building on Apollonius's epicycles, and using the precise observations of his predecessor, Hipparchus of Nicaea (190–120), Ptolemaeus developed a geocentric model that remained scientific orthodoxy until the Renaissance. His system, as expounded in his thirteen-volume opus *The Almagest,* had much influence both in Europe and in the Islamic world, and was later adopted as dogma by the Catholic Church. This was unfortunate not only because Ptolemaeus's system was wrong, but because it seemed to endorse a measurement of the earth's circumference of 18,000 miles—a significant underestimate.

Ptolemaeus's epochal influence has had the effect of making ancient astronomy seem, to us, a lot less diverse than it was. By the third century BCE, Eratosthenes was heir to a rich heritage of possible universes. His earth could have been a flat disk (Thales), disklike with a raised rim (Anaximenes), a cylinder (Anaximander), an object shaped like a snare drum (Leucippus), a body extending infinitely downward (Xenophanes), a shallow funnel (Democritus), or a sphere (Pythagoras). His sun could have been located just beyond the moon (Pythagoras, Anaxagoras, et al.) or farther away than Saturn (Leucippus); it could have been a nearby object just

---

★This person is often referred to as "Ptolemy." Here he will be called Claudius Ptolemaeus, or Ptolemaeus, to avoid confusion with the royal Ptolemies.

one foot across (Heraclitus), or a distant window on a vast wheel of fire (Anaximander). Eratosthenes' cosmos could have been geocentric (Thales and others), heliocentric (Aristarchus), centered on "pure fire" (Pythagoras), floating on air (Anaximenes), formed from a set of nested spheres (Eudoxus), characterized by epicycles (Apollonius), or something else that has not come down to us.

Admittedly, most of these older ideas would have seemed decidedly quaint by Eratosthenes' time. There is a famous story, recounted by the Roman-era writer Plutarch, of how Pericles (495–429) reassured the helmsman of his ship during a solar eclipse by demonstrating the prosaic reality behind the spectacle. Holding up his cloak between the helmsman and the sun, he asked, "Do you find *this* frightening? Then why fear the other?" Pericles' astronomy lesson, which was probably inspired by the teachings of his friend and mentor, Anaxagoras of Clazomenae (c. 500–428), suggests that modern-sounding conceptions of the universe (for example, that the heavenly bodies are physical objects that move freely in space and may obstruct one another, and that the sun is more distant from the earth than the moon) were current in educated circles by the classical era. By Alexander's time, the rise of major philosophical schools, such as the Academy and Lyceum in Athens, began to introduce a degree of conformity on cosmological questions.

Yet however "quaint" the universes of the archaic or classical sages might have seemed by the third century, they were far from empirically *disproven*. As late as the mid-fourth century, Aristotle felt it worth his time to vigorously engage notions of a flat earth, an earth floating on air or water, and the Pythagorean view of a "central fire" around which the earth moved. The observational data were improving, but still crude; many were still content to paper over theoretical difficulties with teleological nostrums (for example, Aristotle explained why fewer concentric spheres were necessary to account for the motion of the moon than that of Jupiter by asserting that the moon was "more good" than Jupiter). By Eratosthenes' time, most of those who thought seriously about such questions believed in the sphericity of the earth. But as with the reception of ideas of global warming or evolution in our own time, it was not always serious people who dominated public discussion of such issues.

In any case, for the purposes of Eratosthenes' geodesic experiment the only necessary astronomical assumptions were the sphericity of the earth and a relatively distant sun—notions that could be accommodated by a number of competing models. That the sun was larger and more distant than the moon was generally accepted by most contemporary authorities. Aristarchus put the diameter of the sun at about seven times the earth's, and its distance at about two million miles; Eratosthenes' own estimate of the solar distance is unclear from the sources, but may have been as great as ninety million miles—astonishingly close to the truth (see discussion below). From the comfortable vantage of modernity, such magnitudes seem safe bets. But they were hardly the only wares for sale in the heated marketplace that was ancient Greek cosmological debate.

### THE END OF SCIENCE

Before we end this gallop through early astronomy, it's worth asking why the ancient Greeks didn't achieve more in their study of the heavens. We now know that Aristarchus's sun-centered cosmos, with the stars set at a practically infinite distance from the observer, was absolutely correct, yet we have little evidence that anyone else thought his model worth proving. Indeed, not only in astronomy but in other realms of inquiry, notably mechanical technology and medicine, the ancients seem almost perverse in their aversion to stumbling on the truth.

They were certainly ingenious enough to do so; by the time of the Ptolemies the Greeks were on their way to grasping the principles of steam-powered machines; the Roman-era writer Vitruvius tells us that an Alexandrian named Ctesibius had invented devices powered by compressed air, including a siege cannon and a water pump for fighting fires, by early in the third century BCE. In his treatise on pneumatics, the Roman-era engineer Heron of Alexandria describes a fire-powered mechanism for opening heavy temple doors, a steam turbine, and an automated puppet theater that rolled itself out, presented a show, and closed itself, all without human intervention. We will hear of other clever contraptions in our discussion below. Yet the principles behind all these devices, like Aristarchus's heliocentrism, died on the vine.

The answer to the puzzle lies not in the answers ancient minds were capable of producing, but in the questions they asked. Of "truths" like geocentrism, the four elements of the material universe, or the body's four "humors," one classicist has asked

Why prove them? It is self-evident [to the Greeks] that they're there! Greek astronomy is an astonishing achievement. But of course it was based . . . on assumptions that were totally false. There just wasn't sufficient reason to invent, for example, the telescope when you had an astronomical theory which, with extraordinary mathematics, could fit the appearances. You can save the appearances with Ptolemaic astronomy.

To those who called for empirical proof, Plato replied, "He, however, who should attempt to verify all this by experiment, would forget the difference of the human and divine nature. For God only has the knowledge and also the power. . . ."

Thus we confront a characteristic bent of the ancient mind—that tendency to equate what *appears* to be with what *ought* to be, without being distracted along the way with what *is*. In the early third century Herophilus of Chalcedon, the brilliant Alexandrian anatomist, invented a device for timing the pulse. This was essentially a portable water clock. If used as part of a systematic program of research in disease and physiology, Herophilus's timer might have taught ancient doctors much about the circulation of the blood. Yet this assumes that Herophilus was asking modern questions of his data. According to Galen of Pergamum (129–c. 200 CE), Herophilus used the device only to refine his preexisting theory of fever types—differentiating fevers that caused the blood to "caper" like a gazelle, "crawl" like an ant, or "leap" like a goat. This begat a tradition of colorful but useless metaphoric descriptions that preoccupied physicians for centuries.

All of which brings us to the key point: the ancients, particularly in the classical period, had no notion that equates exactly with our modern conception of "science." Men inquired about the nature of the world, to be sure, but they considered such questions to be inseparable from philosophy, and by extension, from ethics. The search for scientific truth was never an end in itself, but a means toward attaining the wisdom necessary to achieve peace of mind. When Plato, for instance, derides "ordinary" geometricians who "have in view practice only, and are always speaking, in a narrow and ridiculous manner, of squaring and extending and applying and the like," he does so because "they confuse the necessities of geometry with those of daily life; whereas *knowledge* is the real object of the whole science." Epicurus likewise declared that "there is no end to the knowledge of things in the sky . . . than peace of mind and firm conviction." Rather than pursuing any single "correct" explanation of some phenomenon, Epicurus advised simultaneous acceptance of any number of explanations, as long as they were all consistent with observation. Indeed, he saw pursuit of a single truth as a symptom of an unbalanced mind, tantamount to superstition!

From our modern perspective, it is easy to dismiss the ancients' qualms about the utility of science. We tend to count the diseases conquered, the planets explored, the drudgeries banished, and to assert that the greater good is served by seeing things our way. Indeed, it is more or less taken as modern gospel that profound scientific truth frequently accomplishes the opposite of what Epicurus recommended, costing us peace of mind. The disconcerting lessons of heliocentrism, of evolutionary theory, and of relativity and quantum theory are frequently cited cases in point. These constructs may mock our self-importance, but approaching the world in any other way seems painfully naïve.

The ancient philosopher would have had a ready answer. While impressed by the expertise that has given the world air-conditioning, TiVo, and nuclear weapons, he would still argue that pursuing scientific truth as an end in itself, shorn of its purpose to soothe our uncertainties, is at best a profoundly inhuman activity. At worst, it is a path to madness. And if we are being honest, we would have to agree he has a point. A couple of centuries of material progress haven't been long enough for us to see the final bill for our triumphs.

### SHADES OF ALEXANDER

For all the achievements of Alexander the Great (356–323), dying young in Babylon was perhaps his wisest career move. With his passing, he evaded the overwhelming consequence of his success: the challenge of consolidating a polyglot empire unprecedented in size and comprising peoples who, by and large, despised each other.

His corps of generals and provincial governors was filled with ambitious men with access to manpower and vast amounts of cash. The Persians, of course, were only defeated on the battlefield (defeat and conquest are, alas, not the same thing; other Persian empires would arise in time). On the eastern borders of Alexander's domain, the brilliant Chandragupta (in Greek, Sandrocottus, c. 340–298) would amass an army that dwarfed that of Porus, the minor Indian rajah who gave the Macedonians such a difficult fight at the battle of the Hydaspes. (According to Pliny, Chandragupta's army included six hundred thousand infantry, thirty thousand cavalry, and *nine thousand* war elephants.) Chandragupta's defeat of Alexander's successors in northwest India and modern Afghanistan established the northwest frontier of his Mauryan Empire; how Alexander himself, had he lived, would have dealt with this challenge is one of ancient history's great what-if's. Given all this, it is perhaps understandable that Alexander dreamed instead of going in the other direction—that is, of building a thousand ships and invading Carthage and Italy. If such a campaign had succeeded, it would only have increased the difficulty of holding his domain together.

As it happened, the death of Alexander unleashed a pack of contenders who spent the next several decades fighting over his legacy. Alexander's official descendants, his infant son Alexander IV and his "half-wit" half brother Philip Arridaeus, were quickly pushed aside. One by one Alexander's "successors" (in Greek, *diadochi*) such as Perdiccas, Craterus, Eumenes, Antipater, Cassander, Antigonus One-Eye, Demetrius the Besieger, Lysimachus, and Seleucus, among others, entered, had their moments on the grand stage, and departed, mostly under violent circumstances.

One conspicuous exception was Ptolemy, son of Lagus (367–283). Soon after the conqueror's death, Ptolemy, a childhood companion, advisor, and officer in long service to Alexander, solicited the fiefdom of Egypt. From his rich and secure base in the new capital of Alexandria, Ptolemy watched the antagonists eliminate one another, occasionally throwing his weight behind the opponents of anyone who seemed to be dangerously ahead in the game. By the early third century the situation had stabilized along essentially continental lines: in Europe, the descendants of Antigonus One-Eye (the Antigonids) took over the throne at Pella and ruled Macedon and most of Greece; in Asia, the dynasty begun by Seleucus I Nicator ("the Victor") ruled over most of Alexander's eastern domain from the new foundation of Antioch; in Africa, Ptolemy was content to milk the cash cow of Egypt, hold the line against the Seleucids in Syria, and engage only occasionally in foreign adventures (he annexed the city of Cyrene in Libya, Eratosthenes' birthplace, in 320). Though self-aggrandizement was de rigueur among the generalissimos of the time, he remained ever cautious. Only after Antigonus One-Eye took a crown did Ptolemy finally proclaim himself pharaoh of Egypt in 305. Those last to the party were the last to leave: the Ptolemaic Empire outlived its rivals, largely with the same borders, until the Romans defeated Queen Cleopatra VII and her lover Antony in 30.

## AN EXQUISITE CORPSE?

We're used to seeing the Egypt of the Ptolemies through the eyes of her eventual conquerors. She is rich but decadent, a writhing vipers' nest of savagery and toxic allure. We see straight-arrow Rex Harrison disdaining Alexandria in the 1963 film *Cleopatra,* until he is beguiled by Elizabeth Taylor. We watch Hollywood heroine turn to heroin chic in the 2005 BBC/HBO TV series *Rome,* in which another Cleopatra (Lyndsay Marshal) literally sucks a smack pipe during her exile from the capital. This Ptolemaic Egypt is an exquisite corpse, a dead polity that is somehow still ambulatory, only waiting for a stake to be put through its heart by the legions of Augustus.

That was certainly the Roman view. The received wisdom was, in fact, long in the making: the man who produced the most comprehensive surviving history of the period, Polybius (c. 200–118), was a patriotic Greek who spent much of his life as a political hostage in Rome. To a readership obliged to watch in disbelief as the legions toppled one Greek-speaking kingdom after the other, Polybius begged to offer some historical context. His accounting of (one hesitates to say "apology for") Roman superiority does, now and again, take the form of disparaging the competition: "the savagery of the Egyptians when their passions are roused is indeed terrible," he wrote (as if contemporary Roman mobs were mere knitting circles); he portrays the Ptolemaic court as a gilded cathouse, with its surfeit of flute girls and public prostitutes (though scolds made the same complaint about Periclean Athens); he has Ptolemaic kings regularly lapse into typically oriental debauch, displaying "habitual effeminacy," "corruption," "abandoning all noble pursuits."

Historiographic conceits aside, Polybius was born in Arcadia, notorious throughout antiquity as an irredeemable backwater. His reflections on the character of Alexandria, the brightest and richest of all cities in the Mediterranean, therefore have the suspicious ring of the provincial moralist, like a modern congressional candidate from West Virginia scoring easy debate points at the expense of Hollywood or New York.

The true magnitude of Ptolemaic power is still discernible in Polybius's history, however. He records that Rome sneered at Alexandrian dissipation, yet dreaded the kingdom's fundamental strength: "[The Romans] saw how great the power of the Egyptian kingdom was; and fearing lest, if it ever chanced to obtain a competent head, he would grow too proud." In 224, when Eratosthenes was head librarian, Ptolemy III Euergetes made an enormous donation to the people of Rhodes after an earthquake. His aid package included more than a million bushels of grain, nine tons of silver, thirty tons in bronze coin, three thousand measures of sailcloth, and timber for twenty warships, along with one hundred master builders, 350 workmen, and funds to repair the toppled Colossus of Rhodes. Polybius, interestingly, can't bring himself to laud the monarch's generosity as much as to credit the Rhodians for publicizing their plight so effectively! In any case, we may safely assume that Euergetes' largess did not begin to strain the resources of his supposedly dying kingdom.

Polybius's disdain echoed through the subsequent centuries. The fact that few good histories of the period have survived is often taken by scholars as an unfortunate accident, but likely has as much to do with the low priority placed on them by medieval copyists. Classicists of the nineteenth and early twentieth centuries were happy to concur: George Grote, in the preface to his multivolume *History of Greece* (1846), declared, "After the generation of Alexander, the political action of Greece becomes cramped and degraded—no longer interesting to the reader, or operative on the destinies of the world. . . . As a whole, the period between 300 BC and the absorption of Greece by the Romans is of no interest in itself, and is only so far of value as it helps us to understand the preceding centuries."

Behind this bias lurked a biological analogy that had much appeal to certain Victorian intellectuals, such as Herbert Spencer (1820–1903). This view held that societies, like living organisms, grow, mature, and inevitably decay—a phenomenon for which history provided ready examples. If we stipulate that the fifth century, the time of Themistocles, Pericles, Aeschylus, Sophocles, and Socrates, was the golden age of ancient Greece, then the analogy simply demands that everything that came after must represent a decline. Virtually the same applies in Egyptology, in which the study of the Ptolemaic "late period" has long been the neglected stepchild of a discipline engrossed by the Rameseses and Thutmoses of high antiquity.

The chronological label *Hellenistic* to denote the period between the death of Alexander and the rise of Rome was popularized by the German historian Johann Gustav Droysen in a series of monographs first published in the 1830s. Droysen used the term to refer to the diffusion of Greek culture over previously non-Greek areas, such as Persia, Syria, and Egypt. Droysen himself deserves much credit for pioneering serious scholarly interest in the field; the inevitable reaction to Grote-esque dismissal of everything postclassical, not to mention an explosion of interest in issues of cultural identity in an age of globalization, has lately made the period a legitimate focus of research.

Alas, words can acquire their own semantic momentum through history. Today, the term *Hellenistic* retains an unfocused, wishy-washy feel, if not a whiff of outright condescension. To appreciate its absurdity, one can imagine future historians lumping American history with Canadian, Australian, South African, and later South Asian histories, into a conceptual monstrosity called the "Britishistic" period.

Comparing Plato's Athens to Eratosthenes' Alexandria is not to compare gold to silver, but apples to oranges. By any number of measures, developments in the latter were at least as consequential for us as those in the classical period (or, for that matter, those in New Kingdom Egypt). Hellenistic advances in science and technology are, of course, the substance of this book. In the military arts, Hellenistic armies progressed far beyond the crude set-piece tactics of hoplite warfare. Thanks to the legacies of Philip II and Alexander, and for the first time in the West, shock troops were integrated with mobile forces (cavalry, skirmishers) and missile troops (slingers, archers) into armies that benefitted from the assets of all three (or four, if we include the development of siege artillery). We need look no further than the battle of Raphia in 217 to see that these innovations had become widely established: here an Egyptian army beat the Seleucids in what was essentially a tactical rerun of the Battle of Gaugamela, all under the leadership of Ptolemy IV Philopator, who was surely no Alexander.

In politics, much has been made of the rise of monarchies at the expense of formerly self-governing city-states throughout the Greek world. Hellenistic rulers, it is said, trivialized Greek civic life by reducing it to pompous pageantry and contests over who could best flatter the king. The people responded by withdrawal into political quietism and/or private vices. And indeed, the loss of real autonomy in Athens and other cities had significant consequences. We will have occasion below to consider the effect these changes had on Eratosthenes' own philosophy and work. But it should also be remembered that the balance among the relatively small powers around the Aegean could not last forever; history has a way of alternating periods of political fission and accretion. As the historian Peter Green has noted, "the age of city-states, however remarkable and admirable a phenomenon, was, in historical terms, a marvelous anomaly . . . with the establishment of the Successor kingdoms of the Hellenistic era, the Near East settled back into the age-old patterns it had known from the dawn of civilization."

### THE CITY OF LIGHT

*Well, my child, how long now is it that you've been separated, wearing out your single bed alone? It's ten months since Mandris set off for Egypt, and not a word does he send you; he has forgotten and drunk from a new cup. The home of the goddess is there. For everything in the world that exists and is produced is in Egypt; wealth, wrestling schools, power, tranquility, fame, spectacles, philosophers, gold, youths, the sanctuary of the sibling gods, the King excellent, the Museum, wine, every good thing he could desire. . . .*

—HERODAS, *Mime*, I

The foundation of Alexandria made it something of an oddity in its time. Unlike Naples or Syracuse, it was not the result of a dedicated colonizing effort by a particular parent city. Nor was it an old city with obscure origins draped in chthonic myth, like Athens or Thebes. It was, instead, the fruit of the combined energies of a handful of powerful individuals.

Eratosthenes, in a lost work quoted by the Roman-era geographer Strabo, wrote that of the kingdom of the pharaohs "there was a common saying: 'The way to Egypt is long and vexatious.' . . . [The saying] originated in [the country's] lack of harbors, and in the state of the harbor at Pharos, which was not of free access, but watched and guarded by herdsmen, who were robbers, and attacked those who attempted to sail into it." The old pharaohs, who had a well-founded mistrust of barbarians from across the water, recognized the future site of Alexandria as a tempting spot for invaders to land, and established a guard post there actively to dissuade them from doing so.

Where the native kings saw danger, Alexander the Great saw opportunity. First arriving in Egypt in 332, the young conqueror was on his way to consult the oracle of Zeus-Ammon at Siwah when he first glimpsed the site of Alexandria. Situated on a shallow ridge between the sea and Lake Mareotis, the place could be approached by water both from within Egypt—via the canals joining the lake to the delta and thence the Nile—and from the outside world, on the Mediterranean. It was close to the westernmost of the Nile's seven mouths, the Canopic, but far enough away to avoid having its harbor silted up by the river's outflow. The city was therefore in a position to serve, Janus-like, as an intermediary between the African interior and potential markets overseas. Alexander, says Arrian, "was at once struck by the excellence of the site, and convinced that if a city were built upon it, it would prosper."

Overcome by enthusiasm, Alexander immediately commenced to sketch the city of his dreams, laying down the locations of the walls, the marketplace, the main streets, and the temples, all within an elongated district between sea and lake (see figure 1, page 4). And when the chalk his troops used for surveying ran out, he turned to the grain that was supposed to sustain them on their trip through the desert. As the story goes, when he was done birds flew down and pecked away the outlines—a development that gave

Alexander pause, until someone suggested that it augured well for the town's prosperity. The great man then continued on his way to meet his divine patron at Siwah, destined never to see the place again.

If Alexander was the father of the city, its governor Cleomenes was the midwife. A Greek from the delta trading center of Naucratis, Cleomenes was an ambiguous Boss Tweed–like figure, chiefly remembered for swindling Egyptians and Greeks alike of enormous sums of money. According to one story, he demanded that the people of the city of Canopus abandon their homes to settle in the new capital. When the Canopiotes presented him a large bribe instead, he delayed his plan for a while, then decided their "gift" was but a down payment on another. When they replied that they couldn't pay any more, Cleomenes followed through on the resettlement. In another instance, he informed the priests of the Egyptian temples that they took too much of the people's money, and had to reduce their expenditures—until they handed over their fortunes to him, and his populist scruples vanished.

So brazen was Cleomenes that word of his predations reached Alexander in Babylon. But while the king had proven relentless in punishing corruption on other occasions, he wrote that in this case he was willing to overlook Cleomenes' past misdeeds, and indeed any future ones, on one condition: that a statue to Alexander's recently dead and deified lover, Hephaestion, be erected in Alexandria.

Whether Cleomenes obeyed the order is unknown; the governor was soon deposed and executed by Ptolemy, who was certainly not above dipping deep into the eight thousand talents in bullion (in modern terms, about 242 tons of gold) his predecessor had left behind. On Cleomenes' virtues, or lack of such, the historical record is suspect—post hoc character assassination was not below those who had to justify their part in the dismemberment of Alexander's empire after his death in 323. In any case, Cleomenes could probably point to some positive achievements in realizing

Alexander's dream: a royal mint was operating in Alexandria before Ptolemy arrived; the groundwork for the mole (the Heptastadion or "seven-stader"), a breakwater-causeway to the offshore island of Pharos, was under way. Nor would Alexander have been likely to demand a statue of his lover in Alexandria if no settlement worthy of the honor had yet existed.

In all likelihood, then, Alexandria took shape very quickly in the waning years of the fourth century and early years of the third. As we have seen, the inhabitants of neighboring towns were—to borrow a modern euphemism—"incentivized" to resettle there. The Ptolemies also promoted immigration from elsewhere in the Greek world, offering direct economic rewards as well as the material comforts of a lavish foundation where no expense was spared. Unlike most large Greek towns, which grew gradually and haphazardly, Alexandria had commissioned planners, Deinocrates of Rhodes and Crates of Olynthus, to push through designs for her architecture and waterworks, respectively. The streets were laid out in a gridiron pattern associated with the semimythic visionary Hippodamas of Miletus (c. 500), with avenues of unprecedented width, long colonnades, and orthogonally running streets well situated to channel cool breezes from the sea.

All the administrative machinery it took Athens centuries to develop, such as the arrangement of citizens into units called demes, a citywide legislative assembly (the *ecclesia*), an executive body (the *boule*), and magistrates elected to yearly terms, was put in place at the outset. Unlike in classical Athens, however, the power of the city's civil servants was entirely circumscribed by the king's, preserving only the outward form, not the substance, of self-government. (As we shall see, this wasn't the only aspect of Alexandrian society that was something of a façade.) The foundation was by all measures a complete success, with the city surpassing Athens in size relatively early in her history. Estimates of Alexandria's population in the

Hellenistic era range from four hundred thousand to one million—bigger than any Mediterranean city except Rome.

The city also received an instant tourist attraction with the arrival of Alexander's mortal remains—literally hijacked by Ptolemy's agents on the road to burial in Macedon—and their interment in a splendid tomb (the Soma, "the body") not far from the royal palace. In this sense the place was like modern purpose-built political capitals, such as Washington, D.C., or Canberra, Australia, with sanctifying civic monuments to compensate for a lack of real history.

But the comparison is imperfect, because Alexandria was also meant to be a cultural center. Development of the institutions designed to make the city heir to Athenian intellectual greatness, the Museum and Great Library, was already well under way under the first Ptolemy. As such, Alexandria, along with the Seleucid capital at Antioch, represented the arrival of something new in Western history—vast conurbations at last on a par with the great teeming cities of the east, such as Babylon. A near contemporary of Eratosthenes, the poet Theocritus, likely had firsthand experience of the city when he wrote his fifteenth *Idyll,* and put this description into the mouth of a woman on the streets of Alexandria:

> Ye gods, what a crowd! How on earth are we ever to get through this coil? They are like ants that no one can measure or number. Many a good deed have you done, Ptolemy; since your father joined the Immortals, there's never a malefactor to spoil the passer-by, creeping on him in Egyptian fashion—oh! the tricks those perfect rascals used to play. Birds of a feather, ill jesters, scoundrels all! Dear Gorgo, what will become of us? Here come the King's warhorses! My dear man, don't trample on me. . . .

Such cities "marked a completely new stage in Mediterranean history," writes Peter Green, "culminating, three centuries later, in what Horace was to describe as 'the smoke and wealth and clamor of Rome.'"


## THE GOLDEN LEDGER

Notwithstanding its decadent image, Ptolemaic Egypt was one of the most successful large empires of antiquity. From the time Ptolemy, son of Lagus, took over the governorship of Egypt in 323 to the defeat of the Cleopatra VII nearly three hundred years later, the empire's borders periodically expanded to include parts of modern Jordan and Syria, the Aegean islands, and Anatolia, only to recede again. From the original eight thousand talents left by Cleomenes, the treasury of Ptolemy II Philadelphus mushroomed to 740,000 talents—a handsome 9,150 percent increase. This is profitability even by modern Wall Street standards: if the Dow Jones average had risen a similar amount since World War II, the index would now stand at over twenty thousand.

This increase in wealth is unlikely to have been an accident. How the Ptolemies managed such prosperity, however, is not entirely clear. Egypt's dry, sandy soil preserves papyrus scrolls very well—copious quantities of documents have survived. The trouble is that most of these remains are not from wet, coastal Alexandria or even the southern capital of Ptolemais, but instead from minor localities like Tebtunis, El-Hiba, and Oxyrhynchus. The surviving documents tend to be parochial in nature—the kind of material (deeds, wills, receipts, records of litigation, administrative memoranda, and so on) that most often repose in safe, permanent oblivion in provincial archives. Of course, such material has great value to certain historians, such as those who reconstruct legal and social history. For those interested in tracing the large-scale evolution of Ptolemaic administrative policy, however, studying the papyri is like trying to discern the legislative activities of the United States

Congress from the baptistery records of a few randomly selected country churches in rural Georgia.

The picture is clear only in its broadest strokes. The incomparably ancient kingdom of the pharaohs offered the Macedonian Greeks significant liabilities as well as important assets in their attempt to establish a new ruling dynasty in Egypt. On the plus side, the country had a skilled, well-organized, largely homogeneous population, with a long-standing tradition of civil administration. Its geographic position made the kingdom difficult to reach by both land and sea, but easy to defend by anyone already established there. Policing Egypt was a straightforward matter of controlling its primary transportation channel, the Nile. Above all, the river's reliable yearly inundations had long made the kingdom the breadbasket of the Mediterranean. Making Egypt pay, therefore, depended on keeping up the infrastructure and social institutions that had already existed for millennia, such as irrigation, flood control, and conscripted labor.

On the debit side, the labor pool was of a deeply alien culture, worshipping unfamiliar gods, speaking a language few Greeks understood. The same civil and religious institutions that kept Egypt stable could serve to focus domestic resentment over foreign domination. By the fourth century BCE, years of unrest had depopulated large swaths of the country. Replacing Egyptians with Greek immigrants might solve the manpower shortage in the near term, but would likely heighten native discontent. The empire had defensible borders, yet the vast majority of the population couldn't be trusted in the ranks—the Macedonians had a long-standing reluctance to arm the natives. Greek mercenaries, of course, expected to be paid in coin, not sheaves of wheat. Alas, Egyptian mines were tapped out; the Ptolemies were therefore constantly on the make for gold and silver to pay their soldiers.

The durability of the empire is compelling evidence that the assets outweighed the liabilities. Where specialists argue over the

Ptolemaic record, it is over how deliberately and rationally—in other words, how "Greek"—the dynasty behaved in managing these challenges. How much of its vast bureaucracy was borrowed from the native pharaohs, and how much from the foreign dynasties that preceded Alexander, such as the Persians (525–332) and the Nubians (770–657)? Were the Ptolemies in essence colonial occupiers and exploiters, bent on wringing the last drachma and obol from a captive land regardless of the consequences? Or was their tenure somewhat less cynical, more a matter of improvisation, motivated by the distant but vague object of forging a lasting harmony between Greek and Egyptian?

The answers are complex, not mutually exclusive, and mostly beyond the scope of this book. A few facts are relevant to Eratosthenes' story, however. First, in addition to inviting skilled Greeks to immigrate to the capital, the Ptolemies barred native Egyptians from spending more than twenty days in Alexandria at a time. According to a letter from Philadelphus to Aristeas, an assistant to Demetrius of Phaleron (see below), the king justified this measure as a means of preserving the nation's agricultural output by discouraging mass emigration to the capital. Be that as it may, the policy amounted to a kind of ethnic apartheid, preserving the city's Greek face while excluding Egyptians from the center of imperial power.

The kings also settled Macedonian soldiers on estates throughout the country. These foreign holdings or "cleruchies" not only put underused land back into taxable cultivation, but also afforded the king what was essentially a countrywide system of garrisons. The effectiveness of this levy is beyond any doubt: Appian reports that Ptolemy II Philadelphus had at his disposal as many as 200,000 infantry, 40,000 cavalry, 300 elephants, and a fleet of 1,500 triremes. Even assuming this account is exaggerated by a factor of two, what was left would still have been bigger than anything Alexander commanded against Persia.

But the cleruchies had certain costs. To judge from modern parallels in the Middle East and elsewhere, it is unlikely that the natives approved of having foreign interlopers for neighbors or absentee landlords. Subject to a separate legal system for Greeks only, the settlers were beyond the reach of native courts. They collectively knew very little of the Egyptian language beyond, we imagine, certain commands and curse words; even written translation between Greek and demotic (the common written form of Egyptian, as distinct from hieroglyphics) was, in some cases, nearly impossible. The Macedonian cleruchs were, according to Green, "an occupying imperial minority . . . whose main object was to maintain their own power and privileges, while at the same time making sizable fortunes. To do this involved them in an economically static cycle of extortion, bribery, and sweated labor."

Indeed, there was only a thin tradition for such policies even in Greece. The system harkens instead back to Alexander's settlement of veterans to help control his conquests in Asia. Before him, such a form of colonization had been used in the fifth century by the Athenians, who planted citizen estates in troublesome areas of their Aegean empire. In the latter case the settlements caused deep and abiding resentment.

We find evidence for similar bitterness in the archive of the Greek magistrate Diophanes, who presided over the Arsinoite nome in middle Egypt toward the end of Eratosthenes' lifetime in the late third century. Out of 125 papyri recording contemporary legal cases, fully 20 percent involve personal squabbles between individual Greeks and Egyptians. The disputes were hardly stuff for the ages (an Egyptian attendant allegedly scalds a Greek woman in her bath; a Greek throws an Egyptian man out of his house; an Egyptian woman empties a chamber pot on a Greek man's head). Such cases testify to underlying tensions, however. If the fifth-century Aegean Greeks resented the Athenians for similar policies despite a common language and culture, the Egyptians probably hated the Macedonians even more.

To alleviate this, the Ptolemies legitimized their power by adopting the trappings of old-time pharaonic rule. Traditional notions of the king in society, after all, brooked no possibility of "exploitation" in the modern sense. The country was a single body, with each organ serving its function—to say that Pharaoh exploited the people was therefore as nonsensical as saying that his head "exploited" his hands.

To keep their pharaonic bona fides, the Ptolemies emulated certain of the old practices, such as fraternal incest (Isis, after all, was both sister and wife to Osiris, the Egyptian god of the dead). They took care to engage the temple priesthood, which was essentially a system of religious corporations with their own pecuniary interests. In Eratosthenes' lifetime, Euergetes' bequests to these hierarchs, his additions to existing centers such as the Gate of Ptolemy III at Karnak, and his building of a new temple of Horus at Edfu testify to the importance he attached to mollifying the religious establishment. These efforts bore priceless fruit: in a text known as the Canopus Decree, the assembled priests of Upper and Lower Egypt lauded

King Ptolemaios, the Everliving, the Beloved of Ptah, son of Ptolemaios and Arsinoe, the Sister-gods, and the Ruler Berenike his sister and wife, the Benevolent Gods, have made benefits many and great to the temples of Egypt for all time: since they have ordered very greatly to the gods: since they have taken perpetual care of the things of the glorious Apis, Mnevis, and all animals of the temple which are protected in Egypt, for whom they assigned great things supplying numerous things.

Nor did the kings skimp on eye candy for the home audience of Alexandrian Greeks. Athenaeus of Naucratis, writing in the late second or early third century CE, preserved a contemporary description of the coronation festivities for Ptolemy II Philadelphus in 285. After warming up with a description of the tent set up for the feasters, with columns seventy feet tall, room for 130 couches, and a floor strewn with flowers and the skins of exotic beasts, the account speaks of a sumptuous procession led by

> images of Victory, having golden wings, [bearing] in their hands incense burners nine feet tall . . . next came boys in purple tunics, bearing frankincense and myrrh, and saffron on golden dishes . . . forty Satyrs, crowned with golden ivy garlands, their bodies painted some with purple, some with vermillion . . . four-wheeled wagon twenty feet high and twelve wide, drawn by 180 men, [topped by] an image of Dionysus 15 feet high, pouring libations from a golden goblet, [and fastened with] chaplets and fillets, and ivy wands, drums, turbans, and actor's masks. After it many other wagons came, one 37 feet long and 22 wide; this was drawn by 600 men. On this wagon was a sack, holding 30,000 gallons of wine, and consisting of leopards' skins sewn together. This sack allowed its liquor to escape, and it gradually flowed over the whole road.

For purposes of comparison, the average backyard swimming pool is slightly larger than this Ptolemaic wineskin, containing about forty thousand gallons of water. But most pools are enclosed by something less expensive than leopard skins.

All this was a mere appetizer compared to what followed: a parade of wild beasts including twenty-four chariots each drawn by four elephants, fifteen chariots by buffalo, twelve chariots by antelopes, eight by ostriches, and so on and on. Generations of classics teachers have amused schoolboys with accounts of an enormous phallus, gilded and half a football field long, tumescent but probably not erect given that it would have been taller than any of the surrounding buildings. Topping off the spectacle was a military parade including nearly sixty thousand infantry and more than twenty thousand horsemen. By authentic Ptolemaic standards, then, the procession of Elizabeth Taylor into Rome in the film *Cleopatra* was actually a rather understated affair.

Indeed, the wealth of Egypt had political effects that long outlasted the Hellenistic epoch. Seven centuries later, there were widespread suspicions that the Christian bishop of Alexandria, Cyril (~378 to ~444 CE) had greased many palms in the Byzantine court to remove his rival, Nestorius, bishop of Constantinople. The bribes, which would undoubtedly have been gleaned from the enormous resources of the church in Alexandria, were said to include some 1,500 pounds of gold—worth about sixteen million dollars in 2007. Nestorius was removed from office.

While this kind of stupefying excess seemed to keep the Ptolemies popular in the capital, the rest of the country seems to have submitted to the rule of Alexandria only sullenly, with memories of a better time never far out of mind. "The system didn't work," declares a modern critic: "The administrative checks and controls . . . reflect, not a careful plan established in Alexandria, but rather a desperate attempt on the part of the crown to get some control over a structure that, at the lowest village levels, was practically autonomous." Indeed, when Ptolemy's gem-encrusted boot did lift somewhat, the result was almost instant rebellion. Ptolemy IV Philopater hazarded the use of native Egyptian troops at Raphia, and won the battle with their help; just a few years later, native mercenaries in Thebes used their hard-won martial skills to revolt. From 206 to 186, again around 164, and yet again in 134, great swaths of Upper Egypt were lost to the crown.

Beyond the gated community at Alexandria, then, Hellenistic Egypt was a stewpot of roiling antagonisms, contained only by an elaborate system of regulations, appeasement, and, if necessary, military force. Alienation between rulers and ruled even extended to matters of simple nomenclature: according to one modern authority on demotic-script documents, the natives studiously avoided referring to Alexandria in the language of their conquerors. Instead, they called the city Rhakotis, which might refer to some preexisting Egyptian village on that location, or derive from the term *ra-qed,* the generic term for "building site." The Greeks returned the favor: over the roughly one thousand years of Greco-Roman dominion of Egypt, we have no evidence of any Egyptian word making its way into common Greek usage. (Compare this to the mutual influence of French and English after the Norman Conquest.) Instead of borrowing Egyptian terms, the Greeks preferred to revive abandoned Greek ones. Even after two millennia, the contempt implicit in these linguistic refusals is palpable.

That the Ptolemaic system functioned as well as it did is a tribute as much to the natives' capacity to make do as it is to the regime's skill at making itself as unobjectionable as it could. The picture is not unlike Egypt today, where the government in Cairo keeps power by a combination of tactics, including management of local religious authorities that swerves between heavy-handed intimidation and cynical appeasement. Such policies have today left much of middle Egypt a no-go area for unescorted Westerners. With whole regions of the country's interior seemingly on the edge of revolt throughout Ptolemaic history, it is likely that Greek-speaking travelers faced similar risks in Eratosthenes' time.

# 3. MR. BETA AND THE ANCIENT PLAN B

*Now tell me, Muses, dwellers on Olympus,*
*which goods Dionysus brought here for men on his black ship,*
*from the time when he traded over the wine-dark sea.*
*From Cyrene, the silphium-stalk and ox-hide. . . .*

—HERMIPPUS (Athenian comic playwright,
mid-fifth century BCE)

ERATOSTHENES WAS born in the Greek north African city of Cyrene, in what is now Libya, around 285. His hometown was a wealthy but somewhat peripheral place, analogous in its pleasant remoteness to modern Sydney or Cape Town. According to Herodotus, it was founded in the seventh century BCE by settlers fleeing the drought-stricken island of Thera. The fertility of Cyrene's environs was legendary; according to an inscription, the city single-handedly donated the modern equivalent of more than one million bushels of wheat to various Greek cities during the famine coincident with Alexander's wars.

Cyrene's other principal local export was silphion, a plant that is now extinct but whose products had a universe of uses in antiquity. When used in cooking, its resin lent a pungent, onionlike taste perhaps not unlike modern asafoetida; when taken as medicine, the juice was said to cure sore throats, warts, fever, sour stomach, leprosy, and baldness.

The plant had one other, rather unique use: it ended unwanted pregnancy. Tea brewed from the leaves, or the sap taken orally, or a silphion suppository, was said to prevent conception and/or induce abortion. Perhaps for reasons other than its oniony flavor, then, the plant was in astonishing demand throughout the Greek and the Roman world. Yet because the plant would grow only in a small coastal area in north Africa, it was only available "wild," and therefore worth its weight in gold.

Silphion's export became so integral to the local economy that

the Cyreneans put its image on their coins (see figure 8). It perhaps comes as no surprise that the plant was harvested to extinction by the first century CE. This was a blow from which the city's economy never recovered.

*Fig. 8. Reverse of a gold coin from Cyrene, depicting the city's most important export, the silphium plant*

In its heyday, however, Cyrene was a thriving outpost of Greek civilization in Africa, well able to produce the political, architectural, and educational trappings of Hellenic culture. Wealth generated through trade enabled the natives to attract scholar-teachers from abroad to educate their sons. In an indirect sense, then, Eratosthenes' career—including the first accurate measurement of the earth—was made possible by the demand by ancient women for effective birth control.

Of Eratosthenes' parentage and early life, our sources are almost silent. His biography in the *Suda,* a Byzantine encyclopedia dating from the tenth century CE, states that Eratosthenes' father was named either Aglaos or Ambrosios. The names of neither father nor son are attested much elsewhere. It is tempting to assume, therefore, that Eratosthenes rose from humble origins. His family had to be rich enough to pay for an extensive education, however, so it would be more proper to call his origins obscure rather than lowly.

Though it is a truism to emphasize the stunting of free Greek city life in Hellenistic times, Cyrene in the early third century was no mere political appendage of Alexandria. One of the few local documents to survive from this time, the so-called Constitution of Cyrene, prescribes the kind of political machinery one might expect in a wholly independent *polis.* Citizens had to be born of free parents; to attain membership in the popular assembly, or *politeuma,* a man had to own property worth at least twenty minas—the collective value of a decent house and a few able-bodied slaves. There was also an upper legislative body of five hundred male citizens each at least fifty years old, which had advisory and judicial functions; five of the six *strategoi,* or generals of the city, were elected by the *politeuma,* while the sixth position was always to be held by the king, ex officio. But aside from the latter privilege, and a garrison of Macedonian soldiers quartered in the city, Cyrene was left pretty much to rule herself.

Even this wide latitude wasn't enough for some. In 313, just nine years after the Ptolemaic forces were first invited in by the aristocratic faction, the people were already in revolt. Another uprising followed in 308. Around 300, the stepson of Ptolemy I, Magas, was appointed governor. Apparently a man of some ambition and much patience, Magas bided his time until the death of Ptolemy in 283. He then declared his independent kingship, sending an army to attack Egypt in concert with the Seleucid king Antiochus I's invasion from the east in 274. The combined campaign failed, but Cyrene was not returned to Alexandria's full control for decades. Magas died in 250 after marrying his daughter, Berenice, to the prince who was later to rule as Ptolemy III.

The years of Eratosthenes' birth and childhood, therefore, were marked by defiance of and independence from the distant Ptolemies. And although it is hazardous to assume any of this had formative effects on his character, it is equally an exaggeration to say that Eratosthenes grew up breathing an atmosphere of pure royalist docility. He was well acquainted with how free Greeks ruled themselves.

We have a few more scraps of information about his intellectual pedigree. He took instruction from the native-born grammarian Lysanias. When he came of age, he moved to Athens and heard the philosopher Ariston of Chios, who was a student of Zeno of Citium, a key figure in the history of the Stoic school. No doubt he recalled this period as the most stimulating in his intellectual life: as paraphrased in Strabo's *Geography,* Eratosthenes boasts of Athens, "Never . . . at one period, and in one city, were there so many philosophers fluorishing together as in my time."

Zeno taught that the key to happiness lay in mastering the passions. Ariston, in turn, was something of a reformist within the Stoic school, holding that studies of nature and logic were a waste of time because such truths were fundamentally beyond human understanding. The only proper object of study for the educated man, he declared, was *ethics.*

The virtues of this position aside, it seems remarkable that Ariston, a man who had no use for natural science, a man who insisted on a laserlike concentration on only one branch of philosophical inquiry, produced a student who became one of the most versatile scholars of his age. Indeed, as a natural scientist and a mathematician, the mature Eratosthenes represented the anti-Ariston. His ability to absorb, criticize, and reject the received knowledge of his time—even that of his most renowned teachers—yet to rise unimpeded in his field of endeavor, reflect something of Magas's patience and ambition.

Eratosthenes probably resided in Athens from when he attended Zeno's school before 261, until he left for Alexandria in 245. By this time Athens was well on her way to becoming what she was in Roman times—a spent political force, mindful of her imperial past, but notable mostly as the ancient equivalent of a college town. In residence there for at least sixteen years, Eratosthenes worked his way into the educational establishment, building the reputation that would earn him an invitation to Egypt. We also imagine him imbibing the classical atmosphere the Athenians took pains to cultivate—the revivals of the old tragedies, the ancient round of festivals, the theater of argument in the stoa, and evening walks through the gardens of the Academy. The mix of qualities he cultivated there—an independence of mind, coupled with a respect for tradition—would serve him well in the very different atmosphere at Ptolemy's court in Alexandria.

## THE BOOK REVOLUTION

When many people think of the Periclean age in Athens, their image is often suffused by the pure light of reason—a rationalism that seems as clean and bright as the city's marble remains. The analogy is illusory in two ways: the original buildings were not ghostly white as moderns seem to prefer them, but as garishly painted as a Hindu shrine. Likewise, the celebrated rationality of the fifth century represents a retrospective bleaching of what was actually a complex and contested story.

The rise of literacy, of the culture of writing and reading and bookselling, had reached a critical stage in the classical period. It was not applauded by everyone. To many traditionalists, Plato included, the age of the written word necessarily meant the end of a craft of oral transmission that had long nourished the Greek mind. Bardic recitation was by nature collective and unifying; the reading of books, by contrast, promoted independence, privacy, and the hoarding of knowledge by the privileged few. In this sense, the written word, along with its avid promoters, the Sophists, represented a frightening challenge to the old order. What the digital media revolution is to books today, books themselves were to what preceded them. In his play *The Frogs,* the conservative Aristophanes makes repeated sneering references to Euripides' partiality for books. According to one tradition, when the philosopher Protagoras was convicted on charges of heresy, his books were dumped in the city marketplace and burned.

In sad contrast to the story of Pericles calmly explaining away an eclipse to a frightened sailor, the teaching of scientific astronomy was banned outright in Athens around 432. The picture we have of Socrates from his students, Plato and Xenophon, is of someone perhaps conversant with the natural sciences, but unconvinced of their fundamental importance: "He did not even discuss that topic so favored by other talkers, 'the Nature of the Universe,'" recalls Xenophon. "[He] avoided speculation on the so-called 'Cosmos' of the Professors, how it works, and on the laws that govern the phenomena of the heavens: indeed he would argue that to trouble one's mind with such problems is sheer folly."

As the anecdote from Diogenes Laertius about Anaxagoras (see the epigraph to the preceding chapter) suggests, pursuing natural science at the expense of politics was seen by many as suspicious, if not downright unpatriotic. Anaxagoras, Protagoras, and of course Socrates were hauled up on charges of heresy and impiety. In summarizing the wave of prosecutions of intellectuals in Athens, one modern commentator wrote, "[T]he evidence we have is more than enough to prove that the Great Age of Greek Enlightenment was also, like our own time, an Age of Persecution—banishment of scholars, blinkering of thought, and even (if we can believe the tradition about Protagoras) burning of books." In this sense at least, the original democracy was not the most fertile ground for such inquiries.

Instead, it took the patronage of the "decadent" Ptolemies to put ancient Greek science—and book collecting—on a firm institutional footing. Their predecessors in this included the Sumerians, Babylonians, Assyrians, and Hittites, who all kept significant archives of clay cuneiform tablets in their palaces and temple precincts. The Greeks had direct exposure to these Asian libraries after Alexander's conquest of Mesopotamia; that they were a direct inspiration for Ptolemy's foundation, however, can only be a surmise.

A somewhat more immediate influence was Aristotle himself, whose death in 322 happened to coincide with Ptolemy's accession to the governorship of Egypt. The great philosopher kept a collection of books at his school in Athens, the Lyceum. That an institution of learning should keep a library was not as obvious then as it is now—Plato, for all the reasons we have already discussed, kept no such collection at his Academy. The Peripatetic (Aristotelian) model, which put a value on analysis based on comparison of facts from multiple sources—written if necessary—became the direct rationale for the Alexandrian Library.

That Ptolemy's legitimacy as ruler stemmed from Alexander's, and the great man was a student of Aristotle, was yet another significant factor. Alexander himself had lively intellectual interests, ranging from an amateur enthusiasm for the Homeric epics, to the geography and cultures of the lands he conquered, to natural science (he once conducted a tag-and-release research project on stags). To create an unparalleled center of learning, equipped with the greatest collection of books in the world, was something the Ptolemies, with resources far beyond those of even the richest independent city-states in the fifth century, were uniquely positioned to accomplish. This was the sort of lordly boon they could imagine Alexander looking down upon from his godly vantage, and smiling.

A key figure in the foundation of the Museum and the Library was Demetrius of Phaleron (c. 350–c. 282). Ptolemy I first offered the task of building up the institution to Aristotle's successor as head of the Lyceum, Theophrastus of Lesbos (c. 372–287). He turned the king down, but somehow his ex-pupil Demetrius got wind of the offer. The latter by this time had already had an eventful career: a Macedonian-leaning social conservative, he was already a prolific author when Cassander, the strongman in Pella, installed him as dictator of Athens. Saddling the ex-democracy with the likes of Demetrius suited Cassander's sense of irony. Observes Green, "Cassander . . . must have chuckled at the thought of giving the Athenians, in uncomfortable practice, a taste of their own Platonic—or in this case Aristotelian—medicine, a real philosopher-king."

Demetrius's decade-long tenure, in any case, was marked by relative stability, marred only by his promotion of nanny-state laws that limited citizens' gods-given right to flaunt their wealth in the faces of the destitute majority. Demetrius himself was a notorious dandy. As a well-kitted, bottle-blond bon vivant with a taste for oysters *and* snails, he seems to have pushed hard on the limits of his own sumptuary laws.

When he was finally chased out of Athens in 307, Demetrius was a man of expensive tastes, few friends, and no patron. Taking the opportunity to build up Ptolemy's Museum must therefore have been something of a no-brainer. He made the "philosopher's run" to Alexandria around 297, just as Eratosthenes later would. From our sources, it would be difficult to say whether he got the job more because of influential contacts like Theophrastus, or because his high opinion of himself led him—and others—to believe he was entitled to it.

There were other museums in the Greek world by the third century, such as at Istria, Thespiae, and Stagira (Aristotle's home city). These were foundations more in line with the literal meaning of the word *museum*—that is, places consecrated to the worship of the Muses. The notion of a purely secular center of learning and research was an idea whose time had not yet come; the modern university has a roughly analogous history, originally having much closer ties to religious institutions (for example, Oxford University had its roots in the settlement of various monastic orders in Oxford; Harvard College was founded as a seminary by a clergyman, John Harvard). The Museum at Alexandria, likewise, would have been presented to the public as a religious benefaction from the king. As at the Lyceum, there would have been a sanctuary for the Muses, and an altar for sacrifices, as well as a head priest, in this case appointed by Ptolemy. Regardless of the particular interests of the tenured scholars who worked there, they were understood to represent a community devoted to the larger reverential purpose.

Under Demetrius's guidance, the groundwork was laid for what was to become the preeminent scholarly institution in the Greek world. Having direct knowledge of the Lyceum, he probably helped design arrangements in the Museum; he is credited with urging Ptolemy I to purchase and/or copy books in vast numbers for the Library. Indeed, Demetrius's faith in the power of the written word seems to have been absolute. Displaying a philosophy in exact opposition to that of America's forty-third president, Demetrius advised the prince "to collect books on kingship and the exercise of power, and to read them," presumably because advisors could not be trusted to tell the truth to their bosses. At least one source records that Demetrius was an intimate of the king, and had influence over policy, possibly including the seizure and copying of all incoming manuscripts for the "ships' collection."

If Demetrius did have such influence at court, it appears to have gone to his bleach-blond head. When Ptolemy I started to show evidence of favoring succession to one of his younger sons, the future Ptolemy II Philadelphus, Demetrius opined in favor of the interests of Eurydice, the old king's first wife. The only effect of his interference was to make an enemy of Philadelphus. With the death of the first Ptolemy, Demetrius was placed under house arrest, never to see freedom again. According to Cicero, he was executed some years later when an asp was slipped into his hammock—his end providing a fitting case history for another book on statecraft.


## UMAR'S ANSWER

The questions of the physical location of the Museum, as well as its layout and exact relationship to the Library, have long bedeviled experts. Few of the ancient sources are very specific about these matters, as we would expect when speaking of one of the most visible and famous institutions of their times. (Quick—what's the exact street address of the Jefferson Memorial?) There might perhaps have been a time to undertake excavations that might have comprehensively settled our outstanding questions about the topography of old Alexandria. The growth of the modern city to the ancient municipal limits and beyond, however, has made that prospect a remote dream. Archaeologists today must learn what they can when some parcel of land is briefly exposed by redevelopment. To date no direct remains of the Museum or the Library have come to light.

We do know a thing or two about the physical organization of the city. Its gridiron street pattern was centered on two major avenues: the Canopic Way, running along the major east–west axis between the gates later known as the Gate of the Sun in the east and the Gate of the Moon in the west, and another major street running south from the vicinity of the royal palaces. Alexander's Tomb (the Soma), though obviously not part of Alexander's original town plan (he would have expected to be buried in Macedonia), occupied a central location near the crossroads of two major thoroughfares.

There were five city quarters, designated by the Greek letters alpha through epsilon. The palace complex comprised the Beta quarter and was in the northeast; Alpha quarter housed the courts of justice, and Delta the town's extensive Jewish community. We know the approximate location of many of Alexandria's other streets, and a few of their names—such as the Street of Victory, the Street of Eleusis, the Street of the Fruit Bearer. Like the plethora of byways named Peachtree in modern Atlanta, there were more than a few thoroughfares named in honor of Philadelphus's deified sister-consort, Arsinoe II.

In his description, Strabo unambiguously states, "The Museum is a part of the palaces. It has a public walk and a place furnished with seats, and a large hall, in which the men of learning, who belong to the Museum, take their common meal." The Museum and Library were therefore either located within or adjoining the Beta quarter. This is less helpful than it might seem, however, because the palace complex occupied a large area—as Strabo states elsewhere, up to a third of the extent of the entire city.

One later event appears to offer some hope in pinpointing the location of the Library. In discussions of Julius Caesar's campaign in Alexandria in 48 to 47, Dio Cassius (c. 155–c. 230 CE) and Orosius (c. 385–420 CE) make reference to an earlier lost account of the great Roman historian Livy (c. 59 BCE–17 CE). Here Caesar, having barricaded himself in the palace against a Ptolemaic army, sets fire to his enemy's ships in the Great Harbor. The blaze goes out of control, spreading to buildings onshore and thence to the Library, where it reduces a large number of scrolls to ashes.

This would seem to suggest that the Library lay near the harbor. But as historian Luciano Canfora has compellingly argued, there is nothing in the story to prove that anything other than dockside *warehouses* full of books—possibly stock for export or new additions for transfer to the Library itself—were destroyed in the incident. This hasn't stopped the popular legend from spreading that Caesar destroyed the Great Library, however—in the movie

*Cleopatra,* we watch Hume Cronyn bemoaning Rex Harrison's careless loss of "Aristotle's manuscripts . . . [and] the testament of the Hebrew God."

Another tradition holds that the Museum was set near the Soma, near the confluence of the Canopic Way and its orthogonal counterpart (see figure 1 on page 4). This location seems remote from the Lochias peninsula where the palaces began, but is not impossible if we assume that Strabo's phrase "part of the palaces" means that the Museum was connected with, but not encompassed by, the royal estate. We can imagine it was rendered literally accessible from the palaces, as Cosimo Medici made Florence's Palazzo Vecchio accessible through a special aboveground corridor from his private residence. Or we can assume Strabo simply means that the Museum was adjacent to outlying parks, buildings, and so on, that were affiliated with the palace.

So what was in the Library? When we picture the place, we tend to think of it in modern terms: a dedicated building full of racks of books, in this case papyrus rolls. One of the most famous envisionings was in Carl Sagan's landmark PBS documentary TV series *Cosmos.* That show's Library was a monumental edifice, with towering marbled halls and tinkling fountains, like the lobby of some five-star hotel. (Through the then relatively new magic of digital postproduction, circa 1980, Sagan inserted himself into his creation.)

In point of fact, we have no solid evidence the Great Library was a monument distinct from the Museum. The Greek word for our *library, bibliotheke,* is not an exact equivalent but roughly means "bookshelf." Most scholars now accept that the content of the Library was nothing more than what was accumulated on all the bookshelves in the Museum. Strabo's terse description of "a public walk and a place furnished with seats, and a large hall" can be interpreted to suggest some sort of ambulatory with alcoves to the side, containing the scrolls. The living quarters and dining rooms of the tenured scholars would have been in the very same building, affording easy access to the collections.

For most of the history of the Library the collections were not in the form we are familiar with—the oblong stacks of paper printed on both sides and bound together on one vertical edge that we call "books"—but in the form of papyrus scrolls. The Nile River valley, with its plentiful stands of papyrus plant, was long the primary source of this material in antiquity. To produce a scroll, the stalks of the plant were slit open and laid flat in overlapping fashion; when two layers of these were pressed or pounded, the moisture-laden stalks cohered, producing a sheet. Multiple sheets were then glued together at the edges into documents some ten to twenty feet long, which were then rolled.

The text was written in columns perpendicular to the long axis of the scroll. To read one, the reader would unroll the next column of text on the right side while rerolling the last on the left. Contrary to what is maintained by some scholars, this did not mean that it always required two hands to work with a scroll—ancient readers were perfectly capable of using paperweights to hold their places while reading, searching the text, or taking notes. But scrolls did suffer the disadvantage of holding far less information than bound books (or *codices,* as their inventors, the Romans, called them). Depending on how the text was copied, the twelve thousand verses of Homer's *Odyssey* filled five to ten scrolls of normal length; truly monumental works, such as Callimachus's *Pinakes,* were well over a hundred scrolls long. By contrast, all but the very longest titles could easily be printed in a single codex. For this and other reasons, by late antiquity codices on parchment (a "paper" made from sheep- or goatskin) had gradually supplanted papyrus scrolls all over the Mediterranean world.

With not a scrap of physical evidence to go on, little can be said about the physical arrangement of the scrolls in the Library. Such a large collection would obviously be unusable without some means of locating particular titles. Different genres of writing had to be physically separated. Within each genre, historians believe the scrolls were arranged alphabetically by author, with care taken to include the writer's city of origin on the label (for example, Apollonius of Rhodes versus Apollonius of Perge). To differentiate multiple copies of the same work, the provenance (origin) of each edition would likely have been included (for example, "the *Timaeus* of Plato of Athens, copy of Crates of Rhodes"). As some specific titles, especially in poetry, would have been used in works by multiple authors, it is also likely that some labels included an "incipit"—the first line of the work.

To confuse matters further, the Great Library was not the only one in Alexandria. There was also an annex in the precinct of Serapis, southwest of the city, traditionally called the "daughter" library. This institution, which contained only about one-tenth the number of volumes in the Museum, seems to have been dedicated to public use. Where the parent collection included some 490,000 scrolls at its height, the daughter library held something like 43,000. These were likely just selected copies from the scholars' collection. For his part, Fraser doubts the daughter library contained copies because "duplicates are hardly likely to have been subject to a careful count." But this seems unreasonable: modern libraries, after all, keep records of duplicate volumes, and their ancient counterpart was no less carefully cataloged.

That the Ptolemies maintained a public library suggests that literacy was relatively widespread in the capital, at least among the Greeks. It also indicates enough interest in formal learning to make such a benefaction worthwhile—as opposed, say, to paying more dancers to paint themselves purple and dance on wine-soaked streets.

Like mendicants imagining fantasy meals, scholars have for centuries imagined the lost contents of the Great Library. We know

that the "authorized" versions of the plays of Aeschylus, Sophocles, and Euripides, commissioned by the city of Athens, were
there, as were the complete works of Aristotle, known today only
from sketchy lecture notes compiled by his students. We hear of
a three-volume Babylonian history, derived directly from the
cuneiform records at Babylon, by a Chaldean priest named Berossus.
We'd love a peek at the *Ephemerides,* the official war diary of the
Macedonian army's campaign through Persia, and basis for much
of Eratosthenes' eastern geography. The firsthand account of
Alexander's campaigns by Ptolemy I is almost certainly reflected
in the extant histories by Arrian and Rufus, but the primary
source would be of monumental interest. Resources on Egyptian
history were also no doubt in the Library, such as the original *Ae-
gyptiaca* of Manetho. A universal lexicon by Callimachus of
Cyrene, recording the most prominent authors in every sphere of
knowledge and their works, was not simply a catalog of the Library, but was probably based on an early version of that catalog.
It ran to 120 scrolls.

This inclusiveness is tempered somewhat by the fact that the Library was an entirely monolingual enterprise. It appears that books
from all over the known world were not only collected, but assid-
uously translated into Greek. Some of these efforts were highly
consequential (the first translation of the Hebrew Bible, the Septu-
agint, supposedly by seventy-two invited Jewish scholars) if not
heroic (a complete translation from Persian of Zoroaster's *Avesta,*
with more than two *million* lines—if we imagine a book version
with fifty tightly printed lines per page, the *Avesta* would be forty
thousand pages long). The Ptolemies were liberal in their ambi-
tions, but there was also no dispute over which was the language of
record in the "universal library." That the Greeks sought to understand and rule their foreign subjects by reading their books is obvious; that they declined to learn to read them in their original

languages shows that their ecumenical spirit had limits. (It is tempting to wonder, though, whether untranslated versions were retained, for quality control.)

In short, we can expect that everything worth having from antiquity, and quite a bit that wasn't, was in the Library. Its contents probably did change with time, however—and not always by addition. Conserving such a mass of documents against centuries of use, not to mention in the relatively moist conditions of Alexandria, would have been a stupendous task. Scroll attrition must have been a chronic problem. By the time the collections were destroyed (the daughter library with the rest of the Serapeion in 391 CE, by Christian zealots; the Great Library progressively from the early third to the mid-seventh century CE), they were left mostly with "patristic writings, Acts of Councils, and 'sacred literature' in general." Most of these were probably printed in codices, not the scrolls Eratosthenes or Callisthenes would have known.

In 642 CE, the city's Arab conqueror, General Amrou ibn el-Ass, wrote Caliph Umar ibn al-Khattāb over the disposition of the captured Library. Some say the caliph replied, "If their [the books'] content is in accordance with the book of Allah, we may do without them . . . if, on the other hand, they contain matter not in accordance with the book of Allah, there can be no need to preserve them." Amrou burned the books.

Umar's answer is justly notorious as one of the consummate expressions of ignorance in history. It comes as bittersweet consolation, though, that most of the classical and Hellenistic material was, by then, already long gone.

THE IBIS

From the papyrus documents preserved from the Ptolemaic period, you'd never think Eratosthenes or any other scientist was working in Egypt. Nothing researched or discovered in Alexandria has ever been mentioned in the letters of a contemporary Egyptian; most Greeks, as we have seen, were reciprocally oblivious to the everyday lives of the natives. As one historian has written, the Greeks "were little interested in their Egyptian surroundings, Greek or indigenous, and the surroundings, on their part, went about their own business and ignored the scientists."

We cannot help but wonder if there were other centers of learning in the ancient world that we know nothing about, simply because they were similarly cloistered. That the vast majority of the Library's contents—the fruit of centuries of research and scholarship—were eventually lost to posterity almost certainly had something to do with the Museum's insularity. The consequences were severe: modern astronomy didn't match Alexandrian achievements until well into the Renaissance. Eratosthenes' geodesy itself would have been little attested if not for Cleomedes' fourth century CE summary.

There is no obvious equivalent for the English word *librarian* in *Koine,* the form of ancient Greek spoken through most of the Hellenistic world. We do have a fairly good idea, however, of the identities of the head librarians through the first couple of centuries of the Museum's existence. They were Zenodotus of Ephesus (tenure: c. 285–c. 270); Apollonius of Rhodes (c. 270–245); Eratosthenes (245–c. 204); Aristophanes of Byzantium (c. 204–c. 186); Apollonius the Eidograph or "literary classifier," (c. 186–c.175); and Aristarchus of Samothrace (c. 175–145). Specialists debate whether Demetrius of Phaleron or Callimachus served in any official capacity.

In 145 the newly enthroned King Ptolemy VIII, suspecting disloyalty among his Greek subjects in the capital, expelled many prominent intellectuals from the city, including the head librarian, Aristarchus. For his trouble, the king's epithet was popularly changed from Euergetes ("Benefactor") to Physcon ("Fatty"). Fatty's purge did serious damage to the prestige of the Library in the Greek world—after Aristarchus, the list of head librarians becomes more confused and spotty, with genuine scholars alternating with what seem to be mere political appointees. The last Ptolemaic librarian known is one Onasander, son of Nausicrates, a priest. His tenure ended around the time of Caesar's arrival in Alexandria.

If we characterize each of the known or suspected head librarians by the work he was most renowned for, Eratosthenes represented a clear break from his predecessors. Demetrius of Phaleron, Zenodotus, Callimachus, and Apollonius of Rhodes were, respectively, a philosopher-politician, a Homeric scholar, a scholar-poet, and an epic poet. Eratosthenes was the first librarian whose primary contributions were in mathematics and natural science.

To be sure, few scholars of the period—and least of all Eratosthenes—restricted themselves to a single discipline. The modern division in the university between sciences and humanities (the so-called two cultures) would have been alien to the ancient mind. Thus, in addition to mathematics and astronomy, Eratosthenes produced works of poetry, criticism, history, and philosophy; Callimachus wrote voluminously on diverse natural marvels—on the rivers of Europe, on notable varieties of fish and birds, on the winds. Such sensational material, collectively known as paradoxography, might be called scientific in a loose, descriptive sense.

But the point remains that Eratosthenes was the first in that major post to contribute first-class work in the sciences—and arguably the last, as well. Although the *Suda* names Aristophanes of Byzantium as one of Eratosthenes' pupils, that scholar is overwhelmingly remembered as a critic and for pioneering the use of accent marks in written Greek. Eratosthenes was surely a dominant figure at the Museum in the late third century, yet he had no real successors. It is a paradox we will have occasion to discuss further below.

Of the actual functioning of the Museum we have a few anec-
dotes and many likely suppositions. What is perhaps most important to keep in mind is that it was *not* the ancient equivalent of a
university. True, it had a tenured faculty (with room and board and
stipends free of tax, no less), and lines of scholarly descent that suggest at least informal mentoring. Some of the head librarians did
serve duty as tutors to the crown prince, though there is no clear
evidence Eratosthenes did so. Yet the Museum's educational function was purely incidental; scholars in the Museum were not
obliged to take on students or hold regular classes. If public airing
of research did occur, it was probably in the form of lectures that
may or may not have been open to the ordinary citizen. In this, it
is more closely analogous to a modern private research foundation
or think tank.

That said, the Museum was subject to many of the same petty
political dynamics seen in many modern academic departments—
or indeed anywhere where diverse personalities are obliged to
tolerate one another. Henry Kissinger's famous quip that "University politics are vicious precisely because the stakes are so small"
was nowhere more true than where scholars clashed over the possible spuriousness of this or that single line from Homer. The rarified
atmosphere naturally bred precious, recondite humor: we hear of
one scholar who exercised his wit by rewriting all twelve thousand
lines of the *Odyssey* without once using the letter *s*. In Timon of
Phlius's crack about "scribblers on papyrus, ceaselessly wrangling in
the bird-cage of the Muses," we can hear the distant cacophony of
mutual correction and sneering one-upsmanship, the drone of end-
less seminars, the boozy mixers and their whispered gossip.

Invective, *ad hominem* and otherwise, flew in the form of cheap
pamphlets—the precursor to the intemperately fired-off e-mail.
One scholar, a certain Ptolemaeus, was nicknamed "the Attacker"

on the basis of his relentless crusade against Aristarchus. The most famous feud of all was between Callimachus and Apollonius: the first, who disapproved of bloated epics like Apollonius's *Argonautica,* cleverly likened the author (who appears to have had long, skinny legs) to a street ibis, indiscriminately consuming and spewing forth garbage. Apollonius, in his turn, parodied his rival's lexicon of famous writers (see p. 73) with a mock entry for Callimachus himself as "trash" and "a joke."

And yet the stakes could suddenly turn deadly serious at an institution where the royal patron was immensely more powerful than any modern university dean. Aristophanes of Byzantium, Eratosthenes' successor as head librarian, was imprisoned by Ptolemy V Epiphanes merely on the *rumor* that he was considering defection to the Museum at Pergamon; we've already seen how Ptolemy VIII, "Fatty," opted to eject the entire community of foreign-born Greek intellectuals from the city.

Beneath the petty rivalries, then, there had to be an undercurrent of unease at the Museum that the privileges of membership could not dispel. We can hear this in a fragment from Callimachus's *Aitia,* in which the scholar enjoins himself to observe the better part of wisdom in the company of his patrons:

> Dog, dog! Restrain yourself, my shameless spirit! . . . Much knowledge is a sore ill for anyone who cannot control his tongue; he is like a child with a knife.

Where tenure was no guarantee of safety, obsequiousness, in the form of paeans and dedications to the sovereign, was honed to a fine art. On the plus side, the bane of the modern system, where an academic may earn tenure and elect to coast thereafter, was probably unheard of. While there were certainly creepers and climbers at the Museum, there was probably very little "deadwood."

## THE FUNDAMENTALISTS

The ostensible purpose of the Museum was to honor the Muses—the deities upon whom artistic creation depends. The canonical list of the Muses, which dates only from Hellenistic times, lists nine goddesses: Calliope (muse of epic poetry); Clio (history); Erato (erotic poetry); Euterpe (lyric song); Melpomene (tragedy); Polyhymnia (sacred song); Terpsichore (dance); Thalia (comedy); Urania (astronomy). Insofar as the Muses are associated with creative inspiration, the specialties of the "artistic" eight come as no surprise. The inclusion of astronomy among the arts, however, seems somewhat odd. This has much to do with the fact that today we separate astronomy, the science of the heavens, from astrology. If modern astronomers require inspiration, it is only in a loose sense (or else literally, in the case of writing grant proposals). Astrology, the art of discerning heavenly influence on human affairs, is most definitely helped by divine guidance.

Like the Muses, the Museum was mainly not in the science business. Many of the more lasting contributions of her scholars lay in the recovery, maintenance, and transmission of texts—specifically, Greek ones. With the collapse of the old order of competing city-states, and the incorporation of vast areas of the Old Persian Empire into the Greek *oikoumene* (homeland), there was a general feeling that a critical stage had been reached in Greek history. Exposure to other peoples and other histories, many profoundly ancient, lent a perspective that made Greeks reflect anew on their own deep past. The rise of rationalist skepticism in the fifth century—and the suspicion that the radical criticisms of the Sophists could not be stuffed back into the philosophic bottle whence they came—had a similarly disruptive effect on the old sureties. To many thinking Greeks, the Olympian gods came to seem remote or irrelevant, and the myths nothing more than childish stories. "The old prophecies concerning Laius are fading; already men are setting them at nought, and nowhere is Apollo glorified with honors; the worship of the gods is perishing," lamented the chorus in Sophocles' *Oedipus Tyrannus.*

The response to such crises, then as now, is to pare back to fundamentals and refound tradition on a more secure basis. The root stories that defined Greekness had to be excavated and purified of corruption. The project of fixing the great heritage of the Homeric epics in written form—and removing the anachronisms, errata, and interpolations that had infested the text over hundreds of years of oral transmission—consumed vast amounts of time and energy at the Museum. Zenodotus, perhaps along with Aristarchus, was the first to establish the twenty-four–book structure of *The Iliad* and *The Odyssey* as we know them today. The works of other important poets, such as Hesiod and Pindar, were similarly winnowed and organized.

There was an analogous preoccupation with tracing Greek myths and practices back to their causes, or *aitiai;* Callimachus devoted one of his most renowned poems, also called the *Aitia,* to the task of recounting the causes of a miscellany of obscure rituals, stories, statues, and customs. His *bête noire,* Apollonius of Rhodes, agreed with him on little except to fill his own epic, the *Argonautica,* with similar tidbits of anthropology. We have already had occasion to mention paradoxography—a semiscientific genre of popular writing that collected and presented remarkable "facts" about the world, often uncritically. This, too, can be taken as an attempt to bring a kind of understanding to a world that was suddenly much wider and weirder than that known to Greeks just a few generations before.

Along with purification and synthesis, the scholars of the Great Library sought to rationalize scholarship. They were likely the first to use alphabeticization to organize written material: Zenodotus, the first official head librarian, was the first we know of to compile a dictionary with entries in alphabetical order. It is believed that he also employed this principle in cataloging the scrolls in the Museum, probably by authors' names. This method seems prosaic to us, even obvious, because it has become ubiquitous—by using the alphabet, which is universally known to literate people, as a mnemonic device, Zenodotus hit on a powerful and convenient way to organize the Library's huge holdings.

The Alexandrians also established conventions for orthography and punctuation of written Greek, such as the use of accents and breathing marks. They sorted and categorized poetry into formal genres. They laid the foundations for formal grammar by dividing all Greek words into classes—nouns, verbs, conjunctions, and so on. They theorized about grammatical laws, arguing over their regularity in a dispute that anticipated similar arguments among nineteenth- and twentieth-century linguists. And all along the way, there was a preoccupation with authenticity, purity, Greekness. Callimachus, the most widely quoted author in antiquity besides Homer, famously proclaimed, "I abhor all public things." He might as well have said he abhorred all practical and foreign things as well.

Based on its preoccupation with matters linguistic and literary—in short, on philology—we might regard the Museum as the world's first department of classics. Ironically, though Eratosthenes' range of interests was quite a bit wider, he was the first to call himself *philologos*. As we shall see, he probably meant something quite a bit different than what *philologist* has come to mean today.

### POLYMATH

Eratosthenes' tenure at the Museum brought a different kind of intellect to bear on the vast resources of the Library. As head librarian, he was well positioned to embody wisdom in the new age of books.

The true test of learning, then as now, is not necessarily to have all facts committed to memory, but to know where to find things already written down. As someone equally comfortable in the vagaries of grammar, the forest of myth, and the straight and narrow corridors of mathematics, he was perhaps uniquely capable not only of putting Greekness on a rational footing, but of rationalizing the entire world.

But anyone who would serve as head librarian first had to prove his facility in what we would call the "humanities." His most significant work in the field of literary criticism was *About Ancient Comedy,* a treatise in twelve books that surveyed the history, language, and authenticity of plays from the tradition that culminated with Aristophanes. Now known only from fragments quoted elsewhere, the work appears to have had wide influence. Eratosthenes also wrote several minor works that helped bridge the gap between poetry and the more mundane professions: something called *The Master Builder,* for instance, listed and explained carpentry terms for use by poets. He likewise sought to synthesize divergent fields of inquiry in his *Catasterisms,* a book (again, known only from fragments) on the mythic origins of the constellations. This was more a treasury of lore about the stars than it was a work of astronomy.

Indeed, though Eratosthenes was not a historian in the proper sense, his impact on the discipline of history was enormous. By all accounts he is the effective founder of the discipline of scientific chronology—the placement of historical events and persons in their objective temporal order. "Objective" was an important distinction for Eratosthenes: for his *Chronological Tables,* which ran from the conquest of Troy in 1183 to the death of Alexander in 323, he avoided use of myths and legends as much as possible, rooting his chronology in secure sources such as the roster of Olympic victors and the Spartan king list. In a world where every city had its own calendar, most often based on the tenures of local kings, magistrates, or priests, the importance of such a universal work can hardly be overstated. It was also very much in the spirit of Alexandrian scholarship, with its goal of refounding the Greek legacy on a secure, authentic basis.

His emphasis on nonmythological sources, however, ran counter to ancient instinct. For many of Eratosthenes' contemporaries, to stand against the historicity of Homer's epics, and of the great legendary heroes, was an impious—and radically discomfiting— posture. It was not unlike the explicit rejection of the authority of the Bible for modern devouts. Polybius denounces it explicitly, claiming, "Eratosthenes is wrong in bidding us not judge [Homer's] poems with a view to having any serious meaning, or to seek history in them." Similarly unnerved was Strabo, who hewed to a more cautious position: "For while one must concede to Eratosthenes and Apollodorus that the later writers have shown themselves better acquainted with such matters than the men of early times, yet to proceed beyond all moderation as they do, and particularly in the case of Homer, is a thing for which, as it seems to me, one might justly rebuke them and make the reverse statement: that where they are ignorant themselves, there they reproach the poet with ignorance." It comes as little surprise, then, that later chronologists shrank from Eratosthenes' example, listing the exploits of Jason and Theseus and Heracles among other, demonstrably historical, events. In this, as in his geodesy, the vindication of Eratosthenes' approach lay in the distant future, with the rebirth of so-called critical chronology at the end of the sixteenth century.

The most enduring foundation of Eratosthenes' ancient fame lay in his contributions to geography. Use of the noun *geography* is unattested before him; even Polybius, who is elsewhere critical, concedes, "On matters concerning the country between the Euphrates and India, Eratosthenes is a better authority than Artemidorus." His geodesy was described in his short treatise *On the Measurement of the Earth.* His three-volume magnum opus, entitled

*Geography,* appears to have discussed the topographic and ethno-graphic aspects of the subject with equal ease—not unlike the modern *National Geographic.* It is known today only from scattered fragments quoted elsewhere, such as in Strabo:

> He *[Eratosthenes]* says, that the Nile is distant from the Arabian Gulf towards the west 1000 stadia, and that it resembles (in its course) the letter N reversed. For after flowing, he says, about 2700 stadia from Meroe towards the north, it turns again to the south, and to the winter sunset, continuing its course for about 3700 stadia, when it is almost in the latitude of the places about Meroe. Then entering far into Africa, and having made another bend, it flows towards the north, a distance of 5300 stadia, to the great cataract; and inclining a little to the east, traverses a distance of 1200 stadia to the smaller cataract at Syene, and 5300 stadia more to the sea. . . . The lower parts of the country on each side of Meroe, along the Nile towards the Red Sea, are occupied by Megabari and Blemmyes, who are subject to the Ethiopians, and border upon the Egyptians; about the sea are Troglodytae. The Troglodytae, in the latitude of Meroe, are distant ten or twelve days' journey from the Nile. On the left of the course of the Nile live Nubae in Libya, a populous nation. They begin from Meroe, and extend as far as the bends (of the river). They are not subject to the Ethiopians, but live independently, being distributed into several sovereignties. . . . The extent of Egypt along the sea, from the Pelusiac to the Canopic mouth, is 1300 stadia.

In his geographic writings, Eratosthenes shared with the Alexandrian paradoxologists a fascination with exotic details of foreign places. In book 1 of the *Geography,* he ponders some puzzling discoveries deep in the deserts of western Egypt, some three hundred miles from the coast:

This question in particular has presented a research problem: how does it come about that large quantities of mussel-shells, oyster-shells, scallop-shells, and also salt-marshes are found in many places in the interior at a distance of two thousand or three thousand stades from the sea—for instance in the neighborhood of the temple of Ammon and along the road, three thousand stades in length, that leads to it? At that place there is a large deposit of oyster-shells . . . besides that, pieces of wreckage from seafaring ships are shown which the natives said had been cast up through a certain chasm. . . .

Unlike the paradoxologists, however, he seems to have evaluated his material with a decidedly critical eye:

That to repel strangers is a practice common to all barbarians, but that this charge against the Egyptians is derived from fabulous stories related of (one) Busiris and his people in the Busirite Nome, as some persons in later times were disposed to charge the inhabitants of this place with inhospitality, although in truth there was neither king nor tyrant of the name of Busiris. . . .

This skepticism is clothed in a bitingly sarcastic quip preserved from book 1 of the *Geography:* "You will find where Odysseus wandered when you find the [fictitious] cobbler who sewed up the bag of winds." To Eratosthenes, the *Odyssey* was best taken as entertainment, not as a textbook on geography. To take Homeric epic as the wellspring of scientific knowledge, as many of his colleagues did, was to fundamentally misunderstand the nature of poetry, which was actually more about seducing the ear than informing the mind. Insofar as scholars still argue over the reliability of Homer as a historian and geographer, this is an argument that continues today.

Like Eratosthenes' rejection of chronologies based on heroic legends, his skepticism about Homeric topography could not have earned him many friends among the antiquarians and text scholars at the Museum. That his dismissal was a veiled insult—the "bag of winds" hinting at the fatuous emptiness of his opponents' position—bears a tantalizing echo of what must have been a lively subject of dispute around the seminar tables at the Museum. Indeed, when the gloves came off, Eratosthenes the sly provocateur was more than ready to become openly subversive: according to Strabo, he disparaged Homer's verse as " 'old lady idle gossip,' where one has total freedom to fabricate what sounds good in order to captivate." In contemporary terms, this would be like a professor of English literature telling his modernist colleagues that James Joyce was a purveyor of pompous, incontinent drivel.

As radical as Eratosthenes' evaluative powers seem, in other respects he was still a product of his time. This is particularly evident in his efforts to bring deductive, "mathematizing" rigor to what today we would consider the purely descriptive discipline of geography. In a surviving fragment from his poem *Hermes,* Eratosthenes portrays the god flying beyond the farthest of the cosmic spheres and looking back at the whole earth. There he sees that the perfectly rational, perfectly proportionate order that pervades the universe is reflected on the surface of our world, which itself can be resolved into five symmetrical zones disposed around the equator—two "frigid" zones at the poles, a "torrid zone" around the equator, and two temperate zones between them (see figure 17, page 174). It is likely that Eratosthenes expanded on these ideas in book 3 of the *Geography,* which Strabo paraphrases thus:

> Eratosthenes, beginning at the Pillars *[of Heracles]*, divides the inhabited world in half by means of this line, and calls them respectively the Northern Part and the Southern Part, and then attempts to cut each of these parts again into such parts as are

possible; and he calls these parts *sphragides*. And so after called India the First Sphragis of the Southern Part, and Ariana the Second Sphragis, since they had perimeters easy to sketch, he was able to represent not only the length and breadth of both parts but more or less also the shape, as would a geometrician. In the first place, India, he says, is rhomboidal, because the southern and eastern seas, which form shores without very deep gulfs, wash those sides . . . secondly, Ariana, although he sees that it has at least three sides well-suited to the form of a parallelogram, and although he cannot mark off the western side by mathematical points . . . yet he represents that side by a rough line that begins at the Caspian Gates and ends at the edges of Karmania joined to the Persian Gulf.

In other words, Eratosthenes not only sought to describe the shapes of the world's land masses, but also to account for those shapes in geometric terms. His polygonal *sphragides* (literally, "seals") were presumably distributed through the five zones of the earth in regular, proportional fashion, with no zone bestowed with too much or too little land. His persistent concern with distances between points (as in "The extent of Egypt along the sea, from the Pelusiac to the Canopic mouth, is 1,300 stadia") has to be understood in the context of establishing the shape and extent of the *sphragides.*

In this, he was being true to his philosophic training at the Academy in Athens. Following Plato, Eratosthenes believed that a deeper, ideal order must underlay the mass of seemingly disparate, untidy empirical facts. Indeed, the notion that some proportional order must dictate the shape and distribution of the continents lived on far beyond antiquity—it was among the reasons that early geographers long believed another large land mass must exist in the extreme southern reaches of the globe, a "counterworld" to balance the extent of dry land in the northern hemisphere. (Alas, the eventual discoveries of Australia and Antarctica did not quite do the trick; the southern hemisphere turned out to have less than its proper "share" of continent.)

But Eratosthenes' Platonic love of proportion did have a practical benefit: it lay at the heart of the reasoning behind his measurement of the earth.

<br>

PHILOLOGOS

The *New Shorter Oxford English Dictionary* (1993) defines *philology* as "love of learning and literature; the branch of knowledge that deals with (the linguistic, historical, interpretative, and critical aspects of) literature; literary or classical scholarship." As we have seen, Eratosthenes proved his bona fides in this field, and indeed was the first to call himself *philologos*. Exactly what Eratosthenes meant by this claim, however—or even whether he meant any one thing in particular—is less clear.

The word *logos* has powerful, polyvalent meaning in the history of Greek thought. It was derived from the verb *legein*—to speak—and is therefore associated with both the act and the productions of human speech. Given the disputatious nature of the Greeks, it comes as no surprise that *logos* also came to denote "argument," and by assimilation the whole enterprise of reason. In philosophy, to assert the primacy of *logos* came to entail a claim that the world is rationally organized, or even (as in the case among early Christians) that the Creator is the embodiment of reason. The first lines of the Gospel of John are perhaps the most enduring monument of this objectification: "In the beginning was the Word [*logos*], and the Word was with God, and the Word was God."

As historian Rudolf Pfeiffer explains, the classical Sophists were fond of coining words starting with *philo-*: "it may be due to them that we find *philologos* first in Plato . . . and once in a comedy of

Alexis in the later fourth century; it means a man fond of talk, dispute, dialectic in a wide and rather vague or ironical sense." In this sense, by calling himself *philologos* Eratosthenes was being both grand and flip at the same time—rather like calling oneself "citizen of the world." Pfeiffer goes on to suggest that "when Eratosthenes used it . . . the compound word refers (according to Suetonius) to persons who are familiar with various branches of knowledge or even with the whole of the *logos*." Eratosthenes, who was certainly aware of the comedies of Alexis and not beyond facetiousness, may well have embraced all the connotations of the word, from mere facility with words to vague self-deprecation ("the bag of winds") to acquaintance with the profundities of a rational universe.

Eratosthenes was *philologos* in another sense, however, that is directly relevant to his mathematical work and the measurement of the earth. The word *logos* could also be translated as "ratio," the proportional relationship of quantities (for example, the ratio of 3 to 6 and 6 to 12 is 1 : 2 in both cases, though the absolute difference between these pairs is 3 and 6, respectively). In *Timaeus,* a work Eratosthenes almost certainly studied, Plato applies the notion of proportionality to the relationship of the basic elements of the universe: fire, air, water, and earth. Just as the relationship 3 : 6 = 6 : 12, Plato argues for the qualitative proportionality of the worldly substances:

$$Fire : Air = Air : Water = Water : Earth$$

"And for these reasons," Plato wrote, "and out of such elements which are in number four, the body of the world was created, and it was harmonized by proportion . . . ."

In his one major philosophical work, the *Platonicus,* Eratosthenes enlarged upon Plato's use of the *logos* concept. From the fifth century CE philosopher Proclus Lycaeus we hear that Eratosthenes asserted proportionality as the common factor binding together all the quantitative sciences, from the simplest arithmetic to the farthest shores of cosmology. The second century CE mathematician Theon of Smyrna quotes him as proclaiming, "*everything* in mathematics consists of proportions between some quantities" (emphasis added).

By calling himself *philologos,* then, Eratosthenes evoked meanings that operated on different levels for all the denizens of the Museum. For the litterateurs, it suggested his facility with belles lettres. For devotees of fine rhetoric, it suggested his passion for a well-turned argument (and, if necessary, a stinging insult). And for those sufficiently "in the know" to detect it, it also proclaimed his basic Platonism, and his belief that the principle of proportion underlay all of mathematics and, in a literal sense, pervaded reality itself.

### ALL IN DUE PROPORTION

Among those "in the know" was the greatest mathematician of antiquity, Archimedes. Proof that he and Eratosthenes were acquainted in their lifetimes surfaced when the so-called Archimedes Palimpsest was published by the Danish philologist Johan Ludvig Heiberg in 1906. This parchment preserved hitherto unknown works by Archimedes, half-erased under a twelfth-century religious text. One of these books, entitled *The Method of Mechanical Theorems,* contained the following dedication:

> Archimedes to Eratosthenes, greeting.
>
> I sent you on a former occasion some of the theorems discovered by me, merely writing out the statements and inviting you to discover the proofs, which at the time I did not give. . . . Seeing moreover in you, as I say, an earnest student, a man of considerable eminence in philosophy, and an admirer of mathematical inquiry, I thought fit to write out for you and explain in detail in the same book the peculiarity of a certain method, by which it

will be possible for you to get a start to enable you to investigate
some of the problems in mathematics by means of mechanics.

The subject of the *Method* is the calculation of areas and volumes of figures by imagining their lines broken up into infinitely
small increments, and applying to them the mechanical notions of
levering, center of gravity, and torque. What is most relevant here,
however, is the familiar manner in which Archimedes addresses
Eratosthenes. The men clearly shared an ongoing correspondence—
indeed, Archimedes' somewhat didactic tone notwithstanding, it appears to have been a correspondence between equals.

From the reminder of the *Method* it is clear that Archimedes did
not consider reasoning based on mechanical properties to amount
to ideal mathematical proof. Resorting to mechanical notions provided at best a kind of provisional truth, offering encouragement
that a purely geometric proof was possible. It appears that Eratosthenes shared this reliance on pragmatic reasoning in his solution
to one of the most famous problems in ancient geometry, the
"doubling of the cube."

The puzzle was also known as the "Delian problem" because,
according to a passage in the *Platonicus* cited by Theon of Smyrna,
it was posed by Apollo himself:

when the god proclaimed to the Delians through the oracle
that, in order to get rid of a plague, they should construct an
altar double that of the existing one, their craftsmen fell into
great perplexity in their efforts to discover how a solid could
be *made* the double of a similar solid; they therefore went to
ask Plato about it, and he replied that the oracle meant, not that
the god wanted an altar of double the size, but that he wished,
in setting them the task, to shame the Greeks for their neglect
of mathematics and their contempt of geometry.

The problem is that we can't double the volume of a cube by simply doubling the length of the sides. Doubling the length, breadth, and height of a $1 \times 1 \times 1$ cube, for instance, would result in a body of 8 cubic meters ($2 \times 2 \times 2$). Instead, to double a 1 m³ cube we must find the number which, multiplied by itself and by itself again, equals 2. In our terms, this is known as the "cube root" of 2.

The Delian problem could not be formally solved under the conditions under which the ancient Greek geometers placed themselves—namely by stepwise reasoning based on drawn lines and circles. In the passage, Eratosthenes refers to a passage from Plato's *Republic* in which the philosopher seems to chastise his contemporaries because "no government patronizes [these problems of solid geometry]; this leads to a want of energy in the pursuit of them, and they are difficult." "Duplicating the cube" therefore took its place among the other outstanding research topics of the time, along with "squaring the circle" (finding its area), trisecting any given angle, or constructing a regular seven-sided figure (the heptagon).

It was not long before the geometer Hippocrates of Chios (c. 470–c. 410) made the first conceptual advance in solving the Delian problem. The details will not detain us here; what is important is that he realized that the key to doubling the square, or the cube, lay in finding a side length that is in *mean proportion* to the side lengths of the original and duplicated figures. Putting this insight into practice, however, was less than obvious.

Had Plato known about Ptolemaic Egypt, he would have found it far from his ideal republic. But it did patronize a man who found a *practical* way to double the cube. According to a letter to King Ptolemy III—possibly written by Eratosthenes himself, and quoted by the sixth century CE mathematician Eutochios of Askalon—Eratosthenes erected a column near the Museum to celebrate his achievement:

And on the dedication the instrument is of bronze and is fastened with a lead filling just under the moulding of the stele, and beneath the instrument is a shortened version of the proof and the figure, and also an epigram. These shall be written out for you so that you have it as it is on the dedication.

The epigram, which is widely accepted as the genuine work of Eratosthenes, follows:

*Friend, if you're thinking to render a minimal cube to its double, or*
*Even whatever in shape, Formed as solid, you must*
*Metamorphose, this [device] is ready for use;*
*when you've laid out the measure of*
*Deep-sunken grain-pit or byre, Hollowed-out vault of wide well,*
*Using this system, and once you have taken the two-fold concurrent of*
*Means, they are found on the points, Topping interior rods.*

*Nor should you seek for the difficult way of Archutas cut cylinders,*
*Neither for Menaichmos's "Three" (Lines from the conics produced);*
*Further, the line which the pious Eudoxos constructed by bending you*
*  Need not resort to for means; All are far harder than this.*
*Thus you may easily render a myriad means on this "Mid-Graph,"*
*  Starting from origin small, Using these tablets of mine.*

*Fortunate man Ptolemaios, as father in prime with his son and him*
*  All that is dear to the Muse, Royally favored as well,*
*Freely you granted; lord Zeus who are heavenly, hereafter let him in*
*  Quest for the scepter of kings Take it from Your hand alone;*
*All of this, let it come true; and let everyone say he is gazing at*
*  What Eratosthenes placed, making Cyrene his home.*

What Eratosthenes appears to be describing here is a kind of ancient slide rule or mesolabe. The details are sketchy, but it appears to have been a structure with two horizontal, parallel frames, between which slid the "tablets" Eratosthenes mentions in his epigram. The method looks complex at first blush but has a simple, straightforward result: without needing to know the underlying proof, anyone could slide the tablets into position, lower the swing arm, and produce as many segments of mean proportional length as one wished. Indeed, Eratosthenes pointedly does not claim to have found an original solution to the Delian problem in his dedication. He only claims to have invented one that is easy to use.

To be sure, the procedural simplicity of Eratosthenes' method had deep roots in his identity as a *philologos* ("lover of proportion"). The linear mean proportionals calculated by his machine are reminiscent of the elemental proportions described by Plato:

*Fire* : *Air* : *Water* : *Earth*

Indeed, the use of proportions to solve this bedeviling problem must have represented clear evidence of the pervasive importance of *logos* in its mathematical guise.

Eratosthenes was not unique in erecting a monument to his intellectual breakthroughs. We know of other so-called dedicated inventions in the Greek world, such as the head of the Egyptian god Bes erected on a column by Ctesibius of Alexandria (mid-third century), which included a pneumatic mechanism to make the head "speak"; or the engraved sundial set up by Apollonius of Heracleia, dedicated to Ptolemy II Philadelphus. Eratosthenes' celebration of a purely pragmatic method of duplicating the cube, however, did not necessarily sit well with the theoretical purists of his time. It was an attitude reflected by Plutarch (46–127 CE), when he recounts,

Plato reproached the disciples of Eudoxus, Archytas and Menaechmus for resorting to mechanics and instrumental means for resolving the problem of duplication of volume; for in their desire to find in some fashion, two mean proportionals, they resorted to a method that was irrational. In proceeding in this way, did not one lose irredeemably the best of geometry, by a *regression to a level of the senses*, which prevents one from creating and even perceiving the eternal and incorporeal images among which God is eternally god.

Seen against this background, Eratosthenes' invention and even celebration of practical methods like the mesolabe and his so-called Sieve (his handy-dandy method for generating prime numbers) represented a break from academic fundamentalism. We may put this down to the same independence of mind he showed back in Athens, with respect to the know-nothing ethical Stoicism of Ariston. Perhaps as important, it could not have harmed Eratosthenes' standing in the Ptolemaic court to advertise just such a tangible return on the king's investment.

Indeed, despite the high-minded misgivings of the Platonists, Alexandria was a gadget-crazy place. Just how far this ancient passion for gizmos went only started to become clear early in the twentieth century, when something extraordinary was salvaged from the deep waters off the Greek mainland.

### GIFTS FROM RHODES

In the autumn of 1900, the captain of a small fishing vessel decided to try his luck collecting sponges in the deep waters off the northeast coast of the island of Antikythera. In that part of the Aegean, the age-old practice of diving naked had recently given way to Victorian-vintage helmet diving, with the sponge harvesters dressed in the clumsy suits of armor, their air pumped from the surface through an air hose. At the 180-foot depth the crew would visit that day, each diver could only stay down for about five minutes before risking death from the bends. The first man winched down that October morning was one Elias Stadiatos, an experienced diver.

Stadiatos was in a panic when he was pulled back to the surface. When they finally got his helmet off, he began to jabber about seeing the sea floor littered by "a heap of dead naked women, rotting and syphilitic," horse carcasses, and "corpses" green with putrefaction. The captain, Dimitrios Kondos, immediately had the diving gear stripped from Stadiatos and went down himself. When he surfaced, Kondos was likely in a far more cheerful state of mind than his rattled employee: in his hands was the arm of a Greek bronze statue he had plucked from the bottom. Kondos and his men had stumbled on a major find—the first significant archaeological discovery made by Greeks in their homeland since independence.

Investigation and salvage from the Antikythera wreck proved it to be one of the richest maritime hoards ever found. The "corpses" green with putrefaction were a treasure trove of Greek bronzes from the fourth century; massive marble statues, rendered grotesque by the accumulation of underwater growth, as well as fragments of ancient furniture, glassware, wine jars, and other metal objects, were also recovered. Subsequent examination of the pottery suggested that the ship had originated in Rhodes, and had made its last journey sometime early in the first century BCE. Historians now suspect that it was part of the fleet the Roman general Sulla used to ship booty home from his eastern campaigns of the 80s. Though other treasure ships got through to Italy, this one went down in a storm that drove it too close to the rugged shores of Antikythera.

Among the other metal objects was a find that was to prove far more significant than any of the artworks. A shoebox-size device, broken into three major pieces and obscured by marine accretions, was discovered among Sulla's trophies. By all appearances this mechanism, with its complex arrangement of gears and dials, had to be modern; the suggestion was seriously made that some eighteenth-century clock or navigational instrument had been accidentally dropped into the wreck zone. But epigraphic examination conclusively showed that the Greek inscriptions on the device dated from the early first century. All research conducted on it since, which now includes sophisticated X-ray tomography of its hidden details, has confirmed the verdict: the Antikythera mechanism is a truly ancient artifact of heretofore undreamed sophistication—an analog computer two thousand years before its time.

Modern reconstructions indicate that the crank-driven mechanism was a kind of celestial simulator, utilizing a complex arrangement of differential gears to represent the movements of the sun, moon, and planets (see figure 9). One of its faces represented the passages of the sun and moon; the device could not only be used to predict eclipses, but indicated in what part of the zodiac the event would occur. The front dial includes a slip ring that could be adjusted to compensate for the quarter-day difference between the old Egyptian calendar year (365 days, with no leap years) and the ac-

*Fig. 9. Derek de Solla Price's reconstruction of the Antikythera mechanism*

tual time it takes the earth to revolve around the sun (about 365.24 days). In this way the user could adjust the computer to represent the positions of the celestial bodies at any time in the past or future, much as in a modern planetarium.

A number of repairs on the mechanism suggest that it was actually in use for several years before it was lost. The scheme of its movement pushes back the history of such devices by at least a millennium; some of the details anticipate the "planetary gears" in modern automobile transmissions. The mechanism's constructor is unknown, but one of the inscriptions is known to have been authored by the astronomer Geminus of Rhodes (c. 110–40). We also have references to similar devices in the contemporary literature: Cicero, for instance, mentions "the orrery recently constructed by our friend Poseidonius, which at each revolution reproduces the same motions of the sun, the moon, and the five planets. . . ."

The discovery of the Antikythera computer has deep implications for our woefully low estimate of ancient Greek technology. References to similar and earlier mechanisms can no longer be easily dismissed as errors or exaggerations. Cicero elsewhere mentions another device constructed by Archimedes, taken by the Roman general Marcellus after the conquest of Syracuse in 212. This device, like the differential gear system of the Antikythera machine, demonstrated "how a single revolution should maintain unequal and diversified progressions in dissimilar motions."

Ptolemaic Egypt, too, had its share of mechanical marvels. Egyptian agriculture was revolutionized—or at least improved—by the introduction of water-lifting mechanisms such as the screw pump popularly attributed to Archimedes, but probably refined at the Museum. The Pharos, of course, was renowned for its colossal height, its far-reaching beacon, and possibly for a system of mirrors that allowed lookouts to scan over the horizon from ground level. Athenaeus is the source of a description of a similarly massive dreadnought, constructed in the reign of Philopator, that was 420 feet long, had forty banks of oars counterweighted with lead, and a crew of 7,250. Even more outrageous, Pliny describes how the

Arsinoeion in Alexandria was roofed with magnetic stones so that the iron cult statue of the queen would "have the appearance of hanging suspended in the air." A similar contraption is reported at the Temple of Serapis, where the lodestones were supposedly hidden in flat panels on the ceiling, allowing iron statues of the gods to mysteriously levitate. The source for this story, a Christian monk named Rufinus of Aquileia (c. 345–410 CE) was unsympathetic to such pagan "trickery," yet even he would not dispute its ingeniousness.

On the other end of the physical scale, we've already had occasion to mention the water-driven pulse timer of Herophilus. Athenaeus has also preserved an account of a kind of android that appeared at Philadelphus's ascension festivities; the automaton was twelve feet tall, "had on a yellow tunic with gold spangles, and was wrapped in a Laconian shawl. Moreover, this image would rise up automatically without anyone putting his hands to it, and after pouring a libation of milk from a gold saucer it would sit down again" (shades of the "animatronic" presidents at Disneyland!).

The construction of such gizmos contrasts sharply with the presumed disdain of the ancients for complex technology. Their alleged technophobia was diagnosed by classicist Moses Finley in a series of influential but flawed publications starting in the mid-1960s. According to Finley, the Greeks and Romans eschewed technological innovation in part because their societies were poor in mechanical know-how, but awash in cheap human muscle power. To a certain class of contemporary intellectuals, "hands-on" labor, including the tinkering of inventors, was something worse than common, having about as much prestige then as working the fry station at McDonald's does today.

To them, armchair speculation or, if necessary, the kind of informed observation practiced by Aristotle, was the preferred mode. The proper goal of science, argued Plato in his *Republic,* is knowledge of the eternal, unchanging verities accessible to minds undistracted by the transient, imperfect objects of the sensory world. "Nothing of that sort," he declared, "is matter for science." The point applies even to the planets and stars, notwithstanding their ethereal nature: "The true astronomer . . . will never imagine . . . that [things] material and visible can also be eternal and subject to no deviation—that would be absurd; and it is equally absurd to take so much pains in investigating their exact truth. . . . Let us leave the heavens alone."

Similar sentiment is detectible even in the most sophisticated model of the universe the Greeks had until late antiquity. Though Eudoxus's theory of concentric spheres attempted to account for the observed movements of the heavens, "there was nothing mechanical about it." The model lay in the realm of pure geometric fantasy, meant only to derive planetary motion without tackling practical issues (for example, what are the spheres made of? How are they connected? What keeps them moving?).

Finley's arguments were so effective that technophobia came to characterize the ancient world in the popular mind as thoroughly as swords and sandals. (Carl Sagan accepted them uncritically in *Cosmos*.) Yet the Antikythera mechanism proves that, by Hellenistic times at least, the ancients had a tradition of constructing sophisticated scientific instruments. The philosophic bias against the practical occupations likewise must have softened—thanks in part to such figures as Archimedes, Eratosthenes, and Poseidonius. As we have seen, at least some mechanical contraptions, such as Eratosthenes' mesolabe, were seen as worthy of dedication to the sovereign. Putting aside Plutarch's assertion that Archimedes viewed practical research as "ignoble and vulgar," the great mathematician also appears to have indulged the theatricality afforded by some mechanisms, such as when he used a system of compound pulleys to single-handedly pull a loaded cargo ship.

At the very least, this evidence suggests that Finley and his followers have grossly underestimated whole swaths of ancient technical culture. At most, it hints that the prominence of writers such as Plato and Plutarch in the surviving literature—and the archaeology-averse, text-based tradition of classical studies that emerged to interpret them—have not given us an accurate picture of antiquity, but instead led us seriously astray.

Indeed, there can be little doubt that such proto-Luddite idealism resonated with certain prejudices on the part of early modern classicists. The latter were, in the main, donnish types more comfortable with noun declensions than differential gears. For the Victorians, the study of antiquity was not just a matter of idle historical inquiry, but a formative influence on the ruling class of their own time. In this view, the ancients more or less prefigured the hale and hearty collegians who studied them later—they were "fellows of another college," as the old Oxford saying goes. Not for them was the study of puttering mechanics with dirt under their fingernails.

On my way to Alexandria, I stopped at the National Archaeological Museum in Athens to see the real Antikythera mechanism. The fragments are each no more than a handsbreadth wide—I almost missed them among the other, more obviously impressive, artifacts nearby. But the mechanism has its own strange allure. Arranged there in its three pieces, its delicate gears pancaked in verdigris gunk, it looks more like a forlorn remnant of our civilization, not of antiquity. One imagines it used as a prop in *Planet of the Apes,* brandished by Charlton Heston to prove that yes, an advanced culture did exist in the distant past.

The remains are on display beside a full-scale reconstruction of the original device (see figure 9 on page 97). This replica, made thirty years ago by Derek de Solla Price, does not take into account the more sophisticated forms of digital imaging that have been developed since the 1970s, and so is not the last word on the mechanism's true appearance. It is safe to say, however, that it would have been about the size of a shoebox, with a dial representing the movements of sun and moon on one side, and two dials on the reverse showing the positions of other heavenly bodies. Newly fashioned, it would have gleamed like a bronze mirror, reflecting the face of its user as he oiled the gears, set the slip ring, and operated the works with a knob at the mechanism's side. It almost seems presumptuous, the image of our ancient operator watching himself as he wound the crank. For if the Antikythera mechanism is a kind of model universe, the bronze knob is surely a fitting place for the hand of God.

### DENOUEMENT

Like silphion, Eratosthenes was good for many things. By the end of his eighty-two years, he had achieved renown as a mathematician, geographer, astronomer, poet, historian, literary critic, and ethnographer. Yet while this diversity of talents makes for an interesting biography, it almost certainly did not endear him to contemporary specialists in each of these fields. Such resentment was perhaps the inspiration for his nickname in his lifetime: Beta, meaning "second best" in every field, with the implication being much like the modern phrase "jack of all trades, master of none."

Eratosthenes inevitably would have attracted critics, given his intellectual pedigree. His formative studies with the Stoic Ariston and the skeptical Platonist Arcesilaus at Athens have already been mentioned; then, as in many university departments today, such connections provide handy ways to pigeonhole a colleague or adversary. The fact that his *Platonicus* was based on Plato's *Timaeus,* and included Plato himself as a character, suggests that in fact he saw himself largely as a follower of Plato. According to the *Suda,* another of his nicknames was "a second or new Plato"—a nickname that, like Beta, had semiderogatory implications, given the Aristotelian ("Peripatetic") philosophy that lay at the roots of the

Museum and Library. Writes Solmsen, "it is easy to imagine that his less philosophical colleagues in Alexandria found his Platonism just as irritating as the universality of his interests."

As we have seen, Eratosthenes did make contributions to what we would call the "humanities," from literary criticism to poetry to historiography. Yet he was famous in antiquity and remains so today mainly for his quantitative geography. This he accomplished despite the fact that he was head librarian in an institution rooted in an Aristotelian tradition that was hostile to the use of mathematics in science.

In a system rooted in royal patronage, however, the sovereign's priorities weighed heaviest of all, and the Ptolemies were most certainly interested in practical geography. Trade with the African interior constituted a major source of Alexandria's wealth. The continent was also a source of elephants—a military asset roughly equivalent to the tanks of modern armies. These were essential to Egypt's efforts to keep up with the rival kingdom to the east, the vast Seleucid Empire, which had relatively easy access to the elephants of south Asia. It was not lost on the Ptolemies that the four hundred elephants given to Seleucus by Chandragupta as part of a peace treaty in 303 figured prominently in the former's victory over Antigonus One-Eye at Ipsus in 301. African elephants would later figure again in Ptolemy IV's victory over the Seleucids at Raphia in 217.

The circumference of the earth, and by inference the length and extent of African trade routes, would therefore have been of keen interest to the crown. Enthusiasm for Eratosthenes' geodesic project was almost certainly greater in the royal palace than among his jealous peers in the Museum.

## 4. GREEKS AND BARBARIANS

THE ANCIENT Greeks prided themselves on their freedom, but that didn't mean they cared about anybody else's. Their attitude toward the vanquished peoples of the former Persian Empire, and indeed toward anyone who didn't speak Greek, was typically contemptuous. From his first appearance on stage in Aeschylus's *The Persians* through Hellenistic times and beyond—when the Romans echoed the prejudice—the stereotypical barbarian was morally torpid, unfettered by modesty or reason, too selfish and/or ignorant of the craft of politics to govern himself.

The pattern is reflected in the legendary character of Medea, princess of Colchis beyond the Black Sea, who is so in thrall to her passion for Jason that she murders her children in revenge when he abandons her. We see it again in Herodotus's portrayal of the Persian king Xerxes who, on his way to enslaving Greece, childishly flogs the Hellespont straits when a storm wrecks some of his ships. And we hear it in Aristotle, when he supposedly advised the young Alexander to "to have regard for the Greeks as for friends and kindred, but to conduct himself toward other peoples as though they were plants or animals." Alexander should do so because "the barbarians are more servile in their nature than the Greeks, and the Asiatics than the Europeans, [enduring] despotic rule without any resentment."

In addition to Eratosthenes' heterodox philosophy and the irritating comprehensiveness of his interests, he apparently took a dim view of the ethnic prejudices of most educated Greeks. Strabo reports,

Now, towards the end of his treatise—after withholding praise from those who divide the whole multitude of mankind into two groups, namely, Greeks and Barbarians, and also from those who advised Alexander to treat the Greeks as friends but the Barbarians as enemies—Eratosthenes goes on to say that it would be better to make such divisions according to good qualities and bad qualities; for not only are many of the Greeks bad, but many of the Barbarians are refined—Indians and Arians, for example, and, further, Romans and Carthaginians, who carry on their governments so admirably. And this, he says, is the reason why Alexander, disregarding his advisers, welcomed as many as he could of the men of fair repute and did them favors—just as if those who have made such a division, placing some people in the category of censure, others in that of praise, did so for any other reason than that in some people there prevail the law-abiding and the political instinct, and the qualities associated with education and powers of speech, whereas in other people the opposite characteristics prevail! And so Alexander, not disregarding his advisers, but rather accepting their opinion, did what was consistent with, not contrary to, their advice; for he had regard to the real intent of those who gave him counsel.

In other words, Eratosthenes used Alexander's example to argue that it was better to judge men by their personal qualities—by the psychology of virtue, so to speak—than by the "proto-anthropology" that distinguished between the civilized and the barbaric. These virtues transcended the incidental politics of the moment. Indulging his apparent taste for the perverse, Eratosthenes links the Romans and Carthaginians in enjoying admirable government, even though those powers had only recently stopped slaughtering each other in the First Punic War (264–241).

Eratosthenes' liberality may have had something to do with the fact that he came from Cyrene and resided in Alexandria, near the southern periphery of the Greek world. He therefore had more occasions to encounter those "refined" barbarians. Certainly such views were profoundly subversive: the rationale for Greco-Macedonian hegemony over Alexander's former domains was, after all, rooted in Greek superiority in the arts of civic life. (That the power of the Hellenistic kings rendered the skills of self-government moot was conveniently overlooked.) Eratosthenes made such views seem less provocative by cleverly associating them with the policies of Alexander, who was said to reward virtue regardless of the ethnicity of the men who practiced it. Indeed, in this sense Alexander was wiser than his mentors, such as Aristotle: according to Eratosthenes, the conqueror's "color-blindness" served the real intentions of the Greeks—to reward the good and punish the bad—even if some of his advisors were distracted by the outward trappings of culture or language.

What little biographical information that survives about Eratosthenes does not record whether he practiced what he preached. If we grant that the Egyptians must have counted among the most "refined" of all barbarian races, did he seek to acquire more than a superficial understanding of native politics? Did he pore over specimens of native architecture, literature, decorative arts? Did he learn the Egyptian language?

Given the ubiquity of his interests, it is likely that he absorbed what he could of Egyptian religion, history, and social arrangements. Egyptian accounts of the upper reaches of the Nile, for instance, as well as of the lands and people encountered by expeditions mounted in the Pharaonic period, would have been of great relevance to his geography. Notwithstanding restrictions on the residency of natives in the capital, he likely had occasion to converse and correspond with Hellenized Egyptians, some of whom showed lively interest in Greek scholarship.

That he learned to speak Egyptian or write demotic is perhaps too much to expect, however. Barely any of the other Greeks of Alexandria bothered themselves to do so. Having only arrived in Alexandria at about the age of forty, and with the job of head librarian coming with responsibilities that were not inconsiderable, Eratosthenes probably relied on bilingual assistants to help him wade through research materials in written Egyptian. That such translators were available is beyond any doubt, considering the standing policy of rendering all books in the Library into Greek.

Indeed, it was probably one of those translators who first alerted him to an interesting fact about a certain well in Syene, far to the south in Upper Egypt—a well in which, on but one day a year, the sun cast no shadow.

## THE REFINED BARBARIAN

One of our most durable myths about science in history is that it is a solitary occupation. When we envision Archimedes in his bath, shouting "Eureka!" after he apprehends the principle of buoyancy, or Isaac Newton grasping the notion of universal gravitation when an apple falls on his head, we imagine them as singular figures, grappling alone with the puzzles of the universe.

Insofar as ancient scientists lacked the networks of institutional support—the universities and their faculties, corporations, colleagues, the granting agencies, and the calendars of professional meetings that characterize the careers of modern research scientists—they were indeed quite isolated. But many did have circles of colleagues of a less formal kind. As we have seen, even Archimedes, the archetype of history's secluded geniuses, sought "peer review" of one of his mathematical treatises from his friend Eratosthenes. And Eratosthenes himself, of all figures in the history of ancient science, enjoyed a level of institutional patronage at the

Museum that was unheard of until the advent of the modern university.

As noted above, Eratosthenes probably did not speak or read the Egyptian language, but depended on the Library's staff of professional translators. Turning to the specifics of his geodesy, we might also wonder how much of the work he did for himself.

Eratosthenes' method for measuring the earth depended on the difference in the angle of the sun's rays at noon on the summer solstice at two locations, Alexandria and Syene, and the linear distance between the two cities. The angle at Syene was stipulated to be zero—the sun was supposed to be directly overhead. The linear distance between Alexandria and Syene was likely known (or recoverable) from the work of Ptolemy's royal surveyors. The only original measurement—or in current experimental parlance, the "critical manipulation"—therefore lay in ascertaining the sun's angle at Alexandria. According to several detailed studies of Eratosthenes' method, the measurement at Alexandria was the *only* component of the experiment he did firsthand.

Travel to Syene (modern Aswan), located some 523 miles upriver from the capital, would have been expensive and time consuming. Direct measurement of the precise linear distance between distant places in antiquity was possible, but cumbersome (see below). The angular measurement at Alexandria on the solstice, however, would have required no special expense or travel on Eratosthenes' part.

Yet a skeptical mind such as that of Eratosthenes would not have been content with mere hearsay. It is likely that he would have sought *confirmation* that the sun reached the zenith at Syene on the summer solstice, either simultaneously with the Alexandria measurement or in some other year. For this relatively simple task he may well have done what any busy university professor would do today: delegate the boring stuff to a graduate student. As Syene was located well south of the areas frequented by Greek civilians—indeed, it was a place where Greek was rarely heard—it would have been useful to dispatch someone who could deal with the locals in their own language. In other words, Eratosthenes would have done well to send one of those "refined barbarians."

Before we turn to the specifics of how Eratosthenes and his assistants measured the earth, it's important to consider how Eratosthenes' method was revolutionary in its time. Only then might we understand why the challenge of collecting the basic data for his geodesy—the linear distance between the cities and the sun's angle—was worth tackling in the third century BCE.

## THE SAND RECKONERS

The archaic model of a flat earth almost resists the question of how big it might be. When the continents were imagined to be surrounded by a vast extent of water, with nothing at the boundaries but an unapproachable precipice, the issue of the earth's overall size scarcely seemed a meaningful question. Once the spherical model gained currency—and with that the possibility of traveling around the planet—estimates of its circumference followed quickly.

In his *On the Heavens,* Aristotle quotes a figure of 400,000 stades for the earth's circumference. Based on the Attic standard for the stade, this works out to more than 44,000 miles—a significant overestimate. From Archimedes' writings, we know that the geographer Dicaearchus (c. 300) argued, based on the linear and latitudinal distances between the cities of Syene and Lysimachia in the Propontis, that the earth must be 300,000 stades in circumference (about 33,000 miles, still 25 percent too large). In his *Sand Reckoner,* Archimedes posited an estimate of three million stades (that is, bigger than the modern figure for the planet Jupiter of 279,118 miles), though he did so only for the rhetorical purpose of proving that his numeral system could express very large quantities.

The standard method for estimating the earth's circumference before Eratosthenes was to measure the apparent curvature of the horizon at sea. This could be done in any of a number of ways, including measuring how far out from shore a lighthouse beacon of known height was visible, or the difference in the time of the sunset between ground level and a nearby mountaintop, or, as was probably the case in Dicaearchus's geodesy, the height of a bright star above the horizon at Syene when it had just set at Lysimachia.

The fundamental problem with this method, however, is that light from a distant lighthouse or a setting star does not travel straight to the observer's eye, but is slightly refracted (bent) during its passage through the atmosphere. We see a similar effect when a straight object looks bent when one end is placed obliquely in a swimming pool. In the case of observing the setting of a star, atmospheric refraction allows us to see somewhat over the horizon, so the star *appears* to set later than it actually does.

Without going into the arithmetic, the overall effect is that by this method the earth's circumference is overestimated by at least 20 percent. The effect of refraction could easily have been controlled for, if Dicaearchus and other ancient geographers had had a systematic understanding of it. Alas, such knowledge was lacking: the most sophisticated ancient treatment of refraction—itself incomplete—didn't come until Claudius Ptolemaeus's *Optics* half a millennium later. The unfortunate effect was that many ancient estimates of the earth's circumference were simply too large.

Eratosthenes' method avoided this problem. Its key measurement is the sun's angle at noon, when the light rays would travel more or less straight down to the ground. Just as a stick immersed perpendicular to the surface of the water will not look curved, light rays striking the earth from overhead are minimally affected by atmospheric refraction. Provided the other challenges implicit in his approach could be overcome, Eratosthenes had hit upon the best way yet to obtain an accurate measurement of the size of the earth.

## A STROLL IN THE DESERT

So how did Eratosthenes go about determining the distance between Alexandria and Syene? There's more to the question than meets the eye: people in most traditional societies, after all, have reason to know how far they must travel to get someplace, but rarely need to know the distance *exactly*. Expressions like "two weeks by donkey" or "a hard day's walk" would not do for Eratosthenes' purposes.

Aside from its river-borne traffic, Ptolemaic Egypt had one of the finest road-based postal systems of its time. Dispatches traveled north and south along the Nile, with rest stations set one day's journey apart, or about thirty miles. This necessarily implies that Ptolemy's engineers had good knowledge of road distances to and from the capital. But none of this would have helped Eratosthenes. He needed to know the distance not in road-miles—for the byways of Egypt were oriented to the winding river—but linearly, "as the crow flies."

In his landmark monograph on ancient Alexandria, P. M. Fraser argues that the straight-line distance to Syene was determined for Eratosthenes by agents of the king. "[I]t seems likely," he writes, "that [Eratosthenes'] ground measurements were freshly taken for him by pacers put at his disposal by Euergetes or Philopator." And indeed, it is possible—though we have no evidence for it—that Eratosthenes prevailed on Ptolemy to commission a fresh measurement of the distance between Alexandria and Syene. By "pacers," Fraser means that the length of the traverse was measured literally by counting the steps taken by someone on foot. To this method, we might also add the use of some kind of wheeled mechanism, such as the hodometer used later by the Romans. This was essentially a wagon with a geared measuring device mounted on it. When the wheels, which were of known circumference, turned a certain number of times, the mechanism dropped a pebble into a container, indicating that the wagon had traveled exactly one mile.

Alas, we have little evidence for the use of hodometers in Egypt before the Roman conquest. Those were, in any case, good for measuring roads, but not so ideal over rough, broken terrain, wetlands, or any of the three river crossings and one lake crossing the direct passage from Alexandria to Syene required. Fraser's step counters would have faced the same topographic obstacles, along with the challenge of crossing the scorching deserts that yawned on either side of the river, just a few miles beyond the narrow strip of cultivated land. Faced with such challenges, it scarcely seems possible that such direct measurement would have returned anything more than a pretty good approximation of the actual distance.

Though the Alexandrian Greeks may have lacked hodometers, they were heirs to a deep legacy of accurate land survey. The practice of conducting biennial "numberings" of royal properties was as distinctively Egyptian as hieroglyphics, going back at least to the turn of the third millennium. This was a practical necessity in a place sustained by annual flooding of the Nile, which regularly changed both the contours and extent of the arable—and taxable—land around it.

Residing as he did in the administrative capital of the empire, Eratosthenes almost certainly had access to the government's extensive cadastral (tax survey) records. Indeed, it would be more surprising if he didn't, given that the word he uses to describe larger landmasses (*sphragides*) is precisely the term used by the officials of the royal survey to describe parcels of taxable land.

Not a single map of measured land has been discovered from

ancient Egypt. We have a good idea of how such surveys were conducted, however, from paintings on tomb walls, such as in the New Kingdom tombs of Menna and Amenhotep at Thebes. The basic measuring tool was simple: just a hundred-cubit length of rope with knots tied at regular intervals (four or five cubits, or about seven feet). To align the cords, the Egyptians used a device called a *merkhet,* which was basically a plumb bob composed of a pebble suspended by string from a wooden handle. After setting up the merkhet, the so-called rope stretchers would orient the measuring cords by using the split end of a palm leaf as a sight vane.

Even with such crude tools the Egyptians achieved good results. One oft-mentioned example is the precise layout of the foundations of the Great Pyramid of Khufu, which is oriented to about three minutes, or one-twentieth of one degree, from true north. Even more impressive is the surveying done in the fourteenth century BCE for the construction of Pharaoh Akhenaton's new capital Akhetaton, near present-day Tell al-Amarna. Based on fourteen boundary markers that have survived on either side of the river, a modern survey found that the ancient Egyptians had laid out parallel, nearly identical east and west boundaries of 15,075 meters and 15,021 meters respectively. This is better than 99.641 percent accuracy. (Incidentally, even the royal step counters hypothesized by Fraser would have needed surveyors to do their work. For how else would the pacers have kept on an absolutely straight line, along the precise azimuth from Alexandria to Syene?

Such impressive results indicate that, even long before the Ptolemies, the know-how did exist to measure linear distances on the order of ten miles. This was more than adequate to survey nearly all the individual properties in the kingdom. That officials of the time could work up surveys of large areas by measuring them piecemeal is suggested by the deed of the Ptolemaic-era

Temple of Horus at Edfu, which includes the dimensions of multiple triangular and quadrangular parcels. By compiling existing tax maps in similar fashion, Eratosthenes could have determined the overall distance between the cities by simple, albeit laborious, geometrical calculation.

In fact, based on existing knowledge we have no idea how Eratosthenes obtained his linear distance to Syene. The method suggested here at least has the virtue of evoking what the Greeks were good at—survey and plane geometry—without requiring them to take a single step into the desert.

### IN THE VAN OF ERATOSTHENES

The simplicity of Eratosthenes' geodesy has made it the ancient experiment most often reenacted in modern science classes. In August 2006, Melbourne-based RMIT University sponsored a competition between high schools in Australia to most accurately measure the circumference of the earth, using differences in sun angle at local noon. (The winner of the thousand-dollar first prize was Nhulunbuy High School in Northern Territory.) Similar projects have been held by Roanoke High School in Virginia, Sonoma State University in California, the University of British Columbia, the Planetary Society (in conjunction with Bill Nye, the Science Guy), the Institut National de Recherche Pédagogique in Lyon, France, and many other institutions. For the September 2006 Eratosthenes Project organized by Youth.net, a team from Coal Ridge High School in New Castle, Colorado, reported a polar diameter of 24,868.82 miles—just nine miles over the true figure. This astonishing result beat those of competing schools from as far afield as Denmark and India.

One of the most ingenious tributes to Eratosthenes was conducted in the 1980s by the late physicist and educator Philip Morrison. To

find a figure for the earth's circumference, Morrison opted to measure the angle between the horizon and Antares, a prominent double
star in the constellation Scorpio. The measurement was taken at two
points along U.S. Highway 183, a road running north–south
through the American Midwest. Taking their first sighting near Bas-
set, Nebraska, Morrison and his wife, Phyllis, marked the elevation of
Antares on the side of their rental truck with black masking tape.
They then piled into their vehicle (which they christened "the van
of Eratosthenes") and repeated the procedure at a point 370 miles
south, in Coldwater, Kansas. Based on calculations similar to Eratosthenes' (the difference in the angular height of Antares/full circle is
proportional to 370/X, the circumference of the earth), the Morrisons arrived at a figure of 26,500 miles. Only about 1,600 miles
off, this result was not bad—though not in the league of the diligent
students at Coal Ridge High School.

Yet few of the modern reenactments, whether by high school
students or university physicists, accord with Eratosthenes' method
of measuring the angular deflection of the sun from true vertical
on the solstice. In the typical schoolyard case, the angle is taken by
measuring the length of the shadow cast by a vertical stake of
known height. As you may recall from junior high school math, if
we know the lengths of the sides of a right triangle, we can derive
the acute angles by using the basic trigonometric functions, sine,
cosine, and tangent. Here, the equation would be:

$$\tan A = \textit{shadow length} \; / \; \textit{length of stake}$$

Eratosthenes could not have used trigonometry, however, because it was not invented until well after his death. In the Greek
world, the astronomer Hipparchus of Nicaea is generally credited
with compiling the first trigonometric tables in the second century
BCE (though his work did not employ the functions we would

recognize today). The first proper sine table is not attested until the Aryabhata the Elder, an Indian mathematician who lived in the fifth and sixth centuries CE. Europeans gained knowledge of this and later work through Arab mathematicians such as Mohammad Abu'l-Wafa Al-Buzjani (940–998 CE).

One way to get around this is to read the sun's angle directly.

*Fig. 10. A hemispheric sundial* skaphe *similar to the one presumably used by Eratosthenes*
BIBLIOTECA ALEXANDRINA

This could have been done by stretching a string from the top of the stake to the end of the shadow, and reading off the angle of deflection with a protractor. Another is the method actually referenced in Cleomedes' summary of Eratosthenes' experiment. In several places, Cleomedes writes of angles of shadows cast in a "hemispherical bowl of the sundial": "If now we conceive another straight line drawn upwards from the extremity of the shadow of *the gnomon of the bowl at Alexandria,* through the top of the gnomon to the sun, this straight line and the aforesaid straight line will be parallel" (emphasis added).

What Cleomedes appears to be describing here is a *skaphe*—a kind of improved sundial invented by Aristarchus sometime early in the third century BCE (see figure 10). Instead of on a flat surface, the pointer (gnomon) of the skaphe is set at the bottom of a hemisphere. If the inner surface of the bowl had inscriptions of degrees (roughly, "lines of latitude" from the bottom), the precise angle of solar deflection could have been read directly from the tip of the gnomon's shadow—no trigonometry necessary.

This method also has the virtue of befitting the instincts of a true *philologos*. As we have seen, Eratosthenes regarded proportion to be the recurrent theme in the arrangement of the cosmos. Where a flat sundial would bear little resemblance to the surface of the globe, the hemispheric skaphe was, in a sense, a version of the world in miniature. The fact that the gnomon cast a shadow there but not in Syene offered a visual analog to the earth's sphericity that virtually anyone could grasp. In this sense, his geodesy was as much an opportunity for education as it was an experiment.

## TYCHE'S COMPASS

Our sources agree that Eratosthenes measured the solstitial deflection of the sun at Alexandria at 7.2 degrees, or exactly one-fiftieth of a full circle. The linear distance between Alexandria and Syene was taken to be 5,040 stades. According to Strabo, Pliny, and all of our other ancient sources, the fruit of these efforts was a figure of 252,000 stades ($5,040 \times 50$) for the polar circumference of the earth.

Or was it? Cleomedes, writing sometime between the first century BCE and the fourth century CE (no one is sure), clearly reports a figure of "25 myriad stades"—that is, $25 \times 10,000$ or 250,000—which is also what we'd expect if we multiply a linear distance of 5,000 stades by 50. So where did the extra two thousand stades come from?

One explanation for the discrepancy is that Cleomedes opted to report a rounded-off figure, possibly because his treatise was pitched to an undiscriminating audience. Another is that Cleomedes quotes a result that Eratosthenes himself later discarded. And indeed, though we lack Eratosthenes' own account of the experiment, it is possible that he made several attempts over a number of years to get an accurate sun angle. According to Athenaeus, it was Eratosthenes himself who said, "to those who thrice wipe the mouth, the gods give a better portion." (In other words, "the third time's the charm.")

He may also have revised his calculation after later getting more accurate information on the linear distance between Alexandria and Syene. Of all these possibilities, revising the distance seems far more likely—the two-thousand-stade difference amounts to a change of just under 1 percent, which is at least conceivable considering the relatively high precision of cadastral data of the period. On the other hand, that anyone could eyeball a mere 1 percent difference in the angle of a gnomon's shadow (and a *moving* shadow, moreover) strains credulity. In any case, despite the overall usefulness of Cleomedes' account, I prefer to accept Strabo's seemingly more precise figure for the final result.

No experiment, ancient or modern, is free of the possibility of error. Acceptance of the inevitability of uncertainty, and the management of it, is one of the defining characteristics of science, and one that makes it fundamentally different from other sources of knowledge. Eratosthenes' geodesy was no exception.

Some sources of possible error—such as the way the force of the earth's rotation makes a plumb bob point somewhat away from true vertical—are vanishingly minor. More potentially damaging were certain inaccuracies in Eratosthenes' assumptions about the geography of Egypt. Contrary to what he supposed, Syene was not located due south of Alexandria, but about three degrees' latitude east of the line between the cities. (In this regard, he would have done better to take his measurement from the town of Pelusium, on the eastern delta, than from the capital.) This means that the great circle Eratosthenes was measuring was somewhat offset from the geographic poles, and therefore was not the true polar circumference of the earth.

This problem is far from fatal—the difference between the polar circumference and Eratosthenes' oblique one would have been trifling. More troubling is the fact that Syene was not located on the line of latitude beneath which the sun is directly overhead on the summer solstice (otherwise known as the Tropic of Cancer). In 230, the latter would have been at 23° 44' north latitude, or about twenty-four miles *south* of Syene. This means that, rumor notwithstanding, the sun could not have shone directly into the famous well at Syene, but was about a third of a degree off the perpendicular.

One would think that the combined effect of two errors would be more error. But in fact it is less: by using the distance to Syene, a point three degrees of longitude off the north–south line, Eratosthenes managed to compensate for Syene's position somewhat north of the tropic (because the 523-mile distance to Syene, though directionally oblique, is very close to the true north–south distance between Alexandria and the tropic, about 515 miles in 230 BCE (see figure 11).

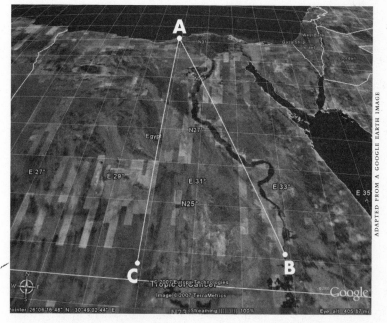

Fig. 11. Eratosthenes used the distance between Alexandria and Syene (A to B) as the basis for his geodesic calculation. However, the actual north-south line to the Tropic of Cancer in his time was A to C. The white line indicates the modern position of the tropic.

Eratosthenes also benefitted from the fact that the sun is not a dimensionless point of light, like the star Antares, but a disk covering approximately half a degree of sky. This necessarily causes some problems in reading sundials precisely, because the sun necessarily makes "fuzzy" shadows. But it also assured that, although the *center* of the solar disk was never directly overhead, for all practical purposes the outer edge of the sun did reach the zenith at Syene.

Though Eratosthenes' method was innovative, the quality of his result is thanks in part to the fact that his errors canceled each other out. In this he was nothing more than an early example of a perennial truth in science: it is not enough to be ingenious. It also helps to be lucky.

### DREAMS OF PRECISION

Some might object that Eratosthenes' final figure still sounds suspiciously round. Why 252,000 stades, and not, for the sake of example, 252,212 stades? Don't those three zeroes suggest that Eratosthenes was really being rather casual in his efforts?

It is a common assumption in the specialist literature that the roundish figure Eratosthenes published was the only one he could derive from his data. In fact, lacking his private notes or even a surviving copy of his monograph, we have no way of discounting the possibility that he did arrive at a more precise number, but simply chose to present a neater version to the public. As several authorities have pointed out, 252,000 is exactly divisible by sixty, and also corresponds to seven hundred stades for every degree of latitude. The implication is that Eratosthenes was only too willing to sacrifice precision for the sake of easy calculation.

This preference is more properly understood in context. When moderns discuss the work of the ancient scientists, they invariably translate all figures into modern numerals. This is a system rooted in ancient India that, with its mere ten basic symbols (0, 1, 2, 3, 4 . . . ) and positional notation (one figure stands for units, second figure to the left stands for tens, third for hundreds, and so on) is fairly easy to use.

Alas, the ancients enjoyed no such advantage. Most of us are familiar with the Roman numeral system, and can imagine how cumbersome it must have been to do arithmetic with it (quick, what's MDCCXCII divided by XVI?). For the period covering the classical period through the early Hellenistic, the Greeks used an even more complex *acrophonic* system, where the first letter of the name of each numeral stood for that number (for example, β = *beta* or 2, Δ = *deka* or 10, X = *xilioi* or 1,000, and so on), and higher numbers consisting of combinations of those numerals (so that 50 would be written ⊓, and 5,000 as ⊓). In this notation, the figure 252,212 would correspond to ⊓⊓⊓⊓⊓XXHHΔII.

After the death of Alexander an *alphabetic* scheme superseded the acrophonic everywhere except Athens. This system used the twenty-four letters of the Greek alphabet (plus three other archaic symbols) to represent the corresponding numbers: letters α through θ stood for 1 to 9, ι through koppa for the decades 10 to 90, and ρ through sampi for the hundreds 100 to 900. For higher numbers, the cycle repeated, with the addition of a small accent mark in the lower left ($'α$ = 1,000, $'β$ = 2,000, etc.). For numbers beyond a myriad (10,000), the letter M was written with a multiplier above ($\overset{\varepsilon}{M}$ = 50,000). The figure 252,212 in the alphabetic system would therefore be $\overset{\kappa\varepsilon}{M},βιβ$.

Both ancient systems were difficult to learn and ungainly to use. Some historians blame the awkwardness of this number system for retarding Greek progress in developing algebra. Where modern schoolchildren only have to memorize nine abstract symbols, the alphabetic system obliged the Greeks to learn more than thirty-seven orthographic correspondences between letters and tiers of various quantities. An analogy would be for us to learn that the expression *fuqd* can only correspond to 6,384 because $f$ is the sixth letter in the thousands tier, $u$ is the third in the hundreds tier, $q$ is the eighth in the decades, and $d$ the fourth in the unit tier. Learning the modern multiplication tables from $1 \times 1$ to $9 \times 9$ is challenge enough for youngsters today; pity unfortunate Greek schoolboys who had to learn methods to handle all the permutations between $1 \times 1$ and $10,000 \times 10,000$!

In a world where arithmetic was cumbersome and scratch paper expensive, avoiding cumbersome figures was not sloppy—it represented the better part of prudence. Indeed, what purpose at all would be served by reporting a conclusion like "252,212 stades"? This is not a question of engineering, where those extra 212 stades might mean the difference between a machine that worked and one that didn't. Supposing such a precise number to be more "scientific" says more about the modern sensibility than it does about the quality of ancient science. It is a modern conceit, after all, to exhibit our prowess with a blizzard of so-called significant figures. (I'm reminded of Mr. Spock in the original *Star Trek,* who would always give gratuitously hyperprecise answers to simple questions, causing his human crewmates to roll their eyes.)

It's also important to remember that Eratosthenes' theory of geography was rooted in his Platonism. In his eyes, the various regions of the earth were not singular creations, entities *sui generis* in the way that moderns perceive, say, South America as unique and worthy of characterization to the minutest degree. Instead, he saw the earth's regions as examples of *types,* polygonal *sphragides* each proportional to the others and all fitting into an overarching rational scheme, like tiles in some great cosmographical mosaic.

To such a mind, dwelling on tiny leftover quantities is counterproductive. It only made the fundamental problem of dividing the whole into its similar parts more difficult. Any preference of

Eratosthenes for citing a more easily expressed, more easily divisible figure for the earth's circumference was therefore not just excusable—by his lights, it was eminently sensible.

## THE STATE OF THE STADE

So much for the precision of Eratosthenes' work. What about its accuracy? Eratosthenes' renown in history is due not only to his clever method of measuring the globe, but to the presumption that he got it right. So, to what distance does 252,000 stades equal in modern units?

This simple-sounding question has bedeviled scholars for decades. Generally speaking, we encounter several traditions that define the stade. According to the folksiest of these, it is the distance covered by one pass of the plow across a field. According to another, it is the linear distance covered by a man taking six hundred heel-to-toe steps. The stade was also the standard length of the premier running race in classical Greek athletic games. Our modern word *stadium* is a direct descendant of the latter meaning, though a modern American football field is far shorter than an ancient running track.

Unfortunately, none of these definitions yields a standard length for the stade. The track at Olympia, for instance, was supposedly laid out by Hercules himself, six hundred of whose heroic strides equaled 192.3 meters or 210.3 yards; six hundred steps by the apparently daintier clogs of the man who laid out the stadium at Delphi yielded only 177.5 meters or 194.1 yards.

As in so many other areas of their civic life, the classical Greeks appear to have been more interested in preserving their regional idiosyncrasies than establishing international standards for currencies, language, or weights and measures. From various authors we hear of still other stades common at other times and places: an Ionic stade of 209.2 meters (229 yards), an Attic of 185 meters (202.3 yards), an Italic of 166.7 meters (182.3 yards), a Philetaeric of 200 meters (219 yards), and a Royal Ptolemaic of 210 meters (230 yards). Hunting down the stade Eratosthenes used in his experiment—his "geodesic stade"—has therefore become favorite prey for classicists with a quantitative bent.

Because it would be impossible (and impossibly dull) to summarize this entire literature here, I shall discuss only the two likeliest candidates for Eratosthenes' stade. The first was originally proposed in a posthumous work published in 1851. Here, the French philologist J. A. Letronne cited the Roman naturalist Pliny to the effect that forty of Eratosthenes' stades were equivalent to one Egyptian schoenus (a unit equivalent to twelve thousand royal cubits, or about four miles). Using measurements from Egyptian buildings, as well as a metrological relief from Libya in the Roman era, archaeologists have established that there were 0.525 meters to the Ptolemaic cubit. According to this reasoning, Eratosthenes' stade had to equal $300 \times 0.525 = 157.5$ meters (172.2 yards).

There is a certain logic to deriving Eratosthenes' geodesic stade from the Egyptian schoenus. He was, after all, residing in Egypt. The surveying records he may have consulted in determining the distance between Alexandria and Syene were based on the work of thousands of low-level government functionaries, many of whom were ethnic Egyptians who might have favored the native unit. A 157.5-meter stade also has the appeal of making Eratosthenes' geodesy look uncannily accurate ($252,000 \times 172.2$ yards $= 24,662.2$ miles, versus the true polar circumference of 24,859.8 miles).

Letronne's stade has therefore endured long in the literature. It was still accepted by at least one commentator writing as recently as 1993, on independent philologic and geographic grounds. Unfortunately, a 157.5-meter stade appears nowhere else in the ancient sources. Pliny, moreover, reports other values for the schoenus used "by other persons," such as one equivalent to thirty-two stades. Because other values appear elsewhere, such as in Strabo, Heron, and Herodotus, ranging from thirty to forty to sixty and even 120 stadia/schoeni, we really have no idea to which schoenus Pliny may have been referring. For these reasons and more, Letronne's seductive conclusion is now rejected by many specialists.

Considering the wide variability of all linear units among Greeks, it would be surprising if "other persons" did *not* find different stade values for the schoenus. In any case, the other leading candidate for Eratosthenes' stade is based on a reading of the whole relevant passage from Pliny, which reads: "by the calculation of Eratosthenes, a schoenus measures 40 stadia, *that is five miles,* but some authorities have made the schoenus 32 stadia" (emphasis added). As the "five miles" Pliny mentions must mean Roman miles, and the modern equivalent of the Roman mile is known with certainty (1 Roman mile = 0.92 miles or 1.48 km), we have the means to root Eratosthenes' stade in a unit far more secure than the Egyptian schoenus. Based on this argument, the stade must be 184.98 meters or 202.3 yards long—which makes it equivalent to the so-called Attic stade (known from the length of the footrace track at Athens). This means Eratosthenes' geodesy works out to 28,965.7 miles, or more than 16 percent too large.

Besides the fact that this argument is based on what Pliny actually said, there are other reasons to favor the Attic stade. In a 1985 article that has profoundly influenced the debate, University of Arkansas classicist Donald Engels suggested that the Ptolemies based their system of linear measurements on the 308.3 mm "Attic foot," exactly six hundred of which equaled one 184.98-meter stade. He also cited accounts of the marches of Alexander the Great in Asia, based on figures published by Eratosthenes. In all cases, assuming that one Roman mile equals eight of Eratosthenes' stades makes his distances very similar to modern ones. To this we might add that publishing in Attic units does have a certain plausibility, insofar as much of Eratosthenes' audience for his writings was in Athens, among the educated circles he got to know during his many years in the city.

Engels, confident that he has laid Letronne's stade to rest at last, concludes "the length of Eratosthenes' stade may be determined by two alternative methods; the first is to accept the ancient evidence for Eratosthenes' use of the Attic stade . . . and the second is to arbitrarily assert that the evidence is wrong and invent our own stade. That a great many in the past have chosen the latter route reveals something about their own attitudes concerning their classical heritage." Many others now agree. Case closed, right?

Not so fast. One innovative study, published in Russian in 1972, used an independent quantitative method to derive the length of Eratosthenes' stade. In a little-cited article (Engels criticizes it but provides no citation), the Soviet classicist L. V. Firsov compiled distances in stades between various places listed in Strabo, all of which were attributed to observations by Eratosthenes. When all such distances are collected, they amount to a significant data set of no fewer than eighty-seven individual linear segments (Firsov counts eighty-one, because he lumps eight segments into two composite ones). By dividing the distances listed in Strabo by the known distances in kilometers, Firsov derived what he thought to be the true value of Eratosthenes' geodesic stade. And voilà, the grand average of all eighty-seven measurements is 157.95 meters or 172.7 yards. This is very close to Letronne's stade.

So what's going on? Engels attempts to discredit Firsov by noting that there is no reason to believe the intercity distances recorded by Eratosthenes and recorded in Strabo were remotely as accurate as modern measurements. He argues that "since Eratosthenes did not have an accurate knowledge of geographical positions, any measurement he gave between two places may be in-accurate, or accurate only coincidentally." Moreover, because Firsov averages over wide variations in the putative stade-distances—from as few as 116 meters to as many as three hundred—it is likely that he is mixing straight-line distances with roundabout voyages by sea. And indeed, the listed 1,400-stade stretch between Trebizond in modern Turkey and Phasis in mod-ern Georgia must reflect an arcing path, since the southeast coast of the Black Sea is curved. "Firsov has averaged giants and pygmies and has obtained a normal average height," declares Engels.

But these objections don't pass quantitative muster. Strictly speaking, it doesn't matter if Eratosthenes' original distances were very accurate in the real world, as long as he introduced no system-atic bias into his figures. In other words, we may gladly stipulate that he got the measurements wrong in the vast majority of cases. As long as Eratosthenes underestimated as often as he overestimated—and there's little reason to think he didn't—Firsov's method should still give us an approximate value for his stade.

Something similar holds for the case of confusing a sea voyage with a road journey or vice versa: as long as no systematic bias creeps in, nudging the average up or down, Firsov's data set can be useful. (Interestingly, though Engels correctly notes that Firsov finds undersize stades for five different coastline measurements, he ne-glects to mention that in his signal example—Trebizond to Phasis—Firsov reports a figure, 171.5 meters, that is well *over* his average.)

Statisticians test for biased sampling before they analyze measure-ments from most phenomena, whether it is the height of a popula-tion of human beings, a census of butterflies, or the concentration of pollutants in a river. When unbiased samples are plotted by their values and frequencies, the result should be a so-called normal dis-tribution, characterized by the classic bell-shaped curve—that is, fat in the middle, trailing off on each end. And indeed, when Firsov's figures are plotted this way, the distribution looks quite normal (see figure 21, page 200).

Engels is correct, however, that calculating a mere average is a crude way to characterize the "central tendencies" of a sample. To test the likelihood of any particular average in the light of observed variation, statisticians employ some basic tests, including determining a range in which we can be confident the average for a population must lie (a so-called confidence interval). When this procedure is applied to Firsov's figures, the result is an interval of 153.50 to 162.39 meters—meaning that we can be 95 percent confident that Eratosthenes' geodesic stade measured between these extremes. Letronne's stade of 157.5 meters is right in the middle of the likely range. The test also indicates that the Attic stade is well outside the confidence interval—so far outside, in fact, that the chance that the real figure is 184.98 meters is less than one in ten thousand.

All this would seem to suggest that Letronne was right after all. But there are additional circumstantial reasons to doubt Eratosthenes used the Attic stade. First, although the Attic stade may have been standard in the Roman period, there is little independent evidence to show it served likewise in the third century BCE. Second, an estimate of 5,040 *Attic* stades for the distance between Alexandria and Syene is simply not very accurate at all—it works out to 579.3 miles, or about 10 percent beyond the actual distance. This compares poorly to a demonstrated accuracy of more than 99 percent for long-distance Egyptian surveying elsewhere; 5,040 Letronnian stades adds up to about 493 miles, or within 5 percent of the true distance to the Tropic of Cancer in 230.

It is undeniable, as Engels points out, that the length of the schoenus varied among Egypt's provincial administrative districts, or nomes. We may take Strabo at his word that the schoenus equaled thirty stades in Lower Egypt, sixty in Upper Egypt, and 120 in the middle of the kingdom. However, this does not necessarily mean that the Ptolemaic administration in the capital had to be similarly befuddled. Charging the same tax for the products of an estate thirty stades square in the Delta and 120 stades square in Syene would seem like a recipe for cadastral catastrophe; placing postal rest stations six schoeni apart in the Delta but twenty-four schoeni apart near Syene would seem like a good way to lose messages. And if the Ptolemies excelled at anything, it was at delivering mail and levying taxes.

For this reason it seems likely that the government, either in the capital or at the level of the local scribes, converted the provincial schoeni to some kind of standard unit for administrative purposes. The forty stade per schoenus figure Pliny quotes for Eratosthenes may even be a reflection of that "official" unit.

But where does this leave our friend Pliny? After all, it can't be true that, as he says, "by the calculation of Eratosthenes, a schoenus measures 40 [Letronnian] stadia, that is five [Roman] miles. . . ." To say he simply got it wrong sounds presumptuous, although it is given to no historian to achieve 100 percent accuracy. Most likely, he was right with respect to both conversions but neglected to add a temporal qualification—that a schoenus was forty stades long based on the unit in Eratosthenes' time (for a total of 6,300 meters), but was five Roman miles long (7,400 meters) several centuries later, when Pliny was writing.

While better-informed minds than ours argue over the evidence of whether Eratosthenes used the Letronnian "short" stade or the Attic "long" one, the most prudent move may be to reserve judgment. Indeed, whether Eratosthenes' geodesy was astoundingly accurate, or just very accurate, we still have reason to admire his achievement.

EXOCEAN

*On the Measurement of the Earth* is the work for which Eratosthenes is best remembered, but it is not the one upon which he would have staked his legacy. That would undoubtedly have been his three-volume *Geography.* Like all his primary works, it is lost, but fortunately Strabo summarizes much of it in the first two books of his own *Geography.* We are therefore in a good position to summarize its contents.

The overarching purpose of Eratosthenes' opus, reports Strabo, was to revise the science of geography in light of contemporary knowledge. For instance, earlier attempts to chart the continents had placed Asia's Taurus Mountains and India too far to the north. Given that the climate in south India and Meroe in Africa are similar, and the roughly equal north–south distances from Athens to Meroe, and from the mountains of north India to her southern coast, Eratosthenes argues that India must extend farther south than previous maps had depicted it. In fact, though Eratosthenes was right on this point, he himself far underestimated the southern extent of India (the parallel of Meroe in modern Sudan is about six hundred miles north of the tip of the subcontinent). But the strict veracity of Eratosthenes' immediate point is not as important as his method. That he advanced data gleaned from firsthand exploration, astronomical observations, and climate reflects a synthesizing intelligence of almost encyclopedic breadth. The result was a treatise that remained the best in its field until Strabo's own time, three centuries later.

Book I of the *Geography* summarizes the history of attempts to chart the habitable world. It is here that Eratosthenes advanced his heterodox views on the practical uselessness of poets as geographic authorities. He also recounts the legacy of past attempts to map the earth, such as that of the philosopher Anaximander, whose circular projection of the known continents (see figure 12) was presented by Aristagoras of Miletus to the Spartan king Cleomenes in 499. The purpose of Aristagoras's lecture was to illustrate the extent of the Persian Empire and the riches the Spartans might gain in making war on it. Cleomenes, for his part, gleaned a different lesson: when he learned that the Persian capital of Susa was no less than three months' march from the sea, he told Aristagoras to get out of Sparta that instant. "There is no argument of such eloquence," declared the king, "that you can use on the Spartans to bring them three months' journey from the sea."

*Fig. 12. The world according to Anaximander, early fifth century BCE*

Cleomenes may have been frightened by the magnitude of Anaximander's world, but it was a small thing compared to the widening horizons of Herodotus and Aristotle in the fifth and fourth centuries. The Hellenistic world of Eratosthenes, which stretched from the semimythical island of Thule in the north to Taprobane (Sri Lanka) in the south, and from Spain in the west to India in the east, was the biggest yet. Building on theoretical and methodological arguments outlined in books II and III, Eratosthenes presented a model of the habitable world that was roughly rectangular in shape, or somewhat more than two times longer than it was wide.

Because it was rooted in the actual measured distances reported by soldiers, traders, and mariners, Eratosthenes attained another distinction: his map was the first *scaled* projection of the known world. His map was hinged on several known parallels and meridians, including the line from Meroe in the south, through Syene and Alexandria in Egypt, to Byzantium and the mouth of the Borysthenes (Dnieper) River. The most prominent parallel was the line from the Pillars of Hercules in the west, through the Straits of Messina, Rhodes, the Gulf of Issus in Asia Minor, and on along the Taurus Mountain chain, which Eratosthenes thought bisected the entire continent of Asia. By adding up the known (or guessed) distances between these points, he was able to estimate the overall dimensions of the habitable earth at 77,800 stades from east to west, and 38,000 from north to south.

We can see at a glance the improvement Eratosthenes' map represented over Anaximander's old version (compare figures 12 on page 131 and 13 on page 134). On the outline and extent of the Mediterranean, the Red Sea, and the Persian Gulf, it was unsurpassed until Roman times. Europe from Spain to Britain was clearly depicted, based in part on the voyages of Pytheas, while the northern reaches of the continent were still conjectural. He had an inkling of the rhomboidal shape of India, though he pointed it too far to the west, and he guessed the proper size of the island of Sri Lanka more accurately than Claudius Ptolemaeus did more than three centuries later.

The shortcomings of his map are also obvious. He subscribed to a common misconception of the time that it was possible to sail from the Caspian Sea into the world-girdling "exocean"; he had no concept of the vast interior of Africa, and the geography of the Far East was entirely unknown to him. For the latter reason, he estimated the east–west extent of Eurasia at about one-third of the total circumference of the planet. The reality is that, at the latitude of Athens, it stretches a little less than halfway around the globe.

It is a commonplace in the scholarly literature to say that the actual result of Eratosthenes' geodesy was less significant than the method—and the deductive logic—he used to find it. Something similar might be said of the relentless empiricism that produced his world map. Unlike geographers before and since, Eratosthenes did not resort to his imagination to fill the gaps in his knowledge. As E. M. Forster observes, his map "represents the world as Eratosthenes thought it was, not as he thought it ought to be. When he knows nothing, he inserts nothing; he is not ashamed to leave blank spaces."

And the blank spaces were immense. Since the map is a measured one, we can project it on a sphere scaled to a circumference of 252,000 stades (see figure 13 on page 134). This shows not only what proportion of the planet was then known, but something potentially more interesting: how insignificant the Greeks themselves must have known their inhabited world to be. Though a certain parochial smugness is often attributed to the ancient mind ("Mediterranean," after all, literally means "center of the world"), educated Greeks and Romans clearly understood that all did not revolve around their little corner of the globe.

This awareness is aptly expressed in a remarkable section of

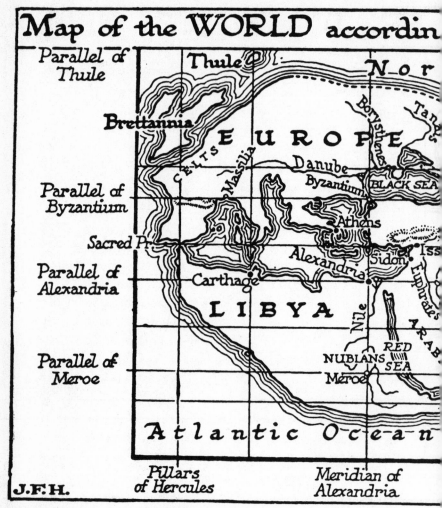

Fig. 13. A modern reconstruction of Erathosthenes' world map

Cicero's *De re publica,* known as "The Dream of Scipio," written around 51. Here Cicero (106–43) imagines that his slumbering hero, Scipio Africanus the Younger (c. 185–129), is given a glimpse of his personal destiny by his adoptive grandfather, Scipio the

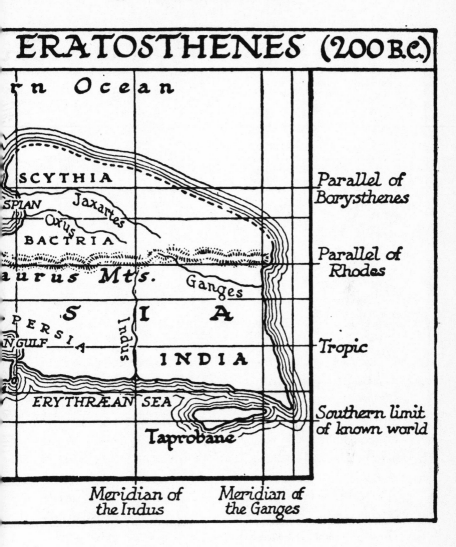

# ERATOSTHENES (200 B.C.)

rn Ocean

SCYTHIA

SPIAN    Jaxartes

Oxus

BACTRIA

aurus Mt's.    Ganges

S        I        A

PERSIA        Indus

N GULF        INDIA

ERYTHRÆAN SEA

Taprobane

Parallel of
Borysthenes

Parallel of
Rhodes

Tropic

Southern limit
of known world

Meridian of        Meridian of
the Indus        the Ganges

Elder (236–183). Part of the dream involves Scipio, like the epony-
mous divinity in Eratosthenes' poem *Hermes,* rising to the sky to
get a god's-eye view of the whole earth. The proportion of it
ruled by Rome is not very impressive:

I was both awestruck and delighted. Nevertheless, I kept looking back to earth. Africanus took note of this and said, "I see you're still stuck on the place where mortals live. Don't you see how insignificant this earth is? Think on the heavenly regions! You should have nothing but scorn for mortal things. For mortals can't give you any fame or glory that is worth seeking or having. Look, the inhabited portions of the earth are tiny and few, the rest is vast desert dividing one inhabited area from another. The inhabitants of earth are so removed from each other that they cannot even communicate with one another. The place where you live is so very far away from other populated areas; some people live in areas on the opposite side of the globe. Do you expect them to honor or glorify your name? . . . If you look at your own northern zone, you can't help but notice how small a section of this region can be regarded as yours. The territory you occupy, your vast Empire, is nothing more than a small island, narrow from north to south, a bit wider east to west, surrounded by the sea which is known as the Atlantic. In spite of the grand name given to this stretch of water, mark how small it really is.

In fact, Eratosthenes had little to say about the possibility of unknown continents beyond Europe, Asia, and Africa. He did note that it is possible, in principle, to sail from the coast of Spain, through the outer ocean, and around to India. Strabo criticized this, suggesting the possibility that some other landmass might prevent such a journey. But the debate was wholly theoretical and thoroughly modern, insofar as both men would have agreed that more evidence was needed.

Contrast this to Claudius Ptolemaeus (see figure 14 on page 158). His map, though more accurate in certain respects, propagated the ancient fable that Asia and Africa were linked by a vast, undiscovered, and wholly fictive southern continent. How many similar misconceptions would have been avoided—and how much more rapid

the progress of geography would have been—if more of Eratosthenes' descendants had followed his example.

TOUCHING THE VOID

Eratosthenes didn't stop at estimating the size and configuration of
the earth. Based on summaries by later writers, we know that he
also attempted to calculate the absolute distance to the moon and
the sun. His reasoning is unclear, but like that of his near contemporary Aristarchus, it probably began with the facts (based on observations of solar eclipses) that the moon is closer to us than the
sun, but has nearly the same angular diameter in the sky. One version of his final figures—780,000 stades to the moon, 804 million
stades to the sun—works out to about 10 and 10,000 times his estimated radius of the earth, and thus betrays the *philologos*'s weakness for whole-number relations.

If we assume that Eratosthenes' stade measured 157.5 meters,
then his lunar distance of more than 76,000 miles is well short of
the true figure (about 240,000 miles); his solar distance, however,
would be surprisingly good at 78.7 million miles, or within 16 percent of the truth. Indeed, Eratosthenes' estimate is a whole order
of magnitude better than those of Claudius Ptolemaeus (fewer
than 5 million miles), Hipparchus (9.8 million), and even Copernicus, two thousand years later (7.5 million). It would have been the
best such estimate until the Italian astronomer Giovanni Domenico
Cassini derived a figure of 87 million miles, using modern techniques, in the late seventeenth century CE.

Without knowing more about his method, we can only attrib-
ute this astounding insight to happy coincidence. Interestingly,
modern critics who argue that Eratosthenes did *not* measure the
earth very well because he used the Attic stade are faced with an
ironic consequence: if we render 804 million stades into Attic

units of 184.98 meters per stade, then Eratosthenes would have gotten a solar distance of 148.7 million km, or 92.4 million miles—that is, within 1 percent of the true figure of just under 93 million miles! If we accept the arguments of Engels and Rawlins about the Ptolemaic stade, then, Eratosthenes would still be renowned, not only for estimating the earth's circumference, but for also being the first to give a correct estimate of the earth-sun distance.

Where his contemporary Aristarchus vaguely speculated that the stars were almost infinitely distant from the earth, Eratosthenes appears to have intuited a largely correct notion of the scale of the "near universe" of the solar system. Much of ancient Greek culture was predicated, more or less, on the sentiment of the pre-Socratic philosopher Protagoras, who declared "Man is the measure of all things. . . ." Eratosthenes and a few of his Hellenistic contemporaries, by contrast, erected a model of the world that called for distances almost inhuman in their infathomability. His astronomical work, coupled with an estimate of $E$ that consigned the entire Greek world to a tiny sliver of the globe, made Eratosthenes a key figure in giving humanity its first plausible—if sobering—picture of the vastness of its universe.

### DEATH

Eratosthenes' *Suda* biography clearly states that he was born during the 126th Olympiad—sometime between 276 and 272—and died at the ripe old age of eighty. There is some disagreement among scholars over his exact birth and death years, however. Since we know from Strabo that he studied in Athens under Zeno of Citium, and the latter died around 262, a birthdate in the mid-270s seems too late, as that would put him in Athens as a teenager.

For these and other reasons, I follow certain authorities who instead put his birthdate in the mid-280s, and his death sometime between 205 and 203.

By this reasoning, Eratosthenes' last years in Alexandria were even more tumultuous than his first. To back up a bit, Ptolemy III Euergetes, the king who had hired Eratosthenes as head librarian, died early in 221. He was succeeded by his twenty-year-old son, who came to be known as Ptolemy IV Philopator ("He Who Loves His Father"). Philopator's two closest advisors were capable, unscrupulous men: the first, Sosibius of Alexandria, had first risen to prominence as an athletic champion in mainland Greece, and held the title of chief priest of the cult of Alexander; the second, Agathocles of Samos, had known Philopator since childhood, and was the brother of Agathocleia, the new king's mistress.

The royal succession appears to have been smooth enough, but Sosibius and Agathocles decided to take no chances. To cement their position, they convinced young Philopator to sanction the executions of his uncle Lysimachus, his younger brother Magas, his mother Berenice II, and his sister, Arsinoe. And while Sosibius and Agathocles got away with these crimes for as long as Philopator was on the throne, it appears that many Alexandrians never forgot that royal blood was on their hands.

The reckoning came in 204, when Philopator died. The king's five-year-old son was his acknowledged successor, but it was widely expected that the queen, Arsinoe III, would rule as regent until he came of age. When the popular queen instead turned up dead, and Sosibius and Agathocles proclaimed themselves guardians of the young Ptolemy V Epiphanes, there was finally a reaction. The governor of Pelusium, Tlepolemus, launched a rebellion that blockaded the capital. Soldiers and ordinary citizens in Alexandria rose in revolt; Polybius describes a scene, similar in its chaos to the fall of Italy's Mussolini or Romania's Ceaușescu, in which Agathocles and his sister at first take the boy king hostage, then release him and plead for their lives before an angry mob. In the end "they were all given up to the populace, who bit, and stabbed them, and knocked out their eyes, and, as soon as any one of them fell, tore them limb from limb, until they had utterly annihilated them."

Eratosthenes—if he was not already dead—could not have been far from this unrest, given that the Museum was either part of or adjoining the palace. Polybius describes a city in turmoil, "with tumult, torches, and running feet." One imagines the old man, who according to the *Suda* was in the process of "starving himself to death since his eyesight failed," listening sadly as his adopted city, a beacon of enlightenment, tore itself apart. Another scholar, the grammarian Aristophanes of Byzantium, would soon be named to succeed Eratosthenes as head librarian; Alexandria herself, and the Ptolemaic Empire in general, would continue to be major forces in Greek culture and politics for years to come. But her best days were behind her.

## I, GNOMON

The Morrisons encompassed the earth with a van and a roll of black masking tape. Generations of schoolchildren have measured solar deflections with stick gnomons and trig tables. Having landed in the city of the original geodesy, I decided that I too would attempt to replicate Eratosthenes' experiment—though some of my surveying equipment would turn out to be even cruder than what was available in the third century BCE.

Not quite by accident, I was in Alexandria for the 2007 vernal equinox. This, the first day of spring in the northern hemisphere, is the day when the earth's axis is perpendicular to the plane of its solar orbit. At local noon on the equator, the sun stands directly overhead (at the zenith); from elsewhere in the northern hemisphere, it is offset southward from the zenith by the angle corresponding to the latitude at which that place is located.

By measuring the angle of solar deflection at noon on the equinox, it is possible to obtain a good measurement of the local latitude. Knowing that, and the distance to the equator, you can calculate the circumference of the earth. Eratosthenes, as we have seen, measured the solar deflection on the summer solstice, not the equinox, when the sun was directly above the Tropic of Cancer instead of the equator. But the principle behind his calculation is essentially the same.

For my gnomon, I planned to use the most prominent vertically plumb object in the city: the ninety-eight-foot-high granite monolith known as Pompey's Pillar. This massive pile was the late medieval city's most prominent landmark, located at the top of the mound the Alexandrians once called—rather grandiosely—their Acropolis. It once shared the hill with the sprawling complex dedicated to Serapis, Alexandria's patron god, as well as the Great Library's public annex. The temple and its fifty-thousand-scroll "daughter library" were obliterated by Christian vandals in 391 CE. The Pillar, however, has been left strangely unscathed by Christians, earthquakes, and other epochal disasters. The sole insult inflicted by time has been a persistent misnomer: the Pillar was raised in honor of the Roman emperor Diocletian in 291 CE, and has nothing at all to do with Pompey. Though it is a relative latecomer, it is just about the only feature left above ground to testify that Alexandria has an ancient past.

The Pillar turned out to be charmless but straight and true. Alas, my plan to use it as a giant gnomon ran into an unexpected obstacle. To measure the angle of the sun at noon, I needed a flat patch of ground beneath the monument on which to measure its shadow. Unfortunately, the "archaeological park" that surrounds the Pillar offered no such thing. All that remains of the Serapaeion is a complex of subsurface galleries and a column or two; to the north of the Pillar, where the equinoctial shadow would be cast, the ground is gouged by trenches like a World War I battlefield.

Standing with tape measure and notebook in hand, the final minutes to noon counting down, I needed to find an object of exactly known height right away. The answer turned out to be literally at my feet, for this writer is five foot, eleven inches tall in socks, six feet in cross-trainers. He is also known, when motivated, to be vertically plumb.

And so Egyptian passersby who happened to look up that day would have seen a frazzled, harried figure on the hillock of Pompey's Pillar. This character—American to judge by his dress but possibly Canadian by his pallor—was seen to be standing absolutely straight, then running out to adjust the position of a coin on the ground, then checking his watch, then standing still again. When this odd exercise was over he measured the distance to the coin with a tape measure, jotted some figures in a notebook, and stole away into the chaos of al-Sawari Street on market day.

It was only when I got home that I checked the accuracy of my personal geodesy. On the equinox, I, a seventy-two-inch tall object, cast a shadow 40⅛ inches long. Getting out my calculator (with the trigonometric functions that were, of course, unavailable to Eratosthenes), I solved for the equation

$$\tan X = 40.125/72$$

X, the angle of solar deflection, turned out to be a shade over 29.2 degrees. This, combined with a linear distance of 2,143.1 miles between Alexandria and the equator (courtesy of Google

Earth—alas, also not available to Eratosthenes), yields the following proportion:

$$\frac{29.13}{360} = \frac{2,143.1 \text{ miles}}{E}$$

Solving for $E$, the circumference of the earth, I got 26,485 miles. This is 1,625 miles over the modern figure, or accurate to within 7 percent.

# 5 . ECLIPSE

*On winter nights I work at camp garb for you, and I sew together lengths of Tyrian wool to make a military cloak; I learn where flows the Araxes that you are to conquer, how many miles a Parthian horse can cover without water; and I am constrained to find out from a map the countries painted on it and the manner of this arrangement by the wise creator, what lands are sluggish with frost, what crumbling with heat, what wind will bring sails safely back to Italy.*

—PROPERTIUS, *Elegy,* IV, 3

BY MID-SEPTEMBER 331, the battle-hardened troops of Alexander the Great had reached Mesopotamia. After completing a laborious crossing of the Tigris River, the Macedonian army, some fifty thousand strong, was ordered to make camp on the east bank. Captured enemy horsemen had informed Alexander that an enormous Persian host was for waiting for him, somewhere to the southeast. There was just enough time for the conqueror to rest his troops and horses before marching out to meet the levy of the great king.

Though they had beaten Darius III twice before, the Macedonians were nervous. Only one other Greek army—the mercenary force described by Xenophon in his *Anabasis* ("the march upcountry")—had ever penetrated that far east, and had achieved immortal fame merely for making it back to Greece intact. This time the Persians, in a bid to starve the invaders, had left behind a scorched landscape, burning not only the villages but even the grass in the fields. A choking haze rose to obscure the daylight. At night, the camp seemed afloat in a sea of embers as numerous as the stars.

Soon another apparition would amplify their unease. On the first night in camp, the full moon rose in the constellation Pisces. Less than an hour after sunset, a faint shadow began to nibble at its lower left extremity. As the Macedonians gathered to watch, the shadow spread across the moon's face, stealing its light and changing its color to a baleful red. By two and a half hours after sunset, the eclipse had reached totality; the once bright moon was now a vaporous absence, like a hole in the sky traced by the glimmer of Hades.

Old timers had witnessed such events before. But the dust and haze from the Persian fires made this eclipse the ruddiest in memory. Its location, just above where the Persians were expected to be, seemed pregnant with meaning. The timing, on the eve of a battle that would decide the fate of Asia, was also less than propitious—as was the proximity of Saturn (known to the Greeks as Phaenon), a planet with its own malefic associations:

> Right on the brink of the decisive battle the men were already in a state of anxiety, and this now struck them with a deep religious awe which precipitated a kind of panic. . . . Mutiny was but a step away when, unperturbed by all this, Alexander summoned a full meeting of his generals and officers in his tent and ordered the Egyptian seers (whom he believed to possess expert knowledge of the sky and the stars) to give their opinion. They were well aware that the annual cycle follows a pattern of changes, that the moon is eclipsed when it passes behind the earth or is blocked by the sun [sic], but they did not give this explanation, which they themselves knew, to the common soldiers. Instead, they declared that the sun represented the

Greeks and the moon the Persians, and that an eclipse of the
moon predicted disaster and slaughter for those nations. . . .
Thus the dissemination of the Egyptians' responses restored
hope and confidence to the dispirited soldiers.

No doubt the Persians saw the eclipse from their camp, too—
though history doesn't record their response. We also know it was
seen almost two thousand miles away, in Carthage on the North
African coast. Due to their position farther west, however, the
Carthaginians saw the moon rise with its eclipse already underway;
totality was reached with the moon just five degrees above the Gulf
of Tunis.

The significance of this eclipse lived well beyond Alexander's
campaigns. At a time when determining longitude was an uncertain
business, the timing of eclipses from different points on the earth offered a ready method for measuring east–west distance. That the
eclipse reached its culmination hours in the evening in Mesopotamia,
but just after sunset in Carthage, reflected the angular distance between the two places over the curved surface of the earth.

Because the event was partly hidden by the horizon from
Carthage, there was some uncertainty over when it began there. As
reported by Claudius Ptolemaeus in his *Geography,* it was widely
assumed that there was a time difference of about three hours between the two observation points. The real difference was closer to
two and a half hours. As we shall see below, this simple error would
have lasting implications for the science of geography in the West.

CIRCULAR REASONING

Though his career was productive, Eratosthenes failed to reproduce
himself in the academy. The disciples listed in his *Suda* biography—
Aristophanes, Mnaseas, Menandros, and Aristis—were, respectively,

a grammarian, a mythographer, a historian, and an unknown profession. Aristophanes succeeded him as head librarian, and we have at least heard of a couple of the others. But in no case did any of these succeed in emulating the breadth of Eratosthenes' interests, or a shadow of his success.

Fraser observes, "It is significant that we hear of no *Erathostheneioi* (followers of Eratosthenes); this versatile man started no formal tradition of scholarship." It is significant, but not surprising. Then and now, a unique founding figure can help in the foundation of a scholarly tradition or school, but his presence is hardly enough. More important is to convey the kind of coherence— today we might even say "brand consistency"—that impressionable young minds can adopt and wear as a badge of intellectual identity. Define yourself as a Platonist, and a certain point of view is expected; count yourself among the Callistheneioi, and at least a slate of literary prejudices is implied. But what would it have meant to be a follower of Eratosthenes—a mercurial figure who leaped with maddening competence among disparate fields, and whose delights lay in upstaging specialists, astute ridicule, and debunking comfortable myths? For all of the master's success, taking up his legacy would probably have bought a young scholar few patrons, and fewer friends.

Though Eratosthenes' like was never again seen at the Museum, his descendants were obliged to reckon with his work. Unsurprisingly, much criticism focused on the specifics of his *Geography,* some details of which—especially at the margins of the known world—were necessarily speculative. In addition to arguing with his dismissal of Homeric geography, Polybius found occasion to criticize Eratosthenes' knowledge of the western Mediterranean. The astronomer Hipparchus published a book in the mid-second century BCE entitled *Against Eratosthenes,* which is sadly lost but summarized in part by Strabo. In it Hipparchus takes Eratosthenes to task for his overly confident estimates of geographic distance, especially with respect to longitude, and condemns as mere guess-work major features on his map, such as the position of the Taurus mountain chain. In the end, Strabo suspects Hipparchus of making a straw man of Eratosthenes, critiquing "geometric arguments that were not even made by Eratosthenes, but conjured by his own imagination," and therefore furnishing "proof of his [Hipparchus'] own bias." In his own candid appraisal of Eratosthenes, Strabo declares, "Thus he is a mathematician in geography, and in mathematics a geographer; and so lies open to the attacks of both parties." This has been the specialist's complaint about gifted dilettantes since scholarship began.

As part of his preparation for his invasion of Gaul, Julius Caesar appears to have thumbed Eratosthenes' *Geography*. Cicero was also a cautious admirer, professing that an update on the Cyrenian's treatise was necessary, but "my mind is repugnant [to it], because the geography I had in mind is a great undertaking."

In its broadest strokes, however, Eratosthenes' magnum opus aged well. That the habitable continents formed a rectilinear zone twice as long as it was wide became such common knowledge in later centuries that few bothered to credit Eratosthenes for it. Strabo compares its shape to that of a chlamys, or soldier's cloak—a term he applies elsewhere to the elongated outline of the city of Alexandria itself. A great map of the Roman imperium, commissioned by Marcus Agrippa (63–12) was displayed in the Porticus of Octavia in Rome at the time of Augustus. This was essentially, but not explicitly, Eratosthenes' map, possibly filled out with details gathered by the legions. One imagines generations of magistrates, curious about the faraway places they were about to be posted to, coming first to the Porticus of Octavia to consult Agrippa's map. Indeed, there seems to have been something of a cartographic craze in Rome in late first century BCE, as exhibited (albeit in a

melancholy key) by an elegy of the poet Propertius (see the epigraph to this chapter on page 144).

Eratosthenes' geodesy survived even better. Despite his reserva-
tions about Eratosthenes' geography, Hipparchus took no exception
to his figure for the globe's circumference. Geminus and Strabo
likewise accepted it; Vitruvius hailed Eratosthenes' "cunning insight," and Pliny the Elder called him "a man of incomparable skill
in all of science's subtleties, and universally accepted as far as I can
see." Plutarch cites an estimate of forty thousand stades for the
earth's radius as about average by his time; this works out to a value
for $E$ of approximately 251,000 stades, quite similar to Eratosthenes'
figure.

One other widely known competing geodesy from antiquity is
attributed to the savant Poseidonius of Apamea (c. 135–51). Like
that of Eratosthenes, his original treatise on the earth's circumference is lost; we only know of his work from the summaries of
Strabo and Cleomedes. His method was to compare the angular
height of the star Canopus at the same time in two locations; where
the star barely cleared the horizon at Rhodes, it rose several degrees
in the southern skies of Alexandria. In principle, this difference in
elevation was the same as the latitudinal difference between the
two places. If this measurement is coupled with the linear distance
between Rhodes and Alexandria, the polar circumference of the
earth may be calculated.

What Poseidonius actually derived from all this is a matter of
confusion. According to Cleomedes, he reckoned the difference in
Canopus's angular height to be 7.5 degrees, and the distance between Rhodes and Alexandria at a round five thousand stades,
yielding the proportion,

$$\frac{7.5}{360} = \frac{5,000 \ stades}{E}$$

In this case $E$, the circumference of the earth, equals 240,000 stades—or within 5 percent of Eratosthenes' estimate. But Poseidonius's result is suspect on two counts. First, the angular height of Canopus at Alexandria is in fact 5.25 degrees, not 7.5. As we discussed earlier, naked-eye observations of star risings and settings are fraught with difficulty because of the effect of atmospheric refraction. Eratosthenes, for his part, reported something very close to the correct angle when he observed differing noontime shadow angles—a method largely unaffected by this problem.

Second, measuring distances at sea was notoriously difficult in antiquity. For obvious reasons, direct measurement was impossible, and ship transit times could yield only rough approximations. By the time of Poseidonius, however, a distance of five thousand stades between Rhodes and Alexandria would have been recognized as an overestimate. Eratosthenes himself correctly put the distance at around 3,750 stades, based on observations with the skaphe and his estimate of the earth's circumference. According to Strabo, Poseidonius later "adopted" a figure of 180,000 stades for the circumference, based on Eratosthenes' shorter estimate of the Rhodes–Alexandria transit. But because the 3,750-stade figure is itself derived from Eratosthenes' figure of 252,000 stades for the circumference, Poseidonius was engaged in circular reasoning. He only obtained a smaller result for $E$ (180,000 stades) because he erroneously took the height of Canopus to be 7.5 degrees.

Poseidonius was a polymath who contributed fruitfully to philosophy and history, as well as to the physical sciences. What may appear to be muddled thinking on his part may only reflect confusion in our sources. Nor is it entirely clear which version of the stade he had in mind. Living as he did at a time when the Greek world was firmly under the thumb of Rome, he probably meant the unit equivalent (according to Pliny) to one-eighth of a Roman mile, or about 185 meters. This would put his circumference, in modern terms, at about 20,700 miles. If he meant Eratosthenes' likely stade of 157.5 meters, he would be well short at about 17,600 miles. Yet another candidate is the Ptolemaic "Royal" stade of 210 meters, yielding a circumference of about 23,500 miles. This gets us nearer the modern figure for $E$.

But in fact we have no idea of the exact value of Poseidonius's 180,000 stades. Most relevant to the rest of this book, however, is that though all his likely estimates are shy of Eratosthenes' estimate, and well short of the real distance, Poseidonius's geodesy came to have far greater influence on future events. This is entirely due to the ancient scientist who cast the longest shadow of all.

### THE GREATEST

Claudius Ptolemaeus (85–165 CE) lived well after the times described in this book, but we have already had occasion to mention him many times. As one of the latest major figures in Greek science, and the one whose works are best preserved, his influence on how we see his predecessors is pervasive.

On the evidence of his royal-sounding surname and the star catalog he published of 1,028 bright stars visible from Alexandria, it is presumed that he lived and worked in that city. The prime of his life was bracketed by the reigns of the Roman emperors Trajan and Marcus Aurelius—one of the most peaceful and prosperous spans of time in the history of the empire (if not the entire Western world). Beyond this, we know precious little about Ptolemaeus. As with Eratosthenes, we lack even a verifiable likeness of him.

In our own era, the only comparable figure might be the linguist Noam Chomsky. Like Chomsky, Ptolemaeus was brilliant, intimidating, with an influence on his discipline too momentous to ignore. Chomsky is perhaps the most widely cited academic of modern times; Ptolemaeus was arguably the most cited before the Renaissance. Both men formulated theories that were ambitious in scope and mathematical in their essential nature. Both Ptolemaic astronomy and Chomskyan linguistics were often revised, abstruse, yet sufficiently adaptable that legions of institutionally secure adherents could readily defend them. As a result, both scholars dominated their fields for generations—despite the fact (or in Chomsky's case, the growing consensus) that their theories had deep problems.

Ptolemaeus's fundamental contribution was to reconcile the prevailing notions of classical cosmology (geocentricity, the sphericity of the earth and the universe, Aristotelian mechanics) with the improved observational data and techniques developed in the intervening centuries by such figures as Hipparchus. So while Ptolemaeus takes it to be self-evident that the earth neither revolves nor rotates, he is sufficiently aware of the empirical shortcomings of Eudoxus's theory of concentric spheres (which was endorsed by Aristotle) to reject that model. Instead, he elects to develop Apollonius of Perga's notion of epicycles—with the sun, moon, and planets conceived as bodies revolving around points in space that, in turn, revolve around the earth. His model was enshrined in a magnum opus published around 150. It was entitled *Mathematical Composition,* but is known today by its amalgamated Arabic-Greek name, *The Almagest* (an amalgam of Arabic definite article *al* and the Greek *megiste:* "the greatest").

The details of the Ptolemaic model of the universe are outside the scope of this discussion in all but one respect: it was not as unreasonable as it is caricatured to be today. Many popular recountings of the history of astronomy portray Ptolemaeus's solar system, with its wheels within wheels, as some kind of cosmic Rube Goldberg device, as manifestly absurd as it was cumbersome. To be sure, making the irregular motions of the planets fit the ancients' prejudice for perfect circles and uniform movements did force Ptolemaeus to propose complexities happily mooted by Copernicus. Nonetheless, by the admittedly crude empirical standards of the day, Ptolemaeus's model explained planetary motion quite well. It was arguably the best anyone could have done without a universal theory of gravitation, which ultimately allowed astronomers to consider the possibility of elliptical orbits and variable rates of motion in the heavens.

Ptolemaeus's other major work was a *Geography.* Building on the work of Eratosthenes and a shadowy figure called Marinus of Tyre, he produced a treatise that matched the cosmographical ambition of Eratosthenes. As in the *Almagest,* he put his trust more in empirical observation—most notably, on astronomical data—than in the collection of conventions, rumors, and travelers' tales he collectively calls "the traditions":

> it is just and right that a geographer about to write a geography
> should lay as the foundation of his work the phenomena known
> to him that have been obtained by a more careful observation,
> and should make the traditions subordinate to these, so that the
> relative positions of localities may be determined with greater
> certainty and be more nearly accurate than is possible by relying
> on primitive traditions.

The basic shape of Ptolemaeus's inhabited world was rectangular. His map rightly reflects the contemporary Romans' awareness of exotic lands, such as the Sahel and China. Though he made other blunders, such as imagining a southern continent that ran from India to Africa, he eliminated at least one of the perennial myths of ancient geography, rightly depicting the Caspian Sea as landlocked instead of open to the northern ocean. He also pioneered the methods of modern cartography, describing how to draft both flat and spherical projections of his universal map.

Ptolemaeus's partiality for observational data did lead him astray on one crucial point. According to Marinus, a lunar eclipse was simultaneously seen on September 20 in 331 by Alexander near the battlefield of Gaugamela *and* by observers nineteen hundred miles west in Carthage. Since the time of the eclipse was eight PM in Iraq but five PM in Carthage, Ptolemaeus reasoned that these two places must be the longitudinal equivalent of three hours apart on the earth's surface, or forty-five degrees. This turned out to be a significant overestimate—Gaugemela and Carthage are actually separated by only about thirty-three degrees of longitude. The effect of this error was to elongate Ptolemaeus's projection of the Near East and Mediterranean basin. This, and the addition of China to the roster of known lands, stretched his version of Eurasia some 180 degrees east to west over the surface of his globe, versus Eratosthenes' 120 degrees.

Equally important is that Ptolemaeus accepted a figure of five hundred stades per degree of longitude, because it is "a measurement which is proved by distances that are known and certain." This figure is noteworthy because it falls well short of Eratosthenes' estimate of seven hundred stades per degree. Five hundred stades multiplied by 360 yields an overall circumference of 180,000 stades—again well short of Eratosthenes' 252,000 stades, but exactly echoing Poseidonius's figure.

Whether Ptolemaeus was endorsing Eratosthenes' high estimate, or Poseidonius's lowball one, depends entirely on the question (yet again) of which unit he was using. It has been suggested that his estimate could be brought into agreement with Eratosthenes' by assuming that Ptolemaeus used not Eratosthenes' stade, but the Egyptian Royal stade of 210 meters (360 degrees × 500 stades/degree × 210 meters/stade = 37,000 km or 23,488 miles). It is certainly tempting to leave the question at that. For some, the idea that Ptolemaeus, an authority with such high regard for empirical observation and such epochal impact on his discipline, would abandon Eratosthenes' well-established figure for Poseidonius's muddled one just seems too implausible to accept.

In fact, the information we need to relate Ptolemaeus's stade to Eratosthenes' is easy to find. Ptolemaeus claims, after all, that his figure of five hundred stades per degree is "a measurement which is proved by distances that are known and certain." As we saw earlier with respect to Firsov's estimate of the Hellenistic stade, Strabo preserves many of Eratosthenes' estimates for distances between known geographical points. In his *Geography,* Ptolemaeus likewise provides a kind of gazetteer for mapmakers, listing hundreds of localities by their position on a coordinate system similar to modern latitude and longitude (except that longitude is measured east of a "prime meridian" located at the Fortunate Islands, known today as the Canaries). By comparing the respective estimates of distances "known and certain" to both men, it should be possible to see if Ptolemaeus used the same unit as Eratosthenes, or a longer one.

As they were both Alexandrians, we may presume that Eratosthenes and Ptolemaeus were most familiar with distances between the capital and other cities in Egypt. Strabo writes, "The extent of Egyptian seacoast, from Pelusiac to Canopic mouth, is 1300 stadia . . . thus says Eratosthenes." Elsewhere Strabo repeats, without referencing Eratosthenes, that "In sailing towards the west, the seacoast from Pelusium to the Canopic mouth of the Nile is about 1300 stadia in extent, and constitutes, as we have said, the base of the Delta. Thence to the island Pharos are 150 stadia more." Thus, according to Strabo-Eratosthenes, the distance by sea from the city of Pelusium to the Pharos at Alexandria is about 1,450 stades.

In the *Geography,* Ptolemaeus places "Alexandria, the metropolis of all Egypt" at 31° north latitude, and 60° 30' east longitude. Pelusium, on the other side of the Delta, is at 31° 10' north, and

63° 15' east. The difference in longitude between Alexandria and Pelusium, therefore, is about 2° 45'. If we multiply this by the ratio of five hundred stades per degree, then Ptolemaeus's distance between the cities is 1,375 stades (or more precisely, 1,377 stades, if we take the small latitudinal difference into account).

The respective estimates, 1,450 versus 1,375 stades, are quite close. Indeed, it would be suspicious if they matched exactly, given that Strabo refers to a sea voyage around the limb of the Delta, and Ptolemaeus's coordinate points yield a straight-line distance. Ptolemaeus's figure should be *somewhat* smaller. On the other hand, if Heath is correct that Ptolemaeus used the Royal stade of 210 meters, and was reporting the same commonly understood intercity distance, then he should have reported a far smaller figure, something like 1,030 stades, not 1,375.

We can therefore tentatively conclude that if Ptolemaeus did not use Eratosthenes' stade, he used something very similar to it. This suggests that the disagreement between Eratosthenes' circumference and Ptolemaeus's (252,000 versus 180,000) can't be blamed on confusion over units. Ptolemaeus really did believe he lived on a much smaller planet.

Considering moreover that Ptolemaeus's inhabited world was broader than Eratosthenes', stretching some sixty degrees of longitude farther east, we can see that these geographers had very different notions of the extent of open ocean lying between China and Western Europe (see figure 14 on page 158). In Eratosthenes' world, a mariner attempting to sail across the exocean would have to traverse two-thirds of the whole circumference, or about 170,000 stades. In Ptolemaeus's, he would expect a journey of only half the circumference of a smaller sphere, or about ninety thousand stades. This discrepancy will figure prominently in arguments preceding one famous attempt at such a crossing, more than thirteen centuries after Ptolemaeus.

## FOOLISH FOR CHRIST

*For [the kings] alone could free the minds of scholars from the daily anxieties for the necessities of life, and stimulate their energies to earn more fame and favor, the yearning for which is the pith and marrow of human nature. The present times, however, are not of this kind. They are the very opposite, and therefore it is quite impossible that a new science or any new kind of research should arise in our days. What we have of sciences is nothing but the scanty remains of bygone better times.*

—ABŪ AL-RAYHĀN AL-BĪRŪNĪ (973–1048)

That Ptolemaeus was largely the last word in Western astronomy until Copernicus begs the question of what caused the long hiatus. Why does the history of ancient empirical astronomy seem to end in the fifth century CE? Why are so many important texts of ancient Greek science known to us only through Arab translations? Was it a matter of mere bad luck that Eratosthenes' original works were lost?

The answers to these questions, especially regarding the role of Christianity in the decline of ancient rationalism, naturally provoke intense controversy. Those seeking to indict early Church authorities for strangling ancient science find ample ammunition in the words of Christians themselves, such as the apostle Paul:

For the preaching of the cross is to them that perish foolishness; but unto us which are saved it is the power of God. For it is written, I will destroy the wisdom of the wise, and will bring to nothing the understanding of the prudent. Where is the wise? Where is the scribe? Where is the disputer of this world? Hath not God made foolish the wisdom of this world? . . . For the Jews require a sign, and the Greeks seek after wisdom. But we

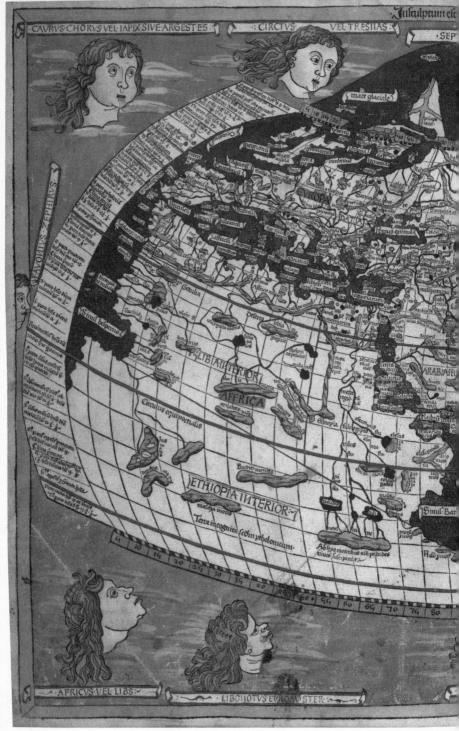

Fig. 14. Ptolemaeus's world map as shown in a medieval geographical text.

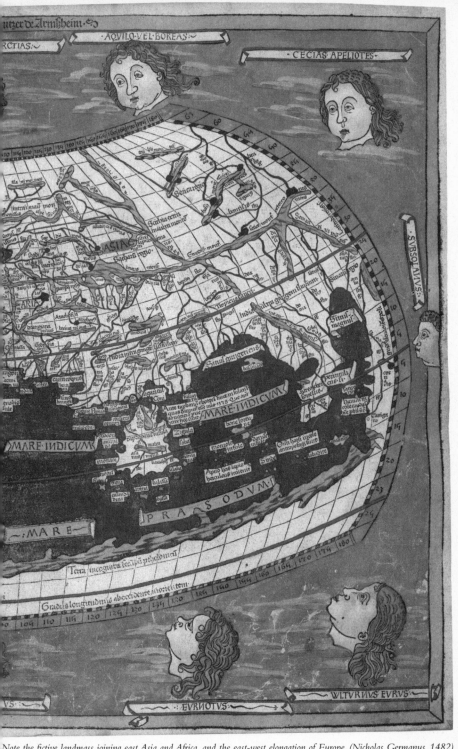

*Note the fictive landmass joining east Asia and Africa, and the east-west elongation of Europe. (Nicholas Germanus, 1482)*

preach Christ crucified, unto the Jews a stumbling block, and unto the Greeks foolishness . . . because the foolishness of God is wiser than men.

It is striking the way Paul not only seems to dismiss the value of Greek "wisdom," but positively to exult in its demise. His lead was enthusiastically followed by Christian apologists such as Tertullian (c. 150–230 CE), who asked

What then has Athens to do with Jerusalem, the Academy with the Church, the heretic with the Christian? Our instruction comes from the Porch of Solomon who himself taught us that the Lord is to be sought in the simplicity of one's heart. . . . We have no need of curiosity after Jesus Christ, nor of research after the gospel. When we believe, we desire to believe nothing more.

The effects of such pronouncements went beyond the merely theoretical. In Egypt, the foot soldiers of Pauline foolishness massed in desert monasteries, at places like the Wadi Natrun. From there they periodically descended on pagan Alexandria. Forster writes

The monks had not been important so long as each lived alone, but by the 4th cent. they had gathered into formidable communities, whence they would occasionally make raids on civilization. . . . The monks had some knowledge of theology and of decorative craft, but they were averse to culture and incapable of thought.

The novelist compares these early Christians to the Bedouins of his time, but a better comparison might be to the Taliban of modern Pakistan and Afghanistan. The contemporary historian Eunapius, a pagan, described them as men in appearance but [who] led the lives of swine, and openly did and allowed countless unspeakable crimes. But this they accounted piety, to show contempt for things [traditionally] divine. For in those days every man who wore a black robe and consented to behave in seemly fashion in public, possessed the power of a tyrant. . . .

Like the Taliban, the monks' ignorance of what they opposed was equaled only by their zeal to destroy it. In 415 CE, outside the Museum, they attacked Hypatia, the forty-five-year-old mathematician and Neoplatonist philosopher, daughter of the last head librarian at Alexandria. Hypatia's *Suda* biography lauds her as a widely respected intellect of her time, a published commentator on the mathematics of Diophantius and Apollonius. Her beauty (probably a figment of retrospective imagination) was matched by legends of her sexual purity: when one of her male students became miserable with love for her, she supposedly shocked him back to his senses by showing him garments stained by her menstrual blood, declaring, "You love this, O youth, and there is nothing beautiful about it!"

Hypatia's chastity earned her little credit with Christian partisans. As Gibbon tells it, she was "torn from her chariot, stripped naked, dragged to the church, and inhumanly butchered by the hands of Peter the Reader and a troop of savage and merciless fanatics: her flesh was scraped from her bones with sharp oyster-shells and her quivering limbs were delivered to the flames." Another tradition holds that Hypatia was flayed not with seashells but with broken shards of pottery (in Greek, *ostraka*), thereby lending a grim new meaning to the word "ostracism."

Hypatia has become something of a secular martyr in recent times; another view suggests her death had more to do with her role in local city politics than with any deliberate attempt to stifle philosophy in the city. Even if that is true, the trend was not encouraging for pagan scholarship in Alexandria. According to the contemporary Greek rhetorician Aphthonius, public access to the rooms of the daughter library containing books on pagan religion was cut off by the early fourth century. In 391, Emperor Theodosius ordered the closure of all pagan temples in the empire, including the Isis Temple at Philae, the oracle of Apollo at Delphi, and the Museum. Within the year, the temple complex dedicated to Serapis, including its famous library, was razed to the ground:

> For these men, girding themselves in their wrath against our sacred places as though against stone and stonemasons, made a raid on the temples, and though they could not allege even a rumor of war to justify them, they demolished the temple of Serapis and made war against the temple offerings, whereby they won a victory without meeting a foe or fighting a battle. . . . Only the floor of the temple of Serapis they did not take, simply because of the weight of the stones. . . .

A monastery was built on the ruins, and the man who ordered the Serapeion's destruction, the Patriarch Theophilus, was declared a saint. It is not hard to imagine that the works of Eratosthenes were among the scrolls burned, buried, or scattered in the destruction of the daughter library. As promised, "the understanding of the prudent" had indeed been brought to nothing.

Against all this, Christian apologists point out that Church institutions were instrumental in preserving many philosophic and scientific texts from antiquity. They also note that certain early Christian thinkers were major philosophic figures in their own right. Some, such as Origen and the so-called Cappadocian fathers, were steeped in the pagan intellectual tradition and were devoted, at least in part, to reconciling the revealed truth of Christianity with secular philosophy. It has also been argued that the decline of ancient science had more to do with its own inherent weakness than anything the Christians did.

The proper responses to these points are, in order, *Not really, Yes and no,* and *Yes, sort of.* It is true that much of what we have of the ancient literature was preserved by the painstaking efforts of Christian manuscript copyists through the centuries. Then again, they were selective in what they chose to copy, tending to favor schools and genres that fit their doctrinal purposes. Plato fared well; Aristotle's massive corpus, on the other hand, was largely lost to the Latin-speaking world after the triumph of Christianity, and survived only because his work was reintroduced to Europe from the Islamic world.

Nor were the Christian copyists particularly interested in scientific treatises per se: as we have seen, several of Archimedes' original works survived only inadvertently, as erased versions fortuitously preserved under religious texts. Compared to the incalculable loss from the destruction of the daughter library at Alexandria—let alone what was allowed to disintegrate in the Great Library from simple neglect—the Christian role in preserving a few tidbits of antiquity seems like nothing to be proud of.

Regarding the new faith's encounter with pagan philosophy, it is indisputable that such Christian thinkers as Clement (c. 150—c. 215 CE) and Origen (184–254 CE), both of Alexandria, were affected by their engagement with their pagan counterparts. These, in turn, shaped the development of Christian theology. Yet again, it's hard to see how ancient secular philosophy, much less science, benefitted from the disputes over doctrine that came to roil the early Church. Beginning in the fourth century CE, Christendom became engrossed not in discussions of moral philosophy, meta-physics, or trivial matters such as the nature of the physical uni-verse, but in an obtuse controversy over the nature of Christ. In the doctrine known as Arianism, Jesus was regarded as the son of God, and therefore not exactly like his divine Father. According to the opposing Monophysite view, Christ and God were of the same na-ture. A third view (Monothelism) tried to bridge this difference by asserting Christ had a different physical nature, but the same divine will.

The dispute between these camps—which raged largely in the churches and streets of Alexandria—seems to modern minds even less fruitful than the question of how many angels can dance on the head of a pin. Yet it consumed the energies of generations, sucking the intellectual oxygen away from other, possibly more fruitful, pursuits.

Most authorities agree that ancient science was in decline after the end of the Hellenistic era. Major figures are thin on the ground after the first century BCE; if not for Galen and Claudius Ptole-maeus, one might have supposed systematic inquiry had ground to a halt. Part of this had to do with the fact that, as today, the rising sophistication of empirical observation never seemed to settle mat-ters, but only led to further questions and more uncertainty. Some became resigned that the truth of such matters as cosmology, dy-namics, and biology was simply beyond the ability of mere mortals to attain. The early Christian fathers happily echoed this despair. Paul, as we have seen, derided the feckless "wisdom of the wise"; Augustine, likewise, called curiosity about the natural world noth-ing more than a "disease . . . which can avail us nothing and which man should not wish to learn."

Perhaps equally damaging, grand syntheses like that of Ptole-maeus may have discouraged research because they subsumed all possible objections, leaving behind few questions to ask. As Keyser and Irby-Massie note,

> Any system in which, by definition, there are no loose ends can only stifle enquiry, for it can never be confronted either by its own defects or by the way the world is. But for some people (then as now), ordered and meaningful wholeness is preferable to loose ends and open questions.

Certainly, the fact that science was more of an avocation than a profession in antiquity—even at the Museum—contributed to its demise. Christian rulers helped ancient science into its grave by institutionalizing this weakness: in 529, the Byzantine emperor Justinian I ordered the regulation or outright closure of all pagan schools throughout the empire, including the Platonic Academy in Athens. The rising prestige and pay gap between academics and churchmen in the Byzantine Empire, with a bishop paid at least five times the salary of a physician or professor, assured that the most ambitious minds devoted their energies not to the problems of secular education, but to the Church. Since much ancient science was done by physicians and professors informally, at their own expense, their relative impoverishment did little to encourage research.

In the end, it is undeniable that science suffered in late antiquity because its role in intellectual life was never placed on a practical basis. As we have previously noted, the chief philosophic justification for science among the Greeks was not a better mousetrap, but a healthier, more secure human mind. Ancient scientists spent so much energy on libation-pouring automatons and levitating statues, and not on the kind of practical laborsaving devices that define modernity, because (with few exceptions) their discipline was meant to be spiritually edifying, not constructive. Providing such comfort is the sort of function better suited to religion. Once the revealed certainties of Christianity, the pagan mystery cults, or Islam were available to soothe ancient spirits, Greek science was destined to be an orphan.

Others, such as Charles Freeman, have surveyed the role of Christianity in the decline of rationalism in antiquity. Given that the disciplines of Greek philosophy and science had roots reaching back well before the birth of Christ, it is ironic that moderns tend to see science as a newcomer "challenging" old-time religion. In fact, it was "old-time religion" that was the subversive force, attacking the foundations of a tradition of rationalism far predating itself. The large and lively corpus of Eratosthenes, which did not survive this long twilight of reason, was but one of its casualties.

## THE HOUSE OF WISDOM

Ptolemaeus may have been the last word in astronomy in the ancient West, but the rest of the world hardly stood still. Everyone knows that the legacy of Greek rationalism was preserved in the Islamic world, but this truism is only half the story: the Arabs, Babylonians, Persians, and Indians did more than simply transmit what they inherited from the Greeks. They refined and enlarged upon it, ultimately bequeathing back to the West a far richer body of knowledge than they received.

Space allows me to mention only a few key figures relevant to the history of geodesy. One of the great pioneers in Indian mathematics was Aryabhata (476–550 CE), who was born the very year the Roman Empire fell in the West. Along with establishing that the ratio between the circumference of a circle and its diameter (*pi*) is an irrational number, inventing the placeholding function of zero, and elaborating a model of the solar system that hinted at heliocentrism, Aryabhata published a figure for $E$ of 4,967 yojanas. Other Indian astronomers, such as Brahmagupta (598–668 CE), basically agreed in putting the figure at 4,800 or 5,000 yojanas. Alas, because the yojana, like the stade, is an ancient unit whose modern equivalent is disputed (most estimates run between five and eight modern miles) it is difficult to ascertain the exact modern value of these geodesies. If the yojana is taken to be five miles long, Aryabhata's estimate is extremely accurate at 24,835 miles.

According to one reading of the seventy-ninth Surah of the *Koran,* verse 30 reads, "[God] made the earth egg-shaped." This could suggest an awareness of the sphericity of the earth among the Arabs of the seventh century CE, but the text is ambiguous. (It can equally be interpreted to mean "oval," "spread-out," or "flat.") In any case, the Muslim caliphs who supplanted Greek rule throughout much of the Near East were very much aware of the legacy of Hellenistic science. The Abbasid caliph Abu Jafar al-Ma'mun ibn Harun (786–833 CE) was one of the most intriguing.

After seizing power from his brother in 813, al-Ma'mun subsidized a program of research inspired by Greek rationalism, inviting scholars from many nations and faiths to his court in Baghdad. (He appointed a non-Muslim, a Zoroastrian, as his vizier—something unthinkable even in most modern Islamic states.) The palace library founded by his father to preserve old Persian texts, the Bait al-hikmah ("House of Wisdom") was expanded into a full-fledged research institution. This new library, supplemented by an observatory and refectory for scholars, was consecrated to translating all major Greek philosophic and scientific texts into Arabic, including those of Ptolemaeus and, one presumes, Eratosthenes. Agents of the caliph were sent to scour the bookstalls of cities all over the Muslim world in search of lost Greek, Persian, and Hindu texts. Al-Ma'mun also demanded manuscripts from the Byzantine Empire as reparations of war. In this sense the caliph was nothing less than a latter-day Ptolemy Philadelphus.

One example of original research conducted under al-Ma'mun's sponsorship was the precise measurement of one degree of arc on the earth's surface (that is, $\frac{1}{360}$th of the meridian). The caliph's experts, like modern scholars, were very much aware of the lack of a clear definition of the stade in the ancient Greek sources, without which neither Eratosthenes' figure of seven hundred stades per degree nor Ptolemy's five hundred stades per degree had any practical meaning. To resolve this ambiguity once and for all, al-Ma'mun sent a team of seventy surveyors and astronomers into the desert to measure the exact distance a man needed to traverse for the North Star (Polaris) to appear to rise or descend one degree in the sky.

With the participation of such eminent Arab astronomers as Muhammad ibn Musa al-Khwarazmi (c. 780–863 CE) and Abu al-Abbas Ahmad ibn Muhammad ibn Kathir al-Farghani (also known, mercifully, as Alfraganus), the experiment was conducted on flat ground north of the Euphrates River. The expedition was divided into two teams, with one dispatched due north and the other due south; each placed an arrow in the ground at regular intervals along their path. Once each team observed the apparent position of Polaris to change by one full degree, they reversed direction and counted the number of arrows back to their starting point.

Their initial result was fifty-six miles per degree. This was revised to fifty-six and two-thirds miles when the experiment was repeated in the Syrian desert near Palmyra. The latter figure yields an accurate 24,276 modern miles for $E$, assuming that one Arabic mile equals 1.19 English miles. One particularly refreshing aspect of al-Ma'mun's geodesic expedition was that it did not just include mathematicians and astronomers. Yahyā ibn Aktham, a magistrate in a Basra religious court, was also invited, most likely for his professional probity. Unlike certain fundamentalist Christians and Muslims, al-Ma'mun and his court did not view the search for scientific and religious truths as contradictory endeavors.

Another giant of Muslim scholarship was Abū al-Rayhān al-Bīrūnī (973–1048 CE). Born in what is now Uzbekistan, he traveled later to undertake research at the House of Wisdom in Baghdad. Because of the tumultuous political environment of the time, al-Bīrūnī developed a skill at diplomacy that almost matched his scientific talents. "I was compelled to participate in worldly affairs," he later confessed, "which excited the envy of fools, but made the wise pity me." Nevertheless, in the early eleventh century he was obliged to join the retinue of the Persian sultan Mahmud of Ghazni as a political prisoner. In this regard he deserves comparison with that other hostage-scholar of antiquity, Polybius.

Al-Bīrūnī made the most of his exile by traveling to India during Mahmud's campaigns on the subcontinent. The fruit of these travels was a massive compendium of Indian geography, history, and linguistics and law, entitled *Ta'rikh al-Hind* (History of India). For this he has been called history's first anthropologist, though of course this is incorrect—classical writers from Aristotle to Eratosthenes to Strabo wrote books of similar scope long before him.

Al-Bīrūnī nevertheless merits inclusion among the great polymaths of all medieval history. Most relevant here are the contributions to mathematical geography, such as his elegant method for determining $E$ using an astrolabe (a kind of manual astronomical computer; see Box 2, "The Astrolabe," on page 171). This involved observing the horizon from the top of a mountain of known height. According to al-Bīrūnī's treatise, *On the Determination of the Coordinates of Cities,* the savant was inspired to try this method when he was living in exile in an Indian fortress: "I observed from an adjacent high mountain standing west of the fort a large plain lying south of the mountain. It occurred to me I should examine this method there." Al-Bīrūnī, who was not above sardonic understatement, takes a jibe at the "big science" approach of al-Ma'mun's manpower-intensive geodesic expeditions by noting, "Here is another method for the determination of the circumference of the earth. It does not require walking in deserts."

The mountaintop method involved sighting the horizon from the summit with the astrolabe, yielding a "dip angle." This angle and the height of the mountain, along with a rather lengthy series of geometrical inferences, yields a distance from the mountain's base to the center of the earth, or the radius. The details need not detain us here, except to note that for al-Bīrūnī the method yielded a figure for $E$ of slightly less than 81 million cubits (20,000 Arabic or 23,800 English miles).

On May 24, 997, al-Bīrūnī made careful observations of a lunar eclipse from his native city of Kath. By prior arrangement, his colleague Abu al-Wafa al-Buzjani observed the same eclipse from Baghdad, 1,200 miles to the west. This was essentially a replication of the simultaneous observation of the Arbela eclipse in 331 from Iraq and Carthage reported in Ptolemaeus's *Geography*. Unlike Ptolemaeus, however, al-Bīrūnī and al-Wafa got the timing of their eclipse correct, and were therefore able to derive accurate longitudes for both cities.

Thanks to these and other studies, Muslim scholars were in a position to correct Ptolemaeus's inaccurate east-west elongation of the Near East and Europe, and forever lay to rest the myth that the Indian Ocean was landlocked. The elegant result—which resembles Eratosthenes' third century BCE map more than Ptolemaeus's—can be seen in the reconstruction in figure 17 on page 176.

Further work in the Islamic east spurred the development of algebra (an Arab word), resulted in improved terrestrial maps and star charts, refined the astrolabe, and promoted the use of the Indian numeral system (mistakenly known in the West as "Arabic" numerals). Like the daughter library in Alexandria, however, the Bait al-hikmah came to a tragic end: in February 1258, it was destroyed along with the rest of Baghdad by the Mongols. The sack was so

## BOX 2: THE ASTROLABE

The astrolabe (in Greek, "star reckoner") is a manual computing and observation device with myriad uses in astronomy, time keeping, surveying, navigation, and astrology. The principles behind the most common variety, the *planispheric* astrolabe, were first laid down in antiquity by the Greeks, who pioneered the notion of projecting three-dimensional images on flat surfaces. The device reached a high degree of refinement in the medieval Islamic world, where it was invaluable for determining prayer times and the direction to Mecca from anywhere in the Muslim world. The astrolabe was introduced to Europe by the eleventh century, where it saw wide use until the Renaissance.

*Fig. 15. A modern reproduction of an Arabic-style astrolabe*

The fundamental innovation underlying the astrolabe was the projection of an image of the sky (usually the northern hemisphere, centered on Polaris) on a plane corresponding to the earth's equator. This image, which was typically etched on a brass plate, was inserted into a round frame (the *mater*) whose circumference was marked in degrees or hours. Over the plate was fitted a lattice-work disk, the *rete,* with pointers to indicate the positions of major stars. A metal hand, similar to those on a clock, was hinged with the rete at the center of the instrument, as was a sighting vane (the *alidade*) for determining the angular height of stars or other features, such as mountaintops. The entire device was usually no more than six to eight inches in diameter and half an inch thick.

One common use of the astrolabe was to determine the time

*continued ...*

of day, even after dark. After suspending the instrument by its ring (see figure 15), the user read the altitude of a prominent star with the alidade. By correlating this figure with the position of the sun in the zodiac, and rotating the rete so that the pointer corresponding to the observed star was in the correct position relative to the altitude and azimuth lines on the plate, the user could read the time from the scale of hours on the mater. A practiced hand could accomplish all this in less than half a minute.

Other uses included the determination of sunrise and sunset times for any date past or future, predicting eclipses, finding important stars or constellations, and (as discussed in the text) measuring the height of earthbound objects and the circumference of the earth. For this and other reasons, the astrolabe has been called "the world's first personal computer."

brutal that the stench of unburied corpses temporarily drove the invaders out of the city. A story is still taught to Baghdadi children of how the Tigris was turned ink-black from the trove of books dumped in the river.

Just as Islamic science went into eclipse, the Christian West was awakening to the need for a modern science of astronomy. The immediate cause was practical. The most important holiday in the Christian calendar, Easter, was decreed in antiquity to fall on the Sunday following the first full moon after the vernal equinox. The day of this moveable feast was easy to discern from year to year, but for various reasons was quite difficult to predict years in advance, as Church administration required. To remedy this, procedures for fixing the date of Easter were worked out by Alexandrian astronomers in the sixth century.

These Alexandrine rules grew less useful as the old calendar drifted noticeably out of sync with the solar year. By the tenth century, with the situation growing dire, the Vatican belatedly launched a program of subsidized astronomical research. Part of this program was the inclusion of mathematics and astronomy in seminary curricula. Improved astronomical instruments were imported from the Arab world, and new translations commissioned of the ancient authorities, notably Ptolemaeus. In one of history's great about-faces, the Church, which was complicit in the decline of science in antiquity, found itself sponsoring the revival of wisdom its founders had once disdained.

It is also one of the great unintended consequences of intellectual history that this sponsorship led directly to the overthrow of the Ptolemaic system long endorsed by the Church. Popular summaries of how Copernicus, Kepler, and Galileo matched and then surpassed the achievements of their ancient predecessors are available elsewhere. One little-known link between Islamic science and the European innovators, though, was Hermannus Contractus ("Herman the Cripple," 1013–1054 CE). Partly paralyzed by a childhood illness, this duke's son was consigned to an isolated monastery on Lake Constance. There he was free to devote himself to diverse academic subjects, including music, history, mathematics, and the introduction of Islamic astronomical methods to Latin Christendom. His *De utilitatibus astrolabii* (On the Uses of the Astrolabe) leaned heavily on an Arabic text by the Persian Jewish, astrologer Mashallah (c. 740–815 CE).

Indeed, Herman's book contained a chapter on the application of the astrolabe to the problem of determining the circumference of the earth. Though his work was influential, it did not settle the controversy simmering in Europe then and in the succeeding centuries—a controversy that served the purposes of an obscure Genoese sea captain with a particularly ambitious project in mind.

## FROM HERE TO CIPANGU

Medieval Europe was something of a prison. When Western merchants and travelers such as Marco Polo wished to travel east, they did so by the sufferance of their powerful, largely suspicious Muslim neighbors. Notwithstanding minor Viking settlements, the north was closed by its frigid climate, while lands to the south had been regarded since antiquity as belonging to an uninhabitable "torrid zone." To the west was the open Atlantic Ocean; contrary winds at European latitudes, though, made passage in that direction virtually impossible by ships of the time.

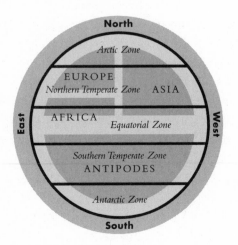

*Fig. 16. The ancient "five-zone" model of earth, as described by Aristotle and reflected in Cicero's* Somnium Scipionis

Yet these limitations were as much psychological as physical. The illusion that a torrid zone encircled the earth, forever dividing the habitable regions of the north and south, had a long pedigree, going back at least to Parmenides and Aristotle (see figure 16). Cicero had

Scipio the Elder describe a five-zone model of the earth, including a *zona torrida,* to his protégé in *The Dream of Scipio.* Eratosthenes, on the other hand, criticized it in his *Geography,* noting that temperate regions did extend toward the equator in some countries. He was followed by Francis Bacon in the sixteenth century, who argued against the conventional wisdom that the southern hemisphere was uninhabitable. Despite such illustrious critics, the specter of the torrid zone still loomed over medieval geographers.

Many Muslims held to an even more radical limitation, believing that the navigable regions of the ocean, which lay near the continents, were enclosed by a gloomy exocean (*al-bahr al-muhit,* or *mare tenebrosum* in Latin) too obscure and forbidding to sail upon (see figure 17). This seems much like the ancient Greco-Roman dread of the storm-tossed waters beyond Gibraltar, generalized in the Muslim case to the more remote "blue-water" ocean.

To be sure, this "sea of gloom" didn't stop Muslim seafarers from gradually venturing farther and farther from shore. Their expeditions found encouragement in the prophetic al-Bīrūnī, who argued in his History of India that additional habitable islands or continents might lie somewhere hidden in the ocean surrounding the known world. The mariners of Islamic Spain and Morocco at least knew what they were getting into when they lit out across the Atlantic: al-Ma'mun's measurement of 56⅔ Arabic miles per degree was a well-known fact, as was the resulting figure of almost 25,000 miles for the whole circumference. Anyone trying to reach the East by sailing west would have to cross many thousands of miles of open ocean, "dark" or otherwise.

Incredibly, there were attempts. A large, heterodox literature exists of pre-Columbian contacts between America and the Islamic world, including accounts from the historians al-Mas'udi (896–956 CE), al-Idrisi (1100–c. 1165 CE), and al-Umari (1300–1384 CE) of sailors striking out west from Muslim lands. A certain Khashkhash ibn Saeed

*Fig. 17. A reconstruction of a Muslim world map of the ninth century CE, compiled by geographers under al-Ma'mun. Note the improvement in accuracy of Ptolemaeus's map. (From Sezgin, pre-Columbian discovery)*

of Cordova supposedly embarked from near Huelva, Spain, in 889, and returned some time later with a hold full of treasure from hitherto unknown territories. According to al-Mas'udi, one Zayn Eddine Ali Ben Fadhel al-Mazandarani sailed from Morocco in 1291 and encountered a "green island" somewhere beyond the Azores. In 1311, an armada of vessels attempted to cross the Atlantic under Emperor Abubakari II, who gave up the throne of Mali to command the expedition himself. Fate did not reward the emperor's sacrifice as well as it did Khashkhash's greed: his fleet was never heard from again.

Exactly where Khashkhash or al-Mazandarani might have landed in America—and indeed, whether they landed there at all—are questions that await hard evidence. There are few projects duller than attempting to extend the list of people (the ancient Egyptians? the Romans? the Chinese?) who *might* have beaten Columbus across the Atlantic. The Muslim accounts have the ring of truth in at least one regard, though: vessels traveling to America from Iberia or West Africa via the Canary Islands are more likely to encounter the favorable northeast trade winds than those striking due west from Christian Europe. Columbus himself sailed by way of the Canaries on his first voyage.

If Strabo is to be believed, the Muslim mariners were relative latecomers to Atlantic navigation. In book 1 of the *Geography,* he clearly implies that deep ocean voyages had already been attempted by Roman times:

> Those who have returned from an attempt to circumnavigate the earth, do not say they have been prevented from continuing their voyage by any opposing continent, for the sea remained perfectly open, but through want of resolution, and the scarcity of provision.

Strabo makes this remark in the context of arguing that the inhabited world is wholly surrounded by one ocean, and that it should be possible to sail directly between Europe and east Asia, because the stretch of water between the two continents is "not much." His confidence on the latter point is somewhat puzzling, given that he seems to accept Eratosthenes' estimate for the whole circumference. "Not much" in that case would amount to some 160,000 stades, or some fifteen thousand miles of open ocean.

This is perhaps a case of Strabo's biases outstripping his reason. To the ancient mind, the notion that the earth was covered mostly by water was plainly counterintuitive—since the summit of creation is man, and man lives on land, why would the gods (or God) make the majority of the earth's surface wet? Though it is apocryphal, the biblical-era Book of Esdras clearly states that the earth is no less than six-sevenths dry land:

> Upon the third day thou didst command that the waters should be gathered in the seventh part of the earth: six parts hast thou dried up, and kept them, to the intent that of these some being planted of God and tilled might serve thee.

Ptolemy's sympathy for this view is evidenced by the massive southern continent he postulated to link east Asia and southern Africa. Declared the Portuguese historian João de Barros (1496–1570), "nature could not have made so disorderly a composition of the globe as to give the element of water preponderance over the land, destined for life and the creation of souls." All this should be a cautionary tale for those who prefer to see "intelligent design" in the physical world—seeing good design depends on what seems intelligent to whom.

In 1492, the German mathematician Martin Behaim presented a globe, now infamous, that placed the half-legendary island of "Cipangu" (Japan) within a few thousand miles of Lisbon (see figure 18). *E* for Behaim could have been no more than sixteen thousand miles—smaller even than Poseidonius's underestimate. Behaim's popularity suggests that educated men all over Europe found this "small, dry Earth" model seductive indeed. One of these educated men was Christopher Columbus.

### ADMIRAL OF AN ABRIDGED SEA

As one of the true "hot-button" figures in history, there is no shortage of opinions about Columbus. Lauded through the nineteenth

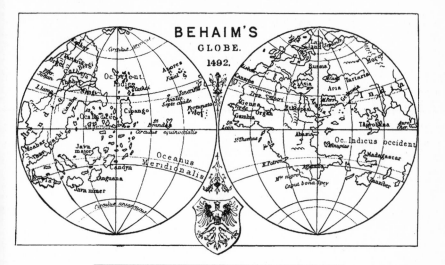

Fig. 18. Martin Behaim's world map, published around the time
of Columbus's first voyage. Note the distance of Japan (Cipangu) from
the Asian mainland and its proximity to known islands in the eastern
Atlantic Ocean.

century as an intrepid explorer and hero of scientific rationalism, his
reputation has lately been battered by accusations that he laid the
foundations for imperialism, slavery, and the environmental devasta-
tion of America. One thing he certainly was not, however, was a
scholar. If Columbus was aware of the geographical writings of
Ptolemy, Strabo, Eratosthenes, or the Arab geographers, his knowledge
was fairly thin, largely limited to combing the literature for support
for his grand project: to reach Asia by sailing west across the Atlantic.

He did know of Eratosthenes, however. One of the sources he
used in his research was an Italian translation of Pliny's *Natural
History*—a book in which Eratosthenes is praised as "a man of incomparable skill." Among the books that apparently sat on his
night table for years was an edition of Aeneas Sylvius's *Historia rerum ubique gestarum,* a summary of Ptolemaic doctrine published in

1477. One of Columbus's marginal notes, preserved in his own hand, enthusiastically seconds a claim by Eratosthenes that portions of the equatorial zone are habitable.

It is perhaps needless to say by now that virtually none of the educated people of fifteenth century Europe believed the earth was flat. The sphericity of the earth had not been in question in learned circles since antiquity. The myth that Columbus had an argument with ignorant flat-earthers was propagated by the writer Washington Irving in his 1828 biography of Columbus, whence it entered popular lore for generations of grade-school children. (Outside the informed minority, all bets are off: by way of analogy, at a time when evolution is an acknowledged fact among all biologists, a majority of U.S. citizens nonetheless fail to accept that human beings have evolved.)

The issue between Columbus and his official critics was never the shape of the planet, but its dimensions. Poseidonius and Ptolemaeus were useful to Columbus insofar as they posited an earth about 30 percent smaller than Eratosthenes' 252,000 stades. But even Ptolemaeus's figure suggested a substantial voyage to reach the Indies— too long, in fact, to trust such an expedition would ever return.

To sell his project to the crowned heads of Europe, Columbus had to out-Ptolemaeus Ptolemaeus in his underestimate of $E$. To this end, he found the claims of Marinus of Tyre, as summarized in the master's *Geography*, to be most congenial. He was also aware of al-Ma'mun's project to measure one degree of the meridian, though as we shall see below, he seems to have seriously misconstrued the results. The accounts of Marco Polo, in which the gold-bedecked island of Cipangu (Japan) was described, promised to extend the Asian continent still farther east; Columbus, like his contemporary Martin Behaim, saw fit not only to accept the existence of Japan, but to place it thousands of miles east of China. By such means the Asian continent was stretched eastward, to mere spitting range of the ports of Iberia. The eminent physician-geographer Paolo dal Pozzo Toscanelli, when asked in 1474 by the king of Portugal to comment on Marco Polo's claims, confidently replied, "A course due west from Lisbon will take you in about 5000 nautical miles to Quinsay, capital of the Chinese province of Mangi." In actuality, such a course would have landed Columbus in the desert of the North American southwest, in the vicinity of what would one day become the town of Eureka, Nevada.

The Arab figure of 56⅔ miles per terrestrial degree might have given Columbus pause. Instead, he was able to rationalize it as support for his scheme by conflating the Arabic mile (about 1.19 statute miles) with a unit more familiar to him, the Roman mile (which was about 5 percent smaller than its modern equivalent). The mistake was self-serving, but understandable insofar as Columbus's ignorance of Arabic metrology was not unusual for his time. Even so, a figure of 56⅔ *Roman* miles per degree yields a figure for $E$ of more than nineteen thousand statute miles—still substantially larger than the shrunken globe advanced by Columbus and Behaim. We can only assume that this inconsistency was simply too inconvenient to have crossed Columbus's mind.

We all know the result: Columbus got his funding and his ships from the Spanish crown, and ran into North America (or more precisely, islands near it) instead of farthest Asia. Yet so tenacious was his idée fixe that Columbus would not admit the possibility that he had discovered a hitherto unknown continent until years later, after his third voyage.

It is tempting to suppose that if Columbus had accepted Eratosthenes' original circumference, he would never had sailed at all. In this sense, mistakes like Columbus's can be very productive. But it would be wrong to assume that everyone agreed with Strabo that nothing but open water lay between Europe and east Asia, and there was nothing of significance left to discover in the world. Al-Bīrūnī speculated on the existence of unknown continents. Almost nine centuries before him, and fifteen before Columbus, the Roman playwright Seneca wrote a version of the tragedy of *Medea*. In this play the chorus sang the following:

*Nothing is left where*
*Once it was; the world is*
*Open to travel. . . .*
*There will be an age,*
*A distant Chinese year when*
*Ocean will lose its*
*Power to limit knowledge,*
*And the gigantic*
*Earth will open to us.*
*Tethys, sea goddess,*
*Will disclose whole new worlds;*
*No more will Iceland*
*Be our far horizon*

### CIRCUMNAVIGATION

Columbus's discoveries had enormous consequences, but they didn't settle the argument over the true circumference of the earth. Doubt that the self-styled "Admiral of the Ocean Sea" had really reached the East began to circulate as early as 1493, when the Italian chronicler Peter "the Martyr" d'Anghiera described his discoveries as occurring not in the Orient, but in a wholly "New World." (Peter was, incidentally, the first to use the phrase "New World" to describe America.) Though Columbus claimed to have reached the eastern extremity of China, and much of Europe was quick to believe him, Peter remarked drily, "the size of the globe seems to suggest otherwise."

Columbus's professional tenacity was matched only by his defensiveness. Indeed, he remained convinced to the end of his days that the golden pagodas of Cipangu were just over the Caribbean horizon, and that the island of Cuba, first surveyed by himself, was really part of the Malay peninsula. His use of celestial navigation to fix his longitude was erroneous and self-serving—one observation of a lunar eclipse from off the coast of the modern Dominican Republic, for instance, led him to conclude he was some eighty degrees west of Portugal, or by his reckoning nearly on the doorstep of Asia. His real position was less than sixty degrees west of Lisbon.

His fourth and final voyage was designed to settle the question once and for all: Columbus informed King Ferdinand and Queen Isabella that he would discover the strait that would lead him to the Indian Ocean. Against the possibility that he would circumnavigate the planet, he bore royal greetings for the Portuguese governor in India, Vasco de Gama, lest they meet on the far side of the globe. The result, of course, is that he discovered there was no passage to Asia in the latitudes he was exploring, though he wore out his ships searching for one. At the end of this, his most ambitious voyage, Columbus had to abandon his storm-battered, worm-eaten vessels. It took a year for his unenthusiastic Spanish sponsors to rescue Columbus and his crew from their makeshift settlement on the coast of Jamaica.

It is fashionable lately to disparage Columbus for his failures as a colonial administrator, his baleful dabbling in the slave trade, and his fixation on showing a profit—preferably in gold—to defray the expenses of his sponsors. As archaeological discoveries of a Viking settlement in Newfoundland have shown, he was not even the first European to glimpse American shores. Why should this latecomer Columbus warrant enshrinement in the history books, let alone a federal holiday? Instead of feting Columbus with a parade in New

York City, shouldn't we all be enjoying pickled herring on Leif Erikson Day?

Columbus's contemporaries in the Spanish Inquisition could hardly outdo his modern detractors for their moral absolutism. In other circumstances, his zeal to justify the investments of the people who believed in him would be taken as evidence of integrity, not personal venality. As historian Samuel Morison has noted, Columbus could have rested on the laurels of his first voyage and lived the rest of his life as a moneyed aristocrat. Unfortunately for him, it was not in his character to walk away from what he had started.

Happily, few serious historians now dispute the fact that Columbus's transatlantic voyages were, if not the first, certainly the most *consequential*. Before Columbus, geography beyond Iceland and the Azores were matters of myth and alehouse conjecture. Though the Arabs, then the Portuguese, explored the Atlantic basin, and might even have anticipated some of Columbus's discoveries, they guarded what they learned as state secrets. Copying nautical charts, or even verbally divulging knowledge of discovered territories, was a criminal offense.

Fortunately, Columbus's Spanish sponsors were eager to establish their *official* sovereignty over the new lands, and were therefore uniquely willing to broadcast their achievements far and wide. Within weeks of Columbus's return from his first voyage, much of southern Europe was aware of his discoveries. After a few more months, the news had traveled as far as Britain and Germany. After Columbus, the existence of the unexplored territories suddenly became known to a vast swath of the human community. The case for his significance is no more or less than that.

For our purposes here, the most important figure sailing for Spain during the so-called Age of Discovery was not Columbus, but the Portuguese émigré Fernão de Magalhães—commonly known by his Anglicized name, Ferdinand Magellan (1480–1521). As everyone learns in elementary school, Magellan led the first expedition to circle the globe by sea. Those who did a little better on their fourth-grade exams may recall that Magellan himself did not survive the trip—he perished in the Philippines after leading his small fleet on an unprecedented crossing of the Pacific Ocean.

His achievement nevertheless stands as the greatest feat of seamanship in history: unlike Columbus, Magellan has no credible or even half credible Phoenician, Roman, Arab, Chinese, or Viking competitors for the title of first circumnavigator. Nor is it likely that the Polynesians, who populated many of the major Pacific islands over many generations, ever launched a single expedition to cross the world's largest ocean. The return of one of Magellan's original five ships to Spain in 1522—not from the west but the east—shocked and delighted his adoptive kingdom. The Atlantic Ocean was known for millennia before it was finally traversed; the much larger Pacific was crossed by Europeans less than a decade after Vasco Nuñez de Balboa cut his way over the isthmus of Panama to glimpse it for the first time.

Like Columbus, Magellan only managed to secure financing for his expedition by lowballing his estimate for $E$. According to an account by the contemporary historian Bartolomé de las Casas, Magellan made his pitch to the king's ministers in Valladolid using a custom-built globe that placed Asia very close to the western rim of America. It seems that by 1518 the exploration of the New World had finally laid to rest Columbus's notion of a dry earth even smaller than Claudius Ptolemaeus's second century CE estimate. Ptolemaeus's original figure of 180,000 ancient stades was, however, still a live possibility—and with the improving blue-water seamanship of the Spanish and Portuguese, not so great an obstacle as it once seemed. For the trip to the Spice Islands of Asia and landfall in lands described by Marco Polo, Magellan estimated a journey of some nine thousand miles.

Like Columbus, Magellan went first to the court of Portugal for money to support his great project. A generation after Columbus's death, however, there was more evidence—albeit hearsay—that a strait existed to the far side of America. Magellan may have been inspired by the Portuguese explorer João de Lisboa, who claimed a few years earlier to have discovered just such a passage far to the south of Brazil. (Storms, Lisboa said, forced him to turn back before he could reach the ocean beyond.) In this sense, then, Magellan's proposal was analogous to Vasco de Gama's mission to circumnavigate Africa, after Bartolomew Dias had proved such a journey possible by rounding the Cape of Good Hope.

However plausible the scheme sounded, the Portuguese king Manuel I was having none of it. Like Columbus, Magellan had better luck in Spain, where the young monarch Charles I was eager to wrest control of the Indonesian spice trade from Portugal. Magellan was given command of a fleet of five ships and about 260 men. On September 20, 1519, the expedition left the Spanish port of Sanlúcar de Barrameda, bound for the half-mythical islands where money—in the form of cloves and cinnamon—literally grew on trees.

Over the next three years, Magellan compelled his little armada across half the planet almost by pure force of will (see figure 19). Two of his five vessels were taken over by mutineers off the coast of Patagonia; by quick and decisive action, Magellan turned the tables on his opponents and regained control of his fleet. The strait that now bears his name is no placid byway, but a storm-tossed maze of glacial inlets, bays, and other dead ends that required weeks to navigate. After rounding South America, what was supposed to be a short and triumphal run to the Spice Islands stretched into the longest open-water voyage yet undertaken by Europeans.

The sense of personal destiny that sustained Magellan through

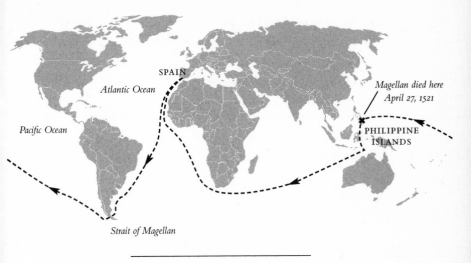

*Fig. 19. Magellan's circumnavigation of the earth*

these trials at last betrayed him off the island of Mactan in the Philippines. Hoping to show off European arms to his native allies, the captain and a handful of men plunged into an ill-considered melee with fifteen hundred Mactanese warriors. Magellan was cut to pieces; not enough of him was left intact to be worth collecting and burying.

Of the five ships and 260 crew who left Spain, only eighteen men in one vessel reached home in 1522. All the survivors, most of whom despised Magellan for his Portuguese origins, his relentless discipline, or both, received honors and titles for their trouble. Magellan's wife and children got nothing.

His voyage did prove, however, that a vast ocean separated Asia and the Americas. The myth that the globe was composed mostly of land was empirically disproven; fully 70 percent of the Lord's terrestrial creation appeared not to be made for human habitation at all. Magellan's logbooks, and those of the captains that succeeded him, showed that the earth was some seven thousand miles wider around than Ptolemaeus had written. Practical experience had at last caught up with what Eratosthenes had shown eighteen centuries earlier.

If the magnitude of the voyage had been understood in 1519, the fleet would never have left port. In this sense, Magellan was the first and last man to sacrifice his life because he chose not to accept Eratosthenes' estimate of the world's circumference.

## THE SIGNIFICANCE OF ERATOSTHENES

"Mr. Beta" notwithstanding, Eratosthenes of Cyrene was one of a handful of truly brilliant figures to work at the Museum in Alexandria. As a scientist with all the prestige and privileges attending the post of head librarian, he was unique. His geodesy was only a small part of what he accomplished, but through sound principles and a bit of luck it turned out to be strikingly accurate. His contributions to the disciplines of geography, chronology, practical mathematics, literary history, and criticism were in most cases quite original, perhaps even modern in spirit. He accomplished these things, moreover, at a time when the philosophic underpinnings and institutions of scientific rationalism had hardly begun to be developed. We can only imagine how large he would loom in Western intellectual history if any of his major works had survived.

One of the paradoxes—if not the frustrations—of surveying Eratosthenes' legacy is that his geodesy seems to have been widely respected, but just as widely disbelieved. In the great marketplace of ideas, lesser products, such as the competing work of Poseidonius, had more appeal. As is so often the case in science and politics, whether a theory is correct is not as important as *when* it is correct. Eratosthenes, despite his reputation, despite the validity of his method, and despite his ideal position as the head of the greatest research institution of his time, was simply right too soon about the dimensions of the earth.

In the end, however, Eratosthenes' figure of 252,000 stades may have been less significant than the spirit in which he pursued all his varied endeavors. His insistence that serious consideration of issues in geography and historical chronology should not include poetry or myth—not uncritically, at least—was as momentous a notion as any ever advanced at the Museum. That his dismissal of the evidentiary power of Homer was universally reviled deep into Roman times was but one measure of its radicalism.

None of this is to suggest that Eratosthenes would have denied the essential role of myth in the functioning of a healthy society. That he was as intimately familiar with mythological material is more than proven by the catalog of his relevant works, including the *Catasterisms* and his best-known poem, *Hermes.* At the very least, Eratosthenes would have agreed with Plato that myths were "falsehoods," but had their uses in maintaining social order. In all likelihood he savored the old stories as thoroughly as the next man around the seminar table.

It is fashionable today to take the division of scholarship into sciences and humanities as unfortunate, even pernicious. In the rarified world of academic celebrity, the poet/physicist and the concert-level pianist/cognitive scientist are often touted in university press releases and at conferences (though they are often the object of contempt by the more specialized colleagues in their departments). The implicit notion is that the "two cultures" distinction is self-defeating—that mastering a sonata will somehow give the psychologist some deeper understanding of the creative process, or conversely, that psychology will lend fresh impetus to creative expression. In anthropology, the principle that such sources as myth and oral history should be used with caution when investigating past events—the very root of Eratosthenes' method in constructing his chronology—currently lies in deep disrepute. On the more radical fringes of the discipline, science itself is held to be nothing more than a Western flavor of mythology, with no more claim to objective validity than Ashanti cosmology or a Zuni creation story.

Be that as it may, Eratosthenes' declaration of what Stephen J. Gould might have called the "nonoverlapping magisteria" of Homeric myth on the one hand and geography on the other was a necessary first step toward the rationalization of scholarship. Just as modern science would later need to separate itself from speculative philosophy, there could have been little objective progress in this field while it remained virtually undifferentiated from poetry. That this innovation earned Eratosthenes few friends and no immediate successors is another consequence of his talent for insight long before the season for truth had arrived.

## THE TABLEMOUNT

This book began by noting the relative lack of material on Eratosthenes at the library. Ironically, though he remains a key figure in the study of the earth, one has to go 240,000 miles away to find his most obvious geographic commemoration. If we look just above and left of the center of the full moon, at the border of the Mare Imbrium (the "Sea of Rains") and the Sinus Aestuum (the "Glowing Bay"), we find the lunar impact crater Eratosthenes. Some thirty-five miles across and two miles deep, the crater retains a well-defined rim and central peak, though it is some 3.2 billion years old. In the history of the moon, its formation marks the beginning of the longest epoch in the selenologic timescale, after the cataclysmic volcanism that formed the lunar "seas"—a period specialists now call the "Eratosthenian epoch."

There is one other feature that bears his name. Though it is far

larger than the crater and much closer to home, it is virtually unknown to all but a few geologists and cartographers. I first learned
of it, ironically, while I was flying across the eastern Mediterranean, on my way home from Alexandria. At the time, I was engaged in one of my typical activities while bored on airplanes:
watching the progress of the flight across the map on my video
screen. This pastime, the geographic equivalent of watching grass
grow, usually amounts to nothing more than a kind of time-killing
self-hypnosis—only this time I noticed something that made me
put down my honey-roasted peanuts. For there, on the bottom of
the sea, about halfway between Egypt and the island of Cyprus,
stood something labeled the "Eratosthenes Tablemount."

Later, I learned that the Tablemount was a huge underwater
massif nearly one hundred miles long. Rising some six thousand
feet above the seafloor, it sprawls over an area equal to the states of
Delaware and Rhode Island put together. It lies amid other geo-
logical features in the eastern Mediterranean—the "Herodotus
Abyssal Plain," the "Hecataeus Ridge," the "Strabo Trench," and
so on—that together amount to a kind of underwater pantheon of
notable ancient figures.

None of these monuments breaks the surface of the sea. The top
of the Tablemount, though as high as Mount Washington, is still
submerged some two thousand feet. Whatever inspired its attach-
ment to Eratosthenes, then, there is poetry in its naming. Like the
man's legacy, it is certainly broad, manifestly massive, and, for all
practical purposes, invisible to terrestrial eyes.

# NOTES

In citing works in the notes, short titles have generally been used. For authors represented in the bibliography by only one work, only the author's last name is given. Complete references may be found in the bibliography.

### CHAPTER 1

2      *the 180-foot-long, 44-foot-wide* Isis      Quoted in Casson, *Travel,* 158–59.

5      *Dedicated in the early third century*      Pliny, 36.18.

6      *Underwater surveys of the area*      Empereur, 64, 82–87.
     *the self-aggrandizing impulse*      Green, 96.
     *More to the point*      All of this begs a question rarely asked in Alexandria scholarship: why was the Pharos built to the height it was? We presume much if we imagine the Greeks meant only to build the tallest tower they could. That it was possible to build higher would have been obvious from the nearby example of the Great Pyramid at Giza, which in its original state exceeded 450 feet. If the object was simply to build a useful landmark, why not make do with a 100- or 200-foot tower? Conversely, if the goal was the *most* useful lighthouse, or the best lookout on the approaches from the sea, or the most physically impressive symbolic structure, why not build taller?

7      *Many are feeding in populous Egypt*      Quoted in Pfeiffer, 97–98.

8      *Strabo offers the best surviving description*      Strabo, 17.6–10.
     *various dwellings and groves*      Strabo, 17.1.8–9.

9      *a scheme that Fraser likens to the Topkapı*      Fraser, 23. Interestingly, the large proportion of Alexandria devoted to its semidivine rulers is in exact agreement with Aristotle's observation that a well-organized city consecrates a quarter to a third of its territory to the gods (*Politics,* 7.10; 2.8).

10      *Achilles Tatius . . . ecstatic description*      Achilles Tatius, 5.1.

11      *The well-traveled Abd al-Malik Ibn Juraij*      Quoted in Delia, 1464.

*Amrou ibn el-Ass . . . wrote a letter to the caliph*    Quoted in Canfora, 83.

*Another Arab visitor reported*    Quoted in Forster, 61–62, 85–86.

12    *She then called on her brother*    Hölbl, 48–50.

15    *That Eratosthenes was the architect*    Geus, 207–10; Forster, 46–47.

21    *Caesar prayed there*    Dio Cassius, 51.

*E. M. Forster complained*    Forster, 112.

23    *Herodotus recounts an earlier voyage*    Herodotus, 4.42.

24    *Pliny the Elder praised Eratosthenes*    Pliny, 2.247.

### CHAPTER 2

29    *The deep antiquity of the Babylonian tradition*    Thurston, 71–81.

30    *Babylonian cosmology*    Williams, vol. 1, part 3.

31    *they were not drawing from some deep well of native wisdom*    Fraser, 336, and Thurston, 82–83; also see Bernal, 247–68, for a conflicting view.

*As Plato wrote in*    Plato, *Timaeus,* 40.

33    *the beginning of scientific astronomy*    Heath, *Aristarchus,* 193.

34    *Aristarchus proposed a universe with the sun at its center*    Lloyd, 57–60.

36    *There is a famous story*    Plutarch, *Pericles,* XXXV.

*the rise of major philosophical schools*    Irby-Massie and Keyser, 9–10.

*Aristotle explained why fewer concentric spheres were necessary*    Aristotle, *On the Heavens,* II, 12.

37    *They were certainly ingenious enough*    White, 235.

38    *Heron of Alexandria describes*    Lloyd, 103–6.

*Why prove them?*    White, 237.

*Plato replied*    Plato, *Timaeus,* 68.

*Herophilus of Chalcedon, invented a device*    Fraser, 353.

39    *The search for scientific truth was never an end in itself*    Lloyd, 31.

*Epicurus likewise declared*    Epicurus, *Letter to Pythocles,* quoted in Lloyd, 21.

*he saw pursuit of a single truth as a symptom*    Lloyd, 25.

40    *Chandragupta . . . would amass an army*    Pliny, frag. 61, VI. 22.

43    *the savagery of the Egyptians*    Polybius, 15.33.

*a gilded cathouse*    Polybius, 14.11.

*typically oriental debauch*    Polybius, 5.87.

*[The Romans] saw how great*    Polybius, 31.18

*Ptolemy III Euergetes made an enormous donation*    Polybius, 5.89.

44    *George Grote . . . declared*    Grote, *History of Greece,* XX.

46    *the age of city-states*    Green, 155–56.

47    *The way to Egypt*    Strabo, 17.1.19.

*Alexander, says Arrian*      Arrian, 149.

48    *Ptolemy, who was certainly not above dipping deep*      Green, 14.
49    *"incentivized" to resettle there*      Rufus, 4.8.5.
50    *a completely new stage in Mediterranean history*      Green, 80.
51    *740,000 talents*      Appian, 10.
      *like trying to discern*      Green, xx.
53    *the king justified this measure*      Canfora, 32.
      *The kings also settled Macedonian soldiers*      Samuel, 175.
      *as many as 200,000 infantry*      Appian, 10.
54    *the settlers were beyond the reach of native courts*      Bagnall, 7.
      *written translation between Greek and demotic*      Samuel, 175.
      *an occupying imperial minority*      Green, 187–98.
      *We find evidence for similar bitterness*      Lewis, 60–61.
55    *King Ptolemaios, the Everliving*      Birch, 83.
56    *the coronation festivities*      adapted from Athenaeus, 5.25.
57    *Cyril . . . had greased many palms*      Freeman, 215; Crake, 423.
      *The system didn't work*      Samuel, 176.
      *native mercenaries in Thebes*      Polybius, v. 107.
58    *Instead of borrowing Egyptian terms*      Lewis, 154–55, quoted in Empereur, 37.


## CHAPTER 3

59    *Now tell me, Muses*      Hermippus, 1.27e–28a.
      *According to Herodotus*      Herodotus, IV.150–59.
      *the city single-handedly donated*      Fraser, 151
60    *Eratosthenes' parentage and early life*      Blomqvist, 58–59; *Suda,* epsilon 2898.
61    *the so-called Constitution of Cyrene*      Bagnall, 28–31.
62    *Never . . . at one period*      Strabo, 1.2.
64    *repeated sneering references to Euripides*      Aristophanes, *The Frogs,* 1.943, 1409.
      *Protagoras was convicted on charges of heresy*      Dodds, 189, 201 n. 66; Pfeiffer, 31–32.
      *the teaching of scientific astronomy*      *Cambridge Ancient History V,* 383.
      *The picture we have of Socrates from his students*      Xenophon, 1.11.
      *one modern commentator wrote*      Dodds, 189.
65    *direct exposure to these Asian libraries*      Pfeiffer, 17–18.
      *The Peripatetic (Aristotelian) model*      Fraser, 320.
      *a tag-and-release research project on stags*      Pliny, VIII, 118–19.
66    *Cassander . . . must have chuckled*      Green, 44.
      *bottle-blond*      Ibid., 46.

other museums in the Greek world    Fraser, 312–19.

67    Demetrius advised the prince    Plutarch, *Sayings,* quoted in Canfora, 18.
Demetrius was an intimate of the king    Aelian, III, 17.
Demetrius was placed under house arrest    Cicero, *Pro Rabirio,* 23.

69    Strabo unambiguously states    Strabo, 17.8.
Luciano Canfora has compellingly argued    Canfora, 66–70.

70    we have no solid evidence    Canfora, 137–44; Delia, 1459.

71    this did not mean that it always required two hands to work with a scroll
Contra Casson, who argues (*Libraries,* 129) that the awkwardness of physically handling scrolls led to their decline vis-à-vis codices for research.
codices on parchment    Casson, 124–35.

72    To differentiate multiple copies    Fraser, 327 and n. 158, p. 483.
some labels included an "incipit"    Pfeiffer, 126.
duplicates are hardly likely    Fraser, 329.
literacy was relatively widespread    Harris, 22. In his study of ancient literacy, Harris opines that the rate of illiteracy was surprisingly high in
the classical period—something over 90 percent—but grants that pop-
ulations in Hellenistic capitals such as Alexandria were probably well
lettered by comparison.

73    the "authorized" versions of the plays    Fraser, 325.
We'd love a peek at the Ephemerides    Blomqvist, 55.
books from all over the known world    Canfora, 24.

74    By the time the collections were destroyed    Canfora, 87.
Some say the caliph replied    Most scholars now dismiss this story as
apocryphal, if for no other reason than that it is corroborated by no
near-contemporary Christian sources. But most medieval Muslim
sources do relate the tale as fact. This amounts to a curious "admission
against interest" for Muslims.

75    As one historian has written    Blomqvist, 66.
no obvious equivalent for the English word librarian    Fraser, 322.
the identities of the head librarians    Ibid., 333.
Ptolemy VIII . . . expelled many prominent intellectuals    Hölbl, 194–95.

77    we hear of one scholar    Forster, 39.
we can hear the distant cacophony    Green, 87; Pfeiffer, 98.
a certain Ptolemaeus, was nicknamed "the Attacker"    Fraser, 467.

78    The most famous feud of all    Forster, 34.
Aristophanes of Byzantium . . . was imprisoned    Fraser, 461.
a fragment from Callimachus's Aitia    Callimachus, frag. 75.4, translated
in Green, 180.

80    The response to such crises    Pfeiffer, 88.
The works of other important poets    Fraser, 477–78.

*similar tidbits of anthropology*   Green, 180, 205.

*alphabeticization*   Casson, *Libraries,* 37.

81   *They theorized about grammatical laws*   Pfeiffer, 202–3.

*Callimachus, the most widely quoted author*   Green, 179.

*the first to call himself* philologos   Suetonius, c. 10; Pfeiffer, 158, n. 8.

82   *Catasterisms*   Pfeiffer, 161, 168; see Pamias and Geus for a German translation of the remains (via Catalan).

*founder of the discipline of scientific chronology*   Blomqvist, 61.

83   *Polybius denounces it explicitly*   Polybius, 34.4.

*Strabo . . . hewed to a more cautious position*   Strabo, 7.3.6

*later chronologists shrank from Eratosthenes' example*   Fraser, 457.

*critical chronology*   Pfeiffer, 163.

*even Polybius . . . concedes*   Polybius, 34.13.

84   *He [Eratosthenes] says that the Nile*   Strabo, 17.1.2.

85   *This question in particular*   Eratosthenes, paraphrased in Strabo, 1.3.4.

*That to repel strangers is a practice common*   Eratosthenes, quoted in Strabo, 17.1.19.

*a bitingly sarcastic quip*   Ibid., 1.2.15.

86   *he disparaged Homer's verse*   Strabo, 1.2.3

*five symmetrical zones*   Cf. Aristotle, *Meteorology,* 2.5.

*Eratosthenes . . . divides the inhabited world*   Strabo, 2.1.22.

87   *Following Plato, Eratosthenes believed*   Solmsen, 208.

88   *the classical Sophists were fond of coining words*   Pfeiffer, 159.

89   *Plato applies the notion of proportionality*   Plato, *Timaeus,* 32.

*Eratosthenes enlarged upon Plato's use*   Solmsen, 194–95.

90   *Archimedes to Eratosthenes, greeting*   Irby-Massie and Keyser, 29.

91   *a passage in the* Platonicus   Quoted in Heath, *Greek Mathematics,* 1, 245.

92   *a passage from Plato's* Republic   Plato, *Republic,* 528.

*a letter to King Ptolemy III*   Quoted in Fraser, 411.

93   *Friend, if you're thinking*   Irby-Massie and Keyser, 31.

95   *Plato reproached the disciples of Eudoxus*   Plutarch, *Symposiacs,* VIII, 2.1 [718e], emphasis added.

96   *Kondos and his men had stumbled on a major find*   Throckmorton, 14, 16, 20; Rice.

97   *the Greek inscriptions*   Price, 61–62.

*X-ray tomography of its hidden details*   Viegas.

98   *the orrery recently constructed*   Cicero, *On the Nature of the Gods,* 2.34–35.

*how a single revolution should maintain*   Cicero, *De re publica,* 1.14.

*Egyptian agriculture was revolutionized*   Oleson, 294; Finley, 36–37.

Archimedes' screw pump—essentially, a rotating screw inside a tube—has since been applied to many technical problems beyond lifting water. At the turn of the century, the mechanism was incorporated in automatic stoking devices for moving fuel into the furnaces of steam railroad engines, relieving trainmen of the task of shoveling vast amounts of coal. Today, snowblowers based on Archimedes' screw save suburban homeowners similar drudgery.

*The Pharos . . . was renowned for its colossal height* · Thiersch, 1909.

*a similarly massive dreadnought* Athenaeus, 5, 203f–204b.

99    *roofed with magnetic stones* Pliny, 34.42.

*A similar contraption* Quoted in Empereur, 93–95.

*Athenaeus has also preserved an account* Athenaeus, 5.198.

*Their alleged technophobia* Finley, 1973.

*The proper goal of science* Plato, *Republic,* book 7.

100    *there was nothing mechanical* Heath, *Aristarchus of Samos,* 217.

*the great mathematician* Lloyd, 95.

100–    *Finley and his followers have grossly underestimated* Ibid.; Greene,
101    29–59; White, 219–20.

103    *it is easy to imagine* Solmsen, 211.

*an institution rooted in an Aristotelian tradition* Solmsen, 207.

## CHAPTER 4

104    *Aristotle . . . advised the young Alexander* Plutarch, *De Alexandri,* I.329.

*the barbarians are more servile* Aristotle, *Politics,* 3.1285a.20.

105    *Now, towards the end of his treatise* Strabo, 1.4.9.

*Eratosthenes links the Romans and Carthaginians* Strabo, 1.4.9; Aujac, ch. 3, n. 57. How much Eratosthenes actually knew about the Romans is open to question; the location of the city of Rome is not even specified in the *Geography* (D. Roller, personal communication). Eratosthenes' acquaintance Archimedes, a Syracusan, may conceivably have been a source for what Eratosthenes knew about Rome.

106    *occasion to converse and correspond with Hellenized Egyptians* Lewis, 123.

108    *According to several detailed studies* E.g., Dutka, Rawlins.

109    *Eratosthenes would have done well* Lewis, 156.

*Once the spherical model gained currency* Diller, 6.

*Aristotle quotes a figure* Aristotle, *On the Heavens,* II, 298a17.

*Archimedes posited an estimate* Heath, *Aristarchus of Samos,* 337–38.

110    *The standard method for estimating the earth's circumference* Rawlins, "Nile Map," 217–18.

*observing the setting of a star* Heilbron, 127–34.

*Claudius Ptolemaeus's Optics* Ptolemaeus, *Optics,* 5.3–6, 5.14–18.

111    *Dispatches traveled north and south* Casson, *Travel,* 182–83.

*[Eratosthenes'] ground measurements*    Fraser, 415.

112    (sphragides) *is precisely the term*    Thalamus, 159.

113    *We have a good idea of how such surveys were conducted*    Lyons, 132–33.
*a modern survey found*    Ibid., 134–35.
*officials of the time could work up surveys*    Van der Waerden, 32.

114    *One of the most ingenious tributes to Eratosthenes*    Morrison, 109–15.

116    *If now we conceive another straight line*    Cleomedes, *De motu circulari corporum caestium,* trans. in Heath, *Greek Astronomy,* 110.

117    *Cleomedes opted to report a rounded-off figure*    Goldstein, 411–12.
*to those who thrice wipe the mouth*    Athenaeus, 1.2.

120    *the outer edge of the sun did reach the zenith at Syene*    Dutka, 61.
*252,000 is exactly divisible by sixty*    Heath, *Aristarchus of Samos,* 339; Gulbekian, 361.

122    *pity unfortunate Greek schoolboys*    Van der Waerden, 46–47.

123    *The stade was also the standard length*    Hornblower, 943, 1437.
*none of these definitions yields a standard length*    Perrottet, 147–48.
*we hear of still other stades*    Gulbekian, 359–60.

124    *Letronne cited . . . Pliny*    The relevant passage is Pliny, 12.53.
*archaeologists have established*    Engels, 305; Ioppolo, 89–98.
*It was still accepted by at least one commentator*    Dutka, 63–64.

125    *other values appear elsewhere*    Gulbekian, 360; Engels, 300.
*Donald Engels suggested*    Engels, 308. Further evidence for the currency of the Attic foot turned up around the time Engels's article was published: in 1985, an ancient relief was discovered on a stone slab that was later built into a church on the island of Salamis, not far from Athens. The relief depicts several standard linear measures, including a "Hellenistic foot" 301 mm long. Cf. Dekoulakou-Sideris, p. 450.

126    *Many others now agree*    E.g., Rawlins, "Eratosthenes' Geodesy unravelled."
*One innovative study*    Firsov, 154–74.

127    *Firsov has averaged giants and pygmies*    Engels, 307–8.

128    *when Firsov's figures are plotted this way*    Note that results for the Kolmogorov/Smirnov normality test ($p < 0.01$) also indicate that the distribution of Firsov's stade data is normal. The parametric test for a range of the likely mean should therefore produce a valid result.
*although the Attic stade may have been standard*    Dutka, 56.

128–    *5,040 Letronnian stades adds up to about 493 miles*    Ibid., 63.

29    *the schoenus equaled . . . in the middle of the kingdom*    Strabo, 17.1.24.

130    *The overarching purpose of Eratosthenes' opus*    Ibid., 2.2.

131    *Anaximander, whose circular projection*    Herodotus, 5.49.

132    *By adding up the known (or guessed) distances*    Tozer, 238.

136    *I was both awestruck and delighted*    Cicero, *Somnium,* 37.

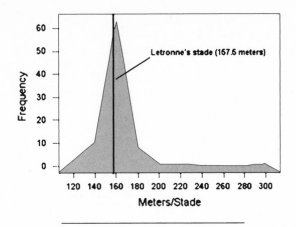

*Fig. 20. Distribution of strade units in Strabo. (From Firsov, 1972)*

He did note that it is possible     Strabo, 1.4.6.

Strabo criticized this     Ibid.

137     he also attempted to calculate     Heath, *Aristarchus of Samos,* 340–41.
There is some dispute over the correct interpretation of the figures in
the *Doxographi,* the texts that summarize supposed opinions of Eratosthenes and other authorities. Heath resolves firmly in favor of the values reported here. If his conclusion is wrong, then the correspondence
between his figure and the real distance to the sun is a truly astounding
coincidence.

139     I follow certain authorities     Blomqvist, 53–54.

Ptolemy III Euergetes . . . died early in 221     Hölbl, 127–28.

140     they were all given up to the populace     Polybius, XV.33.


## CHAPTER 5

144     On winter nights     Propertius, *Elegy,* IV.3, v. 33–40.

145     Right on the brink of the decisive battle     Rufus, 4.10.

146     As reported by Claudius Ptolemaeus     Ptolemaeus, *Geography,* 1.4.

The disciples listed in his Suda *biography*     Blomqvist, 66, n. 4.

147     we hear of no Erathostheneioi     Fraser, 458.

The astronomer Hipparchus published a book     Adapted from Strabo,
2.1.23.

148     Thus he is a mathematician in geography     Strabo, 1.2.41.

Julius Caesar appears to have thumbed     Caesar, VI.24.

Cicero was also a cautious admirer     Cicero, *Letter to Atticus,* II.6.

*Strabo compares its shape to that of a chlamys*   Strabo, 2.5.6.

*a term he applies elsewhere*   Strabo, 17.1.8.

*A great map of the Roman imperium*   Pliny, 3.17.

*something of a cartographic craze*   Propertius, *Elegy*, IV; Aujac, 107.

149   *Vitruvius hailed Eratosthenes' "cunning insight," and Pliny the Elder called him "a man of incomparable skill"*   Vitruvius, I.1.17; Pliny, II.247; Aujac, 115.

*Plutarch cites an estimate*   Plutarch, quoted in Drabkin, 512.

*If this is coupled with the linear distance*   Summarized in Heath, *Aristarchus of Samos,* 345.

150   *Poseidonius later "adopted" a figure*   Strabo, 2.2.2.

*He only obtained a smaller result for E*   Heath, *Aristarchus of Samos,* 343–44; Aujac, 102–4, Drabkin, 509–10.

151   *Yet another candidate*   Heath, *Aristarchus of Samos,* 346.

152   *It was entitled* Mathematical Composition, *but is known today*   Lloyd, 113.

153   *it is just and right that a geographer*   Ptolemaeus, *Geography,* 1.4, 63.

154   *Ptolemaeus reasoned that these two places must be the longitudinal equivalent of three hours apart on the earth's surface*   Ptolemaeus, *Geography,* 1.4.; cf. Pliny, 2.180.

*This, and the addition of China to the roster of known lands*   Aujac, 119.

*a measurement which is proved by distances*   Ptolemaeus, 1.11.12.

155   *The extent of Egyptian seacoast*   Strabo, 17.1.2.

*Thence to the island Pharos*   Strabo, 17.1.6.

157   *For [the kings] alone could free the minds of scholars*   Al-Bīrūnī, *India,* 152.

*Why does the history of ancient empirical astronomy*   Freeman, xix.

*For the preaching of the cross*   1 Corinthians 1:17–25 (King James version).

160   *What then has Athens to do with Jerusalem*   Tertullian, *On Prescriptions against Heretics,* ch. 7, quoted in Lloyd, 168.

*The monks had not been important*   Forster, 55.

161   *men in appearance but [who] lived the lives of swine*   Eunapius, 423.

*Hypatia's Suda biography lauds her*   Suda, upsilon 166.

*torn from her chariot*   Gibbon, 110.

*another view suggests*   Catholic Encyclopedia, IV, 592–93.

*the contemporary Greek rhetorician Aphthonius*   Delius, 1463.

162   *For these men, girding themselves*   Eunapius, 423.

163   *These, in turn, shaped the development of Christian theology*   Chadwick, 94–113.

*Christendom became engrossed*   Forster, 77–83. There are many more scholarly summaries of this controversy (e.g., J. Pelikan, *The Christian Tradition,* 1, ch. 5), but few as incisive and pitch-perfect as that of novelist Forster.

164     *Some became resigned*    Lloyd, 171.

*disease . . . which can avail us nothing*    quoted in Freeman, vii.

*Any system in which, by definition, there are no loose ends*    Irby-Massie and Keyser, 17.

165     *The rising prestige and pay gap*    A. H. M. Jones, *The Later Roman Empire 284–602*, quoted in Lloyd, 171.

*Others, such as Charles Freeman*    Freeman, 6.

166     *Space allow me to mention only a few key figures*    Aryabhata, 29; Al-Bīrūnī, *India*, 312–13.

167     *This new library*    Nasr, 69–70.

*Al-Ma'mun also demanded manuscripts*    Berggren, 23.

*the caliph was nothing less than a latter-day Ptolemy Philadelphus*    Insofar as he promoted a revisionist view of the Koran as an evolving revelation, and not a book composed of literal, timeless truths, he might also be called its Martin Luther.

168     *To resolve this ambiguity once and for all*    Berggren, 8.

*the experiment was conducted*    Hitti, 375.

*Once each team observed the apparent position of Polaris*    Berggren, 8.

*assuming that one Arab ic mile equals 1.19 English ones*    Ibn Battuta, 347; Sezgin, 127; Covington, 6.

*al-Ma'mun and his court did not view*    Berggren, 8.

169     *Al-Bīrūnī . . . takes a jibe at the "big science" approach*    Berggren, 141–43.

170     *On May 24, 997, al-Bīrūnī made careful observations*    Rashed and Moreton, 2, 505.

*This was essentially a repeat*    Ptolemaeus, *Geography*, 1.4.

*The elegant result*    Sezgin, 17.

170 &    *The sack was so brutal*    Hitti, 487.
172

171     "The Astrolabe": *The fundamental innovation underlying the astrolabe* Berggren, 165.

172     *Other uses included the determination of sunrise and sunset times*    Covington, 22–23.

*the world's first personal computer*    James Morrison, "Electric Astrolabe."

*The story is still taught*    Braude, 29.

173     *one of the great unintended consequences of intellectual history*    Heilbron, 3–23.

*One little-known link*    Welborn, 196.

175     *Eratosthenes, on the other hand*    Strabo, 1.3.2.

*He was followed by Francis Bacon*    Phillips and Phillips, 78.

*a gloomy exocean*    Sezgin, 17.

*al-Bīrūnī, who argued*    Ibid.

176    *In 1311, an armada of vessels*    Sezgin, 19; Baxter.

177    *Those who have returned from an attempt*    Strabo, 1.1.8.

178    *Upon the third day thou didst command*    2 Esdras, 6.42.

    *nature could not have made so disorderly a composition*    Quoted in Morison, 71.

179    *his reputation has lately been battered*    Phillips and Phillips, 5–8.

180    *One of Columbus's marginal notes*    Morison, 15, 41.192

    *a majority of U.S. citizens nonetheless fail to accept*    CBS News.

181    *Paolo dal Pozzo Toscanelli*    Quoted in Morison, 34.

    *conflating the Arabic mile*    Sezgin, 37.

    *Yet so tenacious was his* idée fixe    Morison, 54.

182    *Nothing is left where / Once it was*    Seneca, 63–64.

183    *His fourth and final voyage*    Morison, 383, 478, 581–82.

184    *Spanish sponsors were eager*    Bergreen, 24.

185    *According to . . . Bartolomé de las Casas*    Quoted in Bergreen, 32.

186    *Magellan compelled his little armada*    For the full story of Magellan's voyage, I am indebted to Lawrence Bergreen's vivid and heartbreaking history, *Over the Edge of the World.*

190    *On the more radical fringes of the discipline*    Nicastro, part 1.

# BIBLIOGRAPHY

### ANCIENT SOURCES

Achilles Tatius. *Leucippe and Clitophon.* Translated by Tim Whitmarsh. Oxford: Oxford University Press, 2001.

Aelian. *Varia Historia.* Translated by Diane Ostrom Johnson. Lewiston: E. Mellon Press, 1997.

Al Bīrūnī. *Alberuni's India.* Translated by Edward C. Sachau. London: Kegan Paul, Trench, Trübner, 1910.

———. *The Chronology of Ancient Nations.* Translated by Edward C. Sachau. Lahore: Hijra International, 1879.

Appian. *Roman History.* Translated by Horace White. Cambridge: Harvard University Press, 1912.

Aristotle. *Meteorology,* 2d ed. Cambridge: Loeb Classical Library, Harvard University Press, 1962.

———. *On the Heavens, I and II.* Translated by Stuart Leggatt. Warminster: Aris and Phillips, 1995.

———. *Politics.* Translated by Benjamin Jowett. New York: The Modern Library, 1943.

Arrian. *Campaigns of Alexander.* Translated by Aubrey de Sélincourt. London: Penguin Books, 1971.

Aryabhata. *Aryabhatiya.* New Delhi: Indian National Science Academy, 1976.

Athenaeus. *Deipnosophistae.* Translated by Charles Burton Gulick. Cambridge: Harvard University Press, 1927/1941.

Birch, S. *Records of the Past,* series I, volume VIII. London: Samuel Baxter and Sons, 1876.

Caesar. *Gallic War.* Translated by H. J. Edwards. Cambridge: Harvard University Press, 1986.

Cicero. *Cicero's Somnium Scipionis.* White Plains, N.Y.: Longman, 1988.

———. *Letter to Atticus.* Translated by E. O. Winstedt. Cambridge: Harvard University Press, 1953.

———. *De re publica.* Translated by Clinton Walker Keyes. Cambridge: Harvard University Press, 1988.

———. *On the Nature of the Gods*. Translated by H. Rackham. Cambridge: Harvard University Press, 1933.

———. *Pro Rabirio Postumo*. Translated by N. H. Watts. Cambridge: Harvard University Press, 1931.

Curtius Rufus, Quintus. *The History of Alexander*. Translated by John Yardley. London: Penguin Books, 2001.

Dio Cassius. *Roman History*. Translated by Earnest Cary. Cambridge: Harvard University Press, 1914–27.

Diogenes Laertius. *Life of Anaxagoras*. In *The Lives and Opinions of Eminent Philosophers*, book 2. Translated by C. D. Yonge. London: George Bell and Sons, 1895.

Eunapius. *The Lives of the Sophists*. Translated by W. C. Cave. London: Heinemann, 1922.

Herodas. *Mimes*. In *Theophrastus, VI, Theophrastus, Characters. Herodas, Mimes. Sophron and Other Mime Fragments*. Edited and translated by Jeffrey Rusten. Cambridge: Loeb Classical Library, Harvard University Press, 1993.

Herodotus. *History*. Translated by David Grene. Chicago: The University of Chicago Press, 1987.

Ibn Battuta. *Travels in Asia and Africa 1325–1345*. Translated and edited by H. A. R. Gibb. New Delhi: Asian Educational Services, 1997 (reprint of New York: R. M. McBride and Company, 1929).

Plato. *The Dialogues of Plato*. Translated by B. Jowett. New York: Random House, 1937.

Pliny. *Natural History*. Translated by H. Rackham. Cambridge: Harvard University Press, 1991.

Plutarch. *De Alexandri magni fortuna aut virtute*. In *Moralia*, v. IV. Translated by Frank Cole Babbitt. Cambridge: Harvard University Press, 1984.

———. "Life of Pericles." Translated by John Dryden. In *Plutarch: Eight Great Lives*. New York: Holt, Rinehart and Winston, 1960.

———. *Symposiacs*. In *Moralia*, v. IX. Translated by Edwin L. Minar, Jr., F. H. Sandbach, W. C. Helmbold. Cambridge: Harvard University Press, 1961.

Polybius. *The Histories of Polybius*. Translated by Evelyn S. Shuckburgh. Bloomington: Indiana University Press, 1962.

Propertius. *Elegies*. Translated by G. P. Goold. Cambridge: Harvard University Press, 1990.

Ptolemaeus. *Ptolemy's Almagest*. Translated by G. J. Toomer. New York: Springer-Verlag, 1984.

———. *Ptolemy's Geography: An Annotated Translation of the Theoretical Chapters*. Translated by J. Lennart Berggren and Alexander Jones. Princeton, N.J.: Princeton University Press, 2000.

———. *Optics*. Translated by A. Mark Smith. Philadelphia: American Philosophical Society, 1996.

———. *Geography of Cláudius Ptolemy,* translated by Edward Luther Stevenson. The New York Public Library, 1932.

Seneca. *Medea.* Translated by Frederick Ahl. Ithaca, N.Y.: Cornell University Press, 1986.

Strabo. *Geography.* Translated by H. C. Hamilton and W. Falconer. London and New York: G. Bell and Sons, 1889–93.

———. *Geography.* Translated by H. L. Jones. Cambridge: Harvard University Press, 1988.

Suetonius. *De grammaticis et rhetoribus.* Translated by Robert A. Kaster. New York: Oxford University Press, 1995.

Theocritus. *Idylls.* Translated by Andrew Lang. London: Macmillan and Co., 1880.

Vitruvius. *De architectura.* Translated by Frank Granger. Cambridge: Harvard University Press, 1970.

Xenophon. *Memorabilia.* Translated by E. C. Marchant and O. J. Todd. Cambridge: Harvard University Press, 1979–86.


## OTHER SOURCES

Aujac, Germaine. *Ératosthène de Cyrène, le pionnier de la géographie: Sa mesure de la circonférence terrestre.* Paris: Éditions du CTHS, 2001.

Bagnall, Roger S. *The Administration of the Ptolemaic Possessions Outside Egypt.* Leiden: E. J. Brill, 1976.

Baxter, Joan. "Africa's 'greatest explorer.'" *BBC News* Online, 13 December, 2000. http://news.bbc.co.uk/2/low/africa/1068950.stm (accessed April 16, 2008).

Berggren, J. L. *Episodes in the Mathematics of Medieval Islam.* New York: Springer-Verlag, 1986.

Bergreen, Laurence. *Over the Edge of the World: Magellan's Terrifying Circumnavigation of the Globe.* New York: Harper Perennial, 2004.

Bernal, Martin. *Black Athena Writes Back.* Durham, N.C.: Duke University Press, 2001.

Blomqvist, Jerker. "Alexandrian Science: The Case of Eratosthenes." In *Ethnicity in Hellenistic Egypt: Studies in Hellenistic Civilization,* vol. III, edited by Per Bilde, et al. Aarhus, Denmark: Aarhus University Press, 1992.

Braude, Joseph. *The New Iraq: Rebuilding the Country for Its People, the Middle East, and the World.* New York: Basic Books, 2004.

Bury, J. B., S. A. Cook, and F. W. Adcock, eds. *The Cambridge Ancient History,* v. V. London: Cambridge University Press, 1970.

Canfora, Luciano. *The Vanished Library: A Wonder of the Ancient World.* Translated by Martin Ryle. Berkeley and Los Angeles: University of California Press, 1990.

Casson, Lionel. *Travel in the Ancient World.* Baltimore: Johns Hopkins University Press, 1994.

———. *Libraries in the Ancient World.* New Haven: Yale Nota Bene, Yale University Press, 2002.

CBS News, "Poll: Majority Reject Evolution," October 23, 2005. http://www.cbsnews.com/stories/2005/10/22/opinion/polls/main965223.shtml (accessed April 16, 2008).

Chadwick, Henry. *The Early Church.* Penguin: New York, 1967.

Chapman, John. "St. Cyril of Alexandria." In *The Catholic Encyclopedia,* vol. IV. New York: Robert Appleton Co., 1908.

Covington, Richard. "Rediscovering Arabic Science." *Saudi Aramco World* 58, no. 3 (2007): 2–16.

Crake, Augustine David. *History of the Church Under the Roman Empire, A.D. 30–476.* London: Rivingtons, 1879.

Dekoulakou-Sideris, I. "A Metrological Relief from Salamis." *American Journal of Archaeology* 94 (1990): 445–51.

Delia, Diana. "From Romance to Rhetoric: The Alexandrian Library in Classical and Islamic Traditions." *The American Historical Review* 97, no. 5 (1992): 1449–67.

Dershowitz, Nachum, and Edward M. Reingold. *Calendrical Calculations.* Cambridge: Cambridge University Press, 1997.

Dicks, D. R. *Early Greek Astronomy to Aristotle.* Ithaca, N.Y.: Cornell University Press, 1970.

Diller, Aubrey. "The Ancient Measurements of the Earth." *Isis* 40, no. 1 (February 1949): 6–9.

Dodds, E. R. *The Greeks and the Irrational.* Berkeley: University of California Press, 1951.

Drabkin, I. E. "Posidonius and the Circumference of the Earth." *Isis* 34, no. 6 (Autumn 1943): 509–12.

Dukta, Jacques. "Eratosthenes' Measurement of the Earth Reconsidered." *Archives for History of Exact Sciences* 46, no. 1 (1993): 55–66.

Empereur, Jean-Yves. *Alexandria Rediscovered.* Translated by Margaret Maehler. London: British Museum Press, 1998.

Engels, Donald. "The Length of Eratosthenes' Stade." *The American Journal of Philology* 106, no. 3 (Autumn 1985): 298–311.

Finley, M. I. *The Ancient Economy.* Berkeley: University of California Press, 1973.

Firsov, L. V. "Eratosthenes' calculation of the earth's circumference and the length of the Hellenistic stade." *Vestnik Drevnii Istorii* 121 (1972): 154–74.

Forster, E. M. *Alexandria: A History and a Guide.* Garden City, N.Y.: Anchor Books, 1961.

Fraser, P. M. *Ptolemaic Alexandria.* Oxford: Oxford University Press, 1972.

Freeman, Charles. *The Closing of the Western Mind: The Rise of Faith and the Fall of Reason*. New York: Knopf, 2003.

Geus, Klaus. *Eratosthenes von Kyrene: Studien zur hellenistischen Kultur- und Wissenschaftsgeschichte, München Beitrage zur Papyrus Forschung und Antiken Rechtsgeschichte*, vol. 92. Munich Verlag: C. H. Beck, 2001.

Gibbon, Edward. *The History of the Decline and Fall of the Roman Empire*, 2nd ed., vol. 5. London: Methuen, 1901.

Goldstein, Bernard R. "Eratosthenes on the 'Measurement' of the Earth." *Historia Mathematica* 11 (1984): 411–16.

Green, Peter. *Alexander to Actium*. Berkeley: University of California Press, 1990.

Greene, Kevin. "Technological Innovation and Economic Progress in the Ancient World: M. I. Finley Re-Considered." *The Economic History Review*, New Series, 53, no. 1 (February 2000): 29–59.

Grote, George. *A History of Greece*. London: John Murray, 1846.

Gulbekian, Edward. "The Origin and Value of the Stadion Unit Used by Eratosthenes in the Third Century B.C." *Archives for History of Exact Sciences* 37, no. 4 (1987): 359–63.

Harris, William V. *Ancient Literacy*. Cambridge: Harvard University Press, 1989.

Heath, Sir Thomas. *Aristarchus of Samos*. Oxford: Clarendon Press, 1913.

———. *A History of Greek Mathematics*. Oxford: Clarendon Press, 1921.

———. *Greek Astronomy*. New York: Dover, 1991.

Heibron, J. L. *The Sun in the Church: Cathedrals as Solar Observatories*. Cambridge: Harvard University Press, 1999.

Hitti, Philip K. *History of the Arabs*, 7th ed. London: Macmillan, 1961.

Hölbl, Günther. *A History of the Ptolemaic Empire*. Translated by Tina Saavedra. London: Routledge, 2001.

Hornblower, Simon, and Anthony Spawforth, eds. *The Oxford Classical Dictionary*, 3rd rev. ed. New York: Oxford University Press, 2003.

Ioppolo, G. "La tavola della unita di misura nel mercato augusteo di Leptis Magna." *Quaderni di Archeologia della Libia* 5 (1967): 89–98.

Irby-Massie, Georgia L., and Paul T. Keyser. *Greek Science of the Hellenistic Era*. London: Routledge, 2002.

Jacob, Christian. *La Description de la terre habitée de Denys d'Alexandrie, ou, La leçon de géographie*. Paris: Éditions Albin Michael, 1990.

James, T. G. H. *Pharaoh's People: Scenes from Life in Imperial Egypt*. London: Taurisparke, 2003.

Lewis, Naphtali. *Greeks in Ptolemaic Egypt: Case Studies in the Social History of the Hellenistic World*. Oxford: Oxford University Press, 1986.

Lloyd, G. E. R. *Greek Science After Aristotle*. New York: W. W. Norton, 1973.

Lyons, Henry. "Ancient Surveying Instruments." *The Geographical Journal* 69, no. 2 (February 1927): 132–39.

Morison, Samuel Eliot. *Admiral of the Ocean Sea: A Life of Christopher Columbus.* Boston: Little, Brown, 1942.

Morrison, James E. "The Electric Astrolabe," Janus, 2006. http://www.astrolabes.org/electric.htm (accessed April 16, 2008).

Morrison, Philip, and Phylis Morrison. *The Ring of Truth.* New York: Random House, 1987.

Nasr, Seyyed Hossein. *Science and Civilization in Islam.* Cambridge, U.K.: Islamic Texts Society, 2003.

Nicastro, Nicholas. "Why I Am Not a Cultural Anthropologist." *The Bookpress* 10, no. 9 (2000): 4–5, 10.

Oleson, John Peter. *Greek and Roman Mechanical Water-Lifting Devices: The History of Technology.* University of Toronto Press, 1984.

Pàmias, Jordi, and Klaus Geus. *Eratosthenes, Sternsagen (Catasterismi).* Oberhaid, Germany: Utopica, 2007.

Perrottet, Tony. *The Naked Olympics: The True Story of the Ancient Games.* New York: Random House, 2004.

Pfeiffer, Rudolf. *History of Classical Scholarship.* Oxford: Clarendon, 1968.

Phillips, William D., Jr., and Carla Rahn Phillips. *The Worlds of Christopher Columbus.* Cambridge: Cambridge University Press, 1992.

Price, Derek J. de Solla. "An Ancient Greek Computer." *Scientific American* (June 1959): 60–67.

Rashed, Roshdi, and Régis Morelon, eds. *Encyclopedia of the History of Arabic Science.* London: Routledge, 1996.

Rawlins, Dennis. (1982a) "The Eratosthenes-Strabo Nile Map. Is It the Earliest Surviving Instance of Spherical Cartography? Did It Supply the 5000 Stades Arc for Eratosthenes' Experiment?" *Archives for History of Exact Sciences* 26, no. 3 (1982): 211–19.

———. "Eratosthenes' Geodesy Unraveled: Was There a High-Accuracy Hellenistic Astronomy?" *Isis* 73 (June 1982): 259–65.

Rice, Rob S. "The Antikythera Mechanism: Physical and Intellectual Salvage from the 1st Century B.C.," USNA Eleventh Naval History Symposium, 1995. http://ccat.sas.upenn.edu/rrice/usna_pap_fn.html (accessed April 16, 2008).

Sagan, Carl. *Cosmos.* New York: Random House, 1980.

Samuel, A. E. "The Ptolemies and the Ideology of Kingship." In *Hellenistic History and Culture*, edited by P. Green. Berkeley: University of California Press, 1993.

Sezgin, Fuat. "The Pre-Columbian Discovery of the American Continent by Muslim Seafarers." In *Geschichte des Arabischen Schrifttums*, vol. XIII. Frankfurt: Institute for the History of Arabic-Islamic Science, 2006.

Solmsen, Friedrich. "Eratosthenes as Platonist and Poet." *Transactions and Proceedings of the American Philological Association* 73 (1942): 192–213.

Talbert, Richard J. A., ed., in collaboration with Roger S. Bagnall, et al. *Barrington Atlas of the Greek and Roman World*. Princeton, N.J.: Princeton University Press, 2000.

Thalamas, A. *La Géographie d'Ératosthène*. Versailles: Imprimerie Charles Barbier, 1921.

Thiersch, Hermann. *Pharos, Antike, Islam und Occident: Ein Beitrag zur Architekturgeschichte*. Leipzig: B.-G. Teubner, 1909.

Throckmorton, Peter. *The Sea Remembers: Shipwrecks and Archaeology from Homer's Greece to the Rediscovery of the Titanic*. New York: Weidenfeld and Nicolson, 1987.

Thurston, Hugh. *Early Astronomy*. New York: Springer-Verlag, 1994.

Tozer, H. F. *A History of Ancient Geography*, 2nd ed. New York: Biblo and Tannen, 1964.

Van der Waerden, B. L. *Science Awakening*. Translated by Arnold Dresden. New York: Oxford University Press, 1961.

Viegas, Jennifer. "Ancient Astronomy Artifact Bears Hidden Text," Discovery Channel, June 8, 2006. http://dsc.discovery.com/news/afp/20060605/astronomycomp_arc_print.html (accessed April 16, 2008).

Welborn, Mary Catherine. "Lotharingia as a Center of Arabic and Scientific Influence in the Eleventh Century." *Isis* 16 (November 1931): 188–99.

White, K. D. " 'The Base Mechanic Arts?' Some Thoughts on the Contribution of Science (Pure and Applied) to the Culture of the Hellenistic Age." In *Hellenistic History and Culture*, edited by Peter Green. Berkeley: University of California Press, 1993.

Williams, Henry Smith, and Edward Huntington Williams. *A History of Science*. New York: Harper, 1910.

# INDEX

*About Ancient Comedy* (Eratosthenes of Cyrene), 82

*About the Eight-Year Cycle* (Eratosthenes of Cyrene), 14

Abubakari II, 176

Achilles Tatius, 10–11

Aegean, crossing of, 1–3

Africa
  Alexandrian trade with, 104
  circumnavigation of, 23–24, 186

*Against Eratosthenes* (Hipparchus of Nicaea), 147–48

Agathocles of Samos, 139–40

*Aitia* (Callimachus), 78, 80

Alexander the Great
  burial site, 21, 50
  death, 40
  empire-building dreams, 41
  expansion of geographical knowledge, 23
  first sighting of Alexandria, 47–48
  intellectual interests, 65
  Macedonian campaign, 144–46

Alexandria
  Al-Nabi Danyal mosque, 21
  as cultural center, 50–51
  decline, 16–17
  descriptions of, 8–11
  duty collections, 9

  expulsion of intellectuals, 75, 78
  founding of, 46–50
  Greek character of, 7–8, 49
  harbor, 10, 19, 47
  layout, *4,* 20, 49, 68–69
  lighthouse, 3, 5–6, *7,* 19, 98
  as mercantile democracy, 1–2
  in modern day, 16, 18–20
  Pompey's Pillar, 141
  raids by monks, 160–62
  *See also* Great Library and Museum of Alexandria

Alexandrian calendar, 14

Alfraganus, 168

*Almagest, The* (Ptolemaeus), 35, 152

Al-Nabi Danyal mosque, 21

Amarna, Tell-al, 113

Amenhope, 30–31

Amrou ibn el-Ass, 11, 74

Anaxagoras of Clazomenae, 36, 64

Anaximander, 7, 31, 131

Anaximenes, 32

Anghiera, Peter d' "the Martyr," 182

Antikythera computer, *97,* 97–98, 101–2

Antiochus I, 61

Antiochus II, 12

Antipator of Sidon, 6

Apollonius of Heracleia, 94

Apollonius of Perga, 34–35, 152

Apollonius of Rhodes, 75, 76, 80

Apollonius the Eidograph, 75

Appian, 53

Archimedes
  correspondence with Eratosthenes,
    90–91, 107
  geodesy, 109–10
  *Sand Reckoner,* 109–10
  technological innovations, 98, 100

*Argonautica* (Apollonius of Rhodes), 80

Aristagoras of Miletus, 131

Aristarchus of Samos, 34, 37, 116

Aristarchus of Samothrace, 75, 80

Aristis, 146–47

Ariston of Chios, 62

Aristophanes, 64

Aristophanes of Byzantium
  as disciple of Eratosthenes,
    146–47
  as head librarian, 75
  imprisonment, 78
  refinement of written Greek, 76

Aristotelian model of analysis, 65

Aristotle
  book collection at Lyceum, 65
  cosmological theory, 34, 36–37
  five-zone model of earth, *174*
  geodesy, 109
  geographical knowledge, 24
  *On the Heavens,* 109

Arrian, 47

Arsinoeion, 99

Aryabhata the Elder, 116, 166

astrolabe, 169–70, *171,* 171–72, 173

astronomy
  Antikythera computer, *97,*
    97–98

astrolabe, 169–70, *171,* 171–72,
    173

Athenian ban on teaching of, 64

Babylonian, 29–30

Christian sponsorship of research,
    172–73

cosmological models, 31–36

Egyptian, 30–31

Greek, 30–36, 100

Muse of, 79

Athenaeus, 55–56, 98–99, 117

Athens
  literature and writing in classical
    perid, 63–64
  mercantile trade with Egypt, 1–2
  political organization of, 49
  prosecution of intellectuals, 64
  theft of manuscripts from, 13–14

Augustus, 20

Augustine, 164

Babylonian astronomy, 29–30

Bacon, Francis, 175

Bait al-hikmah library and research
    institution, 167, 170–72

Balboa, Vasco Nuñez de, 185

barbarians, 47, 104–6

Barros, João de, 178

Behaim, Martin, 178, *179*

Bīrūnī, Abū al-Rayhān al-
  on decline of scientific inquiry, 157
  *On the Determination of the
    Coordinates of Cities,* 169
  on existence of hidden continents,
    175, 181–82
  geodesy, 169–70
  *Ta'rikh al-Hind* (History of India),
    169, 175

books and literature
  Aristotle's library, 65
  collection by Ptolemies, 9–10,
    13–14, 64–65, 67
  exportation from Athens to
    Alexandria, 2
  in Greek classical period, 63–64
  lexicon of authors, 73
  papyrus scrolls, 71
  See also Great Library and Museum
    of Alexandria
Brahe, Tycho, 35
Brahmagupta, 166–67

Caesar, Gaius Julius, 14–15, 148
calendars
  Alexandrian, 14
  Christian need for revision, 172–73
  Egyptian, 14
  Julian, 14–15
Callimachus of Cyrene
  Aitia, 78, 80
  feud with Apollonius, 78
  as head librarian, 75
  lexicon of authors, 73
  preoccupation with Greek culture,
    81
  scholarly pursuits, 76
Canfora, Luciano, 69
Canopic Way, 21–22, 68
Canopus Decree, 15, 55
Casas, Bartolomé de las, 185
Cassander, 66
Cassini, Giovanni Domenico, 137
Catasterisms (Eratosthenes of Cyrene),
    82, 189
Chandragupta, 40–41
Chomsky, Noam, 151–52

Christians
  astronomical research sponsorship,
    172–73
  destruction of Great Library and
    Museum, 74, 141, 162
  doctrinal disputes, 163–64
  dry-earth notion, 178
  impoverishment of academics, 165
  preservation of philosophic and
    scientific texts, 162–63
  raids by monks on Alexandria,
    160–61
  writings against scientific
    rationalism, 157–60, 164
Chronological Tables (Eratosthenes of
    Cyrene), 82
Cicero
  "Dream of Scipio, The," 134–36,
    175
  five-zone model of earth, 174,
    174–75
  references to technological
    innovations, 98
  rejection of Eratosthenes'
    Geography, 148
circumnavigation of earth, 184–88,
    187
Clement, 163
Cleomedes, 24–25, 116, 117, 149
Cleomenes, 48–49
Columbus, Christopher
  knowledge of geographical
    writings, 178–80
  quest to reach Asia, 181, 183
  significance of discoveries, 183–84
  underestimation of earth's
    circumference, 180–82
Copernicus, 137

cosmology. *See* astronomy
Crates of Olynthus, 49
Ctesibius of Alexandria, 38, 94
Cyrene, 42, 59–61

Deinocrates of Rhodes, 49
Delian problem, 91–94
Demetrius of Phaleron, 65–68, 75, 76
Democritus of Abdera, 32
Dias, Bartolomew, 186
Dicaearchus, 109, 110
Dio Cassius, 69
Diogenes Laertius, 29
"doubling of the cube," 91–94
"Dream of Scipio, The" (Cicero),
    134–36, *174,* 175
Droysen, Johann Gustav, 44–45
dry-earth notion, 177–78

earth, circumnavigation of, 184–88,
    *187*
earth, five-zone model of, 86–87,
    *174,* 174–75
earth, maps of
    Anaximander's, *131*
    Behaim's, 178, *179*
    Eratosthenes', 132–37, *134–35*
    five-zone model, *174,* 174–75
    as known to Herodotus, *23*
    Muslim, 170, *176*
    Ptolemaeus's, 136, 154, *158–59,*
        178
earth, measurement of. *See* geodesy;
    geodesy of Eratosthenes
earth, sphericity of
    common acceptance of, 37, 180
    Eratosthenes' assumption of, 7, 26
    in Koranic interpretation, 167

in Pythagorean model, 32–33
    representation in skaphe design,
        116–17
eclipse observations, 144–46, 154,
    170
Egypt
    astronomy, 30–31
    calendar, 14
    land surveys, 112–14
    postal system, 111
    *See also* Alexandria
*Elegy* (Propertius), 144
Emporion, 9
Engels, Donald, 125–28
Epicurus, 39
Epiphanes, Ptolemy V, 78
Eratosthenes of Cyrene
    *About Ancient Comedy,* 82
    *About the Eight-Year Cycle,* 14
    Archimedes, correspondence with,
        90–91
    on Aristotle's five-zone model of
        earth, 175
    on barbarians, 104–6
    birth and early life, 59, 61–62,
        138–39
    calendar correction, 14–15
    *Catasterisms,* 82, 189
    *Chronological Tables,* 82
    commemorations of, 190–91
    cosmological models known to,
        31–36
    criticism and resentment toward,
        102–3, 148
    death, 138–40
    Egyptian culture, absorption of,
        106–7
    followers, lack of, 146–47

*Geography,* 83–87, 130–31, 147–48
*Hermes,* 86, 189
intellectual development, 62–63
map of habitable world, 132–37,
    *134–35*
*Master Builder, The,* 82
*On the Measurement of the Earth,*
    25, 83
mesolabe invention, epigram
    celebrating, 93–94
on mythology and poetry, 82–83,
    85–86, 189–90
nicknames, 102–3
passage to Alexandria, 1–3
as philologist, 81, 88–90
*Platonicus,* 89, 102
on proportionality, 86–90, 117
scholarly interests and
    contributions, 76, 82–90, 102,
    103, 188
solar and lunar distance
    calculations, 37, 137–38
*See also* geodesy of Eratosthenes
Eratosthenes Crater, 190
Eratosthenes Tablemount, 191
Eudoxus of Cnidus, 33–34, 100, 152
Euergetes, Ptolemy III. *See* Ptolemy
    III Euergetes
Eunapius, 160–61
Eutochios of Askalon, 92

Farghani, Abu'al-Abbas Ahmad ibn
    Muhammad ibn Kathir al-
    (Alfraganus), 168
Finley, Moses, 99
Firsov, L. V., 126–28
five-zone model of earth, 86–87, *174,*
    174–75

Forster, E. M., 21–22, 133, 160
Fort Qaitbey, 19
Fraser, P. M., 111, 147
Freeman, Charles, 166
*Frogs, The* (Aristophanes), 64

Galen of Pergamum, 13, 39
Gama, Vasco da, 186
Geminus of Rhodes, 14, 98
geodesy
    of Archimedes, 109–10
    of Aristotle, 109
    of Aryabhata, 166–67
    astrolabe in, 169–70, 173
    atmospheric refraction and, 110
    of al-Bīrūnī, 169–70
    of Brahmagupta, 166–67
    of Columbus, 180–81
    of Dicaearchus, 109, 110
    hemispheric skaphe in, *116,* 116–17
    of Magellan, 185
    of al-Ma'mun, 167–68, 175
    of Plutarch, 149
    of Poseidonius of Apamea, 149–51
    of Ptolemaeus, 35, 156
geodesy of Eratosthenes
    accuracy, 24–25, 188
    calculation methodology, 25–28,
        110–11
    data collection, 108–14
    errors, 118–20, 127
    imprecision, 120–23
    modern-day replications, 114–15,
        140–43
    principles and assumptions, 7,
        25–28, 37
    solar angle calculation, 117–18,
        *119*

geodesy of Eratosthenes (*continued*)
  solar distance calculation, 37,
      137–38
  stade length, 124–29
  tools, 24
  widespread acceptance of, 149
  widespread disbelief in, 188–89
*Geography* (Eratosthenes of Cyrene),
      83–87, 130–31, 147–48
*Geography* (Marinus of Tyre), 180
*Geography* (Ptolemaeus), 153, 155
*Geography* (Strabo), 62
Gibbon, Edward, 161
Great Harbor of Alexandria, 10, 19, 47
Great Library and Museum of
      Alexandria
  Aristotelian model of analysis, 65
  contents, 9–10, 13–14, 67, 70–74
  daughter library at Temple of
      Serapis, 72
  destruction of, 69, 74, 141, 162
  founding of, 25, 50, 65–67
  functioning of, 77–78
  Greek translations, 73–74
  head librarians, 1, 75–76
  location, 68–70
  organization of materials, 71–72,
      80–81
  scholarly work at, 6, 73–74, 79–81
Great Lighthouse of Alexandria
  depiction on coin, 7
  description of, 5–6
  modern-day site of, 19
  sight of, on approach to
      Alexandria, 3
  as symbol of wealth and political
      confidence, 6
  as technological achievement, 98

Great Pyramid of Khufu, 113
Greece and Greek culture
  Antikythera archaeological
      discovery, 96–97
  astronomy and cosmological
      models, 30–36, 100
  barbarians, mistrust of, 47, 104
  books and literacy, 63
  city life, 2–3, 61
  geographical knowledge, 22–24, *23*
  Hellenism, 44–46, 60–61
  *logos* concept, 88
  mercantile trade with Egypt, 1–2
  number systems, 121–22
  politics, 45–46, 49, 61
  scientific truth in, 37–40, 64,
      99–100, 165
  technology, *97,* 97–101
  theft of manuscripts from, 13–14
Green, Peter, 46, 50–51, 54
Grote, George, 44

Heiberg, Johan Ludvig, 90
Hellenistic period, 44–46, 60–61
hemispheric sundial, *116,* 116–17
Hermannus Contractus "Herman the
      Cripple," 173
*Hermes* (Eratosthenes of Cyrene), 86,
      189
Hermippus, 59
Herodas, 46
Herodotus, *23,* 23–24
Heron of Alexandria, 38
Herophilus of Chalcedon, 38–39,
      99
Hicetas of Syracuse, 33
Hipparchus of Nicaea
  cosmological observations, 35

*Against Eratosthenes,* 147–48
solar distance estimate, 137
trigonometric tables, 115
Hippocrates of Chios, 92
Hippodamas of Miletus, 49
*Historia rerum ubique gestarum*
    (Sylvius), 179
history, discipline of, 82–83
*History of Greece* (Grote), 44
Homer, 3, 83, 85–86
Hypatia, 161

Idrisi al-, 175
*Idylls* (Theocritus), 50
Indian astronomers, 166–67
Ionian schools, 31–32
Irby-Massie, Georgia L., 165
Irving, Washington, 180
*Isis* (grain ship), 2
Islamic world. *See* Muslims

Julian calendar, 14–15
Justinian I, 165

Keyser, Paul T., 165
Khashkhash ibn Saeed, 175–76
Khattāb, Umar ibn al-, 74
Khwarazmi, Muhammad ibn Musa
    al-, 168
Kondos, Dimitrios, 96
Kyrenia ship, 2–3

Letronne, J. A., 124–28
*Leucippe and Clitophon* (Achilles
    Tatius), 10–11
Leucippus, 7, 32
library, Aristotle's, 65
Library at Temple of Serapis, 72

Library of Alexandria. *See* Great
    Library and Museum of
    Alexandria
*Life of Anaxagoras* (Diogenes Laertius),
    29
Lighthouse of Alexandria. *See* Great
    Lighthouse of Alexandria
Lisboa, João de, 186
*logos,* meanings and concepts of,
    88–89
Lucian of Samosata, 2
lunar distance, 137
Lysanias, 62

Magas, 61
Magellan, Ferdinand, 184–88, *187*
Malik Ibn Juraij, Abd al-, 11
Ma'mun ibn Harun, Abu Jafar al-,
    167–68
maps
    Alexandria, *4*
    Anaximander's, *131*
    Behaim's, 178, *179*
    coordinate system, 155
    Eratosthenes', 132–37, *134–35*
    five-zone model, *174,* 174–75
    as known to Herodotus, *23*
    Muslim, 170, *176*
    Ptolemaeus's, 136, 154, *158–59,* 178
    scaled projection, 132
    spherical projection, 153
Marinus, 154, 180
Mashallah, 173
*Master Builder, The* (Eratosthenes of
    Cyrene), 82
Mas'udi al-, 175–76
Mazandarani, Zayn Eddine Ali Ben
    Fadhel al-, 176

mean proportion, 92–94
*Medea* (Seneca), 182
Menandros, 146–47
mercantile trade, 1–2
mesolabe, 94
*Method of Mechanical Theorems*
    (Archimedes), 90–91
*Mime* (Herodas), 46
Mnaseas, 146–47
Morison, Samuel, 184
Morrison, Philip and Phyllis,
    114–15
Muses, 79
Museum of Alexandria. *See* Great
    Library and Museum of
    Alexandria
Muslims
    Bait al-hikmah library and research
        institution, 167, 170–72
    geodesy, 168–70
    navigators, 175–77
    world map, 170, *176*
mythology
    in Egyptian astronomy, 30
    rationalist view of, 79–80
    as scientific knowledge, rejection
        of, 82–83, 85–86, 189–90

Nabi, Danyal al- (mosque), 21
*Natural History* (Pliny), 179
Nearchus, 23
Necho, 23–24
number systems, 120–22
Nye, Bill, 114

*Odyssey, The* (Homer), 3, 85
*Oedipus Tyrannus* (Sophocles), 80
Onasander, 76

*On the Determination of the Coordinates
    of Cities* (al-Bīrūnī), 169
*On the Heavens* (Aristotle), 109
*On the Measurement of the Earth*
    (Eratosthenes of Cyrene), 25, 83
*Optics* (Ptolemaeus), 110
Origen, 162, 163
Orosius, 69

papyrus scrolls, 71
paradoxography, 76, 80
Paul (apostle), 157–60
Pericles, 36, 64
Peripatetic model of analysis, 65
Pfeiffer, Rudolf, 88–89
Pharos of Alexandria. *See* Great
    Lighthouse of Alexandria
Philadelphus, Ptolemy II, *19,* 51, 53,
    56–57
philology, in Eratosthenes' self-
    definition, 81, 88–90
Philopator, Ptolemy IV, 45, 57, 103,
    139
Phoenician circumnavigation of
    Africa, 23–24
Physcon, Ptolemy VIII "Fatty," 75, 78
Plato
    on books and written word, 63, 65
    on concept of empirical proof, 38,
        39
    on importance of cosmological
        models, 31
    on lack of mathematical research, 92
    proportionality of worldly
        substances, 89, 94
    *Republic,* 92, 99–100
    on role of science, 99–100
    *Timaeus,* 31, 89

*Platonicus* (Eratosthenes of Cyrene), 89, 102
Pliny
  on magnitude of Indian army, 41
  *Natural History,* 179
  praise for Eratosthenes, 24, 149
  Seven Wonders of the ancient world, 6
  on value of Eratosthenes' stade, 124–25, 129
Plutarch, 34, 36, 94–95, 149
Polo, Marco, 180–81
Polybius
  description of turmoil in Alexandria, 139–40
  disdain for Ptolemaic Egypt, 42–44
  on Eratosthenes' geographical knowledge, 83, 147
  on Eratosthenes' rejection of Homeric history, 83
Pompey's Pillar, 141
Poseidonius of Apamea, 149–51
Proclus Lycaeus, 89–90
Propertius, 144, 149
proportionality
  as common factor among sciences, 89–90
  device to calculate, 93–94
  in Eratosthenes' geography, 86–88
  mean proportion, in solution to Delian problem, 92
  in Plato's notion of worldly elements, 89, 94
Protagoras, 64, 138
Ptolemaeus, Claudius (astronomer Ptolemy)
  *Almagest, The,* 35, 152
  cosmological model, 35, 152–53

  geodesy, 35, 156
  *Geography,* 153, 155
  influence of, 151–52
  map of world, 136, 154, *158–59,* 178
  mistiming of eclipse observations, 146, 154
  *Optics,* 110
  reliance on observational data, 153–54
  solar distance estimate, 137
  valuation of stade, 154–56
Ptolemies and Ptolemaic Empire
  alienation of natives, 12–13, 57–58, 61
  assumption of power, 41–42
  book collection, 9–10, 13–14, 64–65, 67
  excesses, 55–57
  expansion and prosperity, 12–13, 15, 51–55
  Greek style and character, 8, 49
  interest in practical geography, 103
  Polybius's history of, 42–44
  *See also* Alexandria; *specific Ptolemies*
Ptolemy (astronomer). *See* Ptolemaeus, Claudius (astronomer Ptolemy)
Ptolemy I Soter, *13,* 41–42, 61
Ptolemy II Philadelphus, *19,* 51, 53, 56–57
Ptolemy III Euergetes
  death, 139
  depiction on coin, *13*
  expansion of empire, 12–13, 15
  generosity, 43–44
  hiring of Eratosthenes, 11
  marriage, 61

Ptolemy III Euergetes (*continued*)
  modification of Egyptian calendar, 14
  mollification of religious establishment, 55
  theft of manuscripts from Athens, 13–14
Ptolemy IV Philopator, 45, 57, 103, 139
Ptolemy V Epiphanes, 78
Ptolemy VIII Physcon "Fatty," 75, 78
Pythagoras, 32–33
Pytheas, 23

Raphia, battle of, 45
*Republic* (Plato), 92, 99–100
Romans
  calendar, 14–15
  on Greek character of Alexandria, 7
  opinion of Ptolemaic Egypt, 42–43
  technology, 112
Rufinus of Aquileia, 99

Sagan, Carl, 70, 100
*Sand Reckoner* (Archimedes), 109–10
science and scientific rationalism
  attacks by monks, 160–61
  Christian writings against, 157–60, 164
  in Greek culture, 37–40, 64, 99–100, 165
  impoverishment of academics, 165
  as inspiration for Muslim research, 167–68
  in work at Museum, 79–80
Seleucid Empire, 12

Seleucus of Seleucia, 34
Seneca, 182
Serapis (god), 9
Seven Wonders of the ancient world, 5–6
shipping trade, 1–2
silphion plant, 59–60, *60*
skaphe sundial, *116,* 116–17
Socrates, 64
solar angle, 117–18, *119*
solar distance, 37, 137–38
Solmsen, Friedrich, 103
*Somnium Scipionis* ("The Dream of Scipio") (Cicero), 134–36, *174, 175*
Sophists, 63
Sophocles, 80
Sosibius of Alexandria, 139–40
Soter, Ptolemy I, *13,* 41–42, 61
Spencer, Herbert, 44
sphericity of earth
  common acceptance of, 37, 180
  Eratosthenes' assumption of, 7, 26
  in Koranic interpretation, 167
  in Pythagorean model, 32–33
  representation in skaphe design, 116–17
sphragides, 87, 112, 122
stade
  Eratosthenes', 124–29
  Ptolemaeus's, 154–56
  various definitions, 26–28, 123–24
Stadiatos, Elias, 96
Stoic school, 62
Strabo
  description of Alexandria, 8–9, 69
  on Eratosthenes' vulnerability to criticism, 148

on geodesy of Poseidonius of
    Apamea, 149–50
*Geography,* 62
on Hipparchus's *Against
    Eratosthenes,* 147–48
on pre-Muslim circumnavigation
    of earth, 177
Strabo, summary and commentary on
    Eratosthenes' writings
disparagement of Homer's works,
    83, 86
Egypt's lack of harbor access, 47
*Geography,* 84–85, 86–87, 130
Greek mistrust of barbarians,
    104–5
intellectual stimulation in Athens,
    62
measurement of Egyptian seacoast,
    155
*Suda,* 60
Suetonius, 89
sundial, *116,* 116–17
Sylvius, Aeneas, 179

*Ta'rikh al-Hind* (History of India)
    (al-Bīrūnī), 169, 175
technology, Greek, *97,* 97–101
Temple of Serapis, 99
    daughter library at, 72
Tertullian, 160
Thales of Miletus, 7, 31, 32

Theocritus, 50
Theodosius, 162
Theon of Smyrna, 90, 91
Theophilus, 162
Theophrastus of Lesbos, 65
*Timaeus* (Plato), 31, 89
Timon of Phlius, 7, 77
Toscanelli, Paolo dal Pozzo, 181
trigonometric functions, 115–16

Umari al-, 175

Vitruvius, 38

Wafa al-Buzjani, Abu al-, 116, 170
world maps
    Anaximander's, *131*
    Behaim's, 178, *179*
    Eratosthenes', 132–37, *134–35*
    five-zone model, *174,* 174–75
    as known to Herodotus, *23*
    Muslim, 170, *176*
    Ptolemaeus's, 136, 154, *158–59,*
        178

Xenophon, 64

Yahyā ibn Aktham, 168

Zeno of Citium, 62
Zenodotus of Ephesus, 75, 76, 80–81